Other books in The Best of *Inc.* series:

The Best of *Inc.* Guide to Business Strategy
The Best of *Inc.* Guide to Finding Capital
The Best of *Inc.* Guide to Marketing and Selling

THE BEST OF

GUIDE TO

MANAGING PEOPLE

BY
THE EDITORS OF
 MAGAZINE

PRENTICE HALL PRESS

NEW YORK • LONDON • TORONTO • SYDNEY • TOKYO

PRENTICE HALL PRESS
Gulf+Western Building
One Gulf+Western Plaza
New York, New York 10023

PRENTICE HALL PRESS and colophon are registered
trademarks of Simon & Schuster, Inc.

Library of Congress Cataloging-in-Publication Data

The Best of Inc. guide to managing people / by the editors of Inc.
magazine. — 1st Prentice Hall Press ed.
p.   cm.
Includes index.
ISBN 0-13-073222-2   : $12.95
1. Employee motivation.   2. Leadership.   3. Delegation of
authority.   I. Inc.
HF5549.5.M63B47   1989
658.3—dc19   89-30690
CIP

Designed by Irving Perkins Associates

Manufactured in the United States of America

10 9 8 7 6 5 4 3 2 1

First Edition

CONTENTS

PART
I

MOTIVATION

PART
II

LEADERSHIP 89

PART
III

DELEGATING AUTHORITY

195

THE BEST OF
Inc.
GUIDE TO
MANAGING
PEOPLE

PART

I

MOTIVATION

PREFACE

One of the trickiest aspects of good management is developing and maintaining a mutually beneficial relationship with your employees. There are certain factors that must be agreed on from the start—fair pay, fair benefits and fair work loads, for example—but that is only the beginning. A truly motivated work force is not merely inclined, but positively inspired to contribute to and participate in the goal or goals of the company.

Sound expensive? It's not, really. Developing a motivated team of employees does not necessarily require huge outlays of cash. There are subtle factors at play in the relationship that evolves between employee and employer. Recognizing and understanding them can often mean the difference between a loitering platoon of laborers and a prolific team of professionals.

Motivation, the first part in our book on managing people, looks at some techniques that have been tested in various companies and industries to stimulate productivity and high morale. This collection also offers some insights into what type of managerial behavior most frustrates otherwise valuable employees—and vice versa—and how these behavior patterns can be adjusted.

The first step in initiating good morale is to give employees some measure of certainty and stability. An effective and inexpensive tool for communicating stability in an organization is the employee manual which covers policies such as sick leave, vacation time, benefits, overtime, and the like. Spelling out the company policy shows employees what they can expect from the company and what the company expects from them. Sadly, many small and growing companies overlook the employee manual, figuring they'll deal with vacations and salary increases on an ad hoc basis. What that says to the employee is that you haven't got it all figured out yet, and that can create waves of uncertainty. "How to Write a Personnel Manual," the first piece in this book, lists 29 policy topics that should be covered in any manual, and offers suggestions for other topics as well.

Money, of course, is the carrot that managers often use to motivate workers. In "How to Get More from Your Employees," *Inc.* talks to a consultant with an emphatic belief in the value of financial incentives—relatively small amounts, given frequently, to award superior performance. But such incentive awards are controversial. In "Incentives Can Be Bad for Business," and "Letter to the Editor," two prominent management thinkers—Tom Peters and Alfie Kohn—debate the value of extrinsic awards such as money and prizes.

The right compensation system can motivate employees and speed a company's growth. Re/Max International, Inc., a real estate sales company, rejected the industry practice of requiring agents to split commissions with the company. Instead, agents pay a monthly fee to the company and keep whatever commissions they generate. In "The Ownership Factor," we see that many of the best agents in the business join Re/Max—and stay there. The concept is different but just as innovative at Diedre Moire Corp., a personnel consulting firm featured in "Up from Drudgery." Senior sales reps share the commissions earned by other sales reps they recruit; their compensation and management responsibilities increase as they sustain certain sales levels for a prescribed time.

Cash isn't the only way to motivate employees. In "Why Work?" a review of Michael Maccoby's book of the same name, we hear the argument that companies should de-emphasize carrot-and-stick motivators. Instead, Maccoby says, executives should focus on the internal motivators—such as personal interests and values—that drive people to excel.

Information can be a motivational device as well. In "Show and Tell," one company builder recounts how, when he began to share financial and other information with employees, they began to take a much more intense interest in the company and their jobs. "The Turned-Off Worker: Why John and Mary Won't Work," explores nonmonetary alternatives that work just as well as money in some companies. And "Getting to Know You" shows how a simple but meaningful gesture—spending time with employees to learn what turns them off or on—can pay big dividends for your company.

Which incentives, then, are right for your own company? "Be Sure You Choose the Right Incentives" takes a look at what incentives are designed to do—satisfy or motivate—and how to determine which incentives are the most appropriate for your employees. Zane Tankel, the subject of the next piece, "Zane Tankel Wrote His Own Rules for Managing People," is in some ways the quintessential entrepreneur—he is a mixture of shrewd businessman and understanding employer. He took his company from near-bankruptcy to comfort by looking at the world through the eyes of his employees.

The balance of this collection offers some tips on keeping creative employees on course and facing up to those situations where motivation is *not* the issue: when a loyal employee no longer fits into the changing organization, or when you have to fire someone.

As with all the stories in *The Best of Inc. Guide to Managing People*, we offer these as examples of the creative responses that entrepreneurs have generated to traditional management quandaries.

HOW TO
WRITE A
PERSONNEL
MANUAL

Some executives prefer to make policy decisions on the basis of personal hunches, likes and dislikes, or just plain delight in running the show. They don't want to delegate authority in hiring and firing, or rewarding and punishing employees.

But that's a risky and time-consuming way of managing personnel. Eventually every executive finds that his life would be a lot easier—and his employees a lot happier—if the policies he is constantly being called on to make were written down.

Any company with more than twenty employees, and some with as few as half a dozen, should issue a policy handbook. It should answer some of the most important questions employees ask—questions about salary review, holidays, benefit programs, leaves of absence, and other critical policies that often affect morale and whose absence can create legal problems. The handbook should have two goals: It should keep all employees informed about company regulations and changing policies, and it should give supervisors the support they need when they have to enforce those regulations and policies.

Your lawyer, or a legal expert in the field of labor relations, is the best person to consult before you issue a policy statement to employees. (Remember, a policy handbook may be considered legally binding in the event of a dispute or an unfair employment practice claim.) On the following pages we've outlined some of the major items that should be included in a personnel policy handbook along with some dos and don'ts to consider when you're drafting or revising yours.

—EDGAR S. ELLMAN

5

Policy Item	What it should say	Problems to avoid
Equal opportunity statement	State that an employee's religion, age, sex, national origin, race, or color will have nothing to do with hiring, promotion, pay, or benefits.	Don't include the Affirmative Action Plan, if you're required to have one, in this section. Refer instead to a separate handbook.
Physical examinations	Establish your right to conduct both pre- and post-employment physical exams, at company expense.	Be sure your decisions to conduct a physical are nondiscriminatory—i.e., don't just examine older people or minorities.
Probationary period	Define the period (usually 30, 60, or 90 days) during which a new employee can be dismissed without a hearing on the cause; also indicate when benefits start to accrue.	Avoid a great discrepancy between the probationary period and the period before an employee qualifies for group insurance.
Hiring of relatives	State whether you will allow a married couple or close relatives to work together in the same department.	Too strict policies—e.g., requiring two employees who get married to choose which will remain with the company—are bad for morale.
Work hours	Define the workweek and time allotted for lunch and breaks. Indicate the cut-off time for each pay period.	Provide yourself with the option of rescheduling individual hours of work in any given week at the discretion of the supervisor.
Employee status	Define the nature of each type of employee—full time, part time, temporary, and "exempt" and "non-exempt." Make clear what the benefits each is eligible for.	Be specific to avoid any chance of misconception.
Overtime pay	Establish clearly whether overtime is paid for work more than 40 hours a week or more than 8 hours in a given day, and how much is paid for work on a holiday. Make it clear that pay for overtime must be approved by a supervisor.	Don't say that you are bound to assign overtime on the basis of seniority.
Pay reduction for lateness	The usual policy is to go by the clock, i.e., to dock an employee's pay in units of six minutes or tenths of an hour.	Using too large a unit, such as a quarter of an hour, may cause problems. It may be illegal to dock an employee's pay by that much if he or she is only a few minutes late.

Policy Item	What it should say	Problems to avoid
Severance pay	Determine this on the basis of seniority, e.g., a week's pay for less than three years tenure, two weeks for up to six years, etc. Exclude employees who are released for "cause." You may also exclude those who leave voluntarily.	Unless state law requires it, you don't have to pay for accrued vacation time.
Performance review and merit increases	Review wages either on the anniversary of employment or during a set annual or semiannual period.	This policy is essential— some employees would rather quit than ask for a raise. Don't commit yourself to cost-of-living increases unless required by a union contract. Make all raises based on merit.
Time clock or sign-in systems	Rules should prohibit employees from recording another's time, causing another employee to record for him or her, or failing to record his or her time. They should also forbid signing in too soon or out too late without authorization.	You must keep some sort of record of hours worked by "nonexempt" employees. Early sign-ins or late sign-outs will make you liable for overtime pay in case of a conflict or dispute.
Emergency shutdowns	Consider whether you will pay some minimum "call-in" wage in case you have to close down because of bad weather, a power failure, or some other unforeseen problem. What advance notice will you provide, if possible, in the event of such a shutdown?	Don't lock yourself in too tightly, but be sure you treat everyone the same. If you pay the regular wage to those who don't show up, those who do come in should be paid more.
Group insurance benefits	State coverage generally and briefly, indicating what portion of premium costs the company pays for, how long a new employee has to wait for coverage, and mentioning the conversion privilege.	Don't be too specific, but simply refer to the separate booklet the insurance company provides.
Holidays	List all holidays, and state how long an employee has to work to qualify for a paid holiday. Also indicate that employees have the right to take religious holidays without pay. What happens if the holiday occurs during an employee's vacation? What pay is given for work on a holiday?	Leave some room to reschedule a holiday depending on business conditions. You don't have to pay overtime in a week with a holiday unless more than 40 hours are worked.

Policy Item	What it should say	Problems to avoid
Vacations	Policies should conform with local practices (consult Bureau of Labor Statistics surveys and other published information). How does a new employee qualify for vacation? May a person choose to work instead of taking a vacation? May one take off more than two weeks at a time? As little as a day at a time? Are permanent part-timers given any vacation? Will accrued vacation pay be given at severance? Will a person on leave of absence accrue vacation time?	Don't let vacation scheduling supersede the needs of any individual department. Check state laws regarding payment of accrued vacation time at severance.
Personal time/sick leave	Six to ten days per year is the typical number allowed. Give employees the option of accumulating a reasonable number of days (20 or 30) for the future, or create a payback system for those who don't abuse the privilege.	The advantage of calling it "personal time" rather than "sick leave" is that employees will take sick leave without giving advance notice. Require "proof of illness" if you pay for time off only in the case of illness. Don't let personal time accrue during an extended leave of absence.
Disability leave of absence	Federal law requires leave time for disability due to pregnancy to be equal to that allowed for disabilities that affect only males. You must set some reasonable time limit during which you will guarantee job protection for a disabled worker. A 60 to 90 day period is typical. You may require pregnant women to sign statements of intent to return to work provided you require male workers disabled for other reasons to do the same. You may also reserve the right to require a physical examination by a company-appointed doctor if required of both males and females.	You do not have to have a leave policy at all if you don't want it, but some states have laws requiring a minimum leave time for pregnant women.
Military leave of absence	Required under federal law for National Guard or Reserve service.	Employees may not be compelled to use up vacation or personal time during military leave, and the job must be held open for the employee. He or she

Policy Item	What it should say	Problems to avoid
		must not be discriminated against in pay, promotion, or job assignment.
Personal leave of absence	If you decide to grant such leaves, you may want to specify that they may not exceed 30 (or 60) days, and that they may not be taken to look for or perform another job, or to start another business.	Smaller firms may want to omit this item, and play it by ear. If you plan to grant only discretionary leaves, omit the item.
Jury Service	Required by law, and some local statutes also require you to pay all or a portion of wages. Depending on local laws, you may want to set limits on how many days of jury duty you will pay for, and set a qualifying period of employment before you will pay for jury leave.	Don't require that employees sign over to the company the checks they receive from the court for serving on a jury. This may cause tax problems. Just pay them the difference between the amount of the check and the pay they would have received.
Bereavement pay	Employees expect the company to be very lenient in this matter. Typical policy allows three to five workdays off with pay in the event of a death in the immediate family.	Absence of a policy of some sort is bad for morale, but it's important to be consistent in granting this benefit.
Pension or profit-sharing plans	Mention that you have a plan, when and how the employee becomes qualified for it, whether an employee contribution is permitted or required, and when an employee becomes vested.	Don't go into great detail; refer instead to a separate description of the plan.
Suggestion system	State that the company encourages employees to submit ideas and suggestions to improve operations and reduce costs, and that an employee who submits ideas is considered to be a highly conscientious one. Suggestions should be addressed in writing to a member of top management, not the immediate supervisor.	Small firms should avoid a formal system. Committing yourself to a specific system of reward for ideas is also unwise.
Tuition assistance	Set a length of tenure requirement before the assistance is available. Require proof of course completion and consider awarding a larger percentage of costs for a high grade.	A good policy because it substantiates your desire to provide equal advancement opportunities, but don't commit yourself to paying all costs or fees.

Policy Item	What it should say	Problems to avoid
Bulletin boards	State that this is an official means of communication with employees, and that only authorized people may put up, take down, or alter items on the board.	Though you may think this item unimportant, the bulletin board is looked upon legally as an official "business practice" to keeping employees informed. Don't let items on the board get outdated; otherwise people will stop reading the announcements.
Confidentiality	Make employees aware that they are not to divulge company or customer information to outsiders, including the media and government representatives, without approval from management.	Certain government representatives (OSHA, EEOC) are privileged to speak privately with employees, with advance notice to employers.
Causes for discipline	Some industries, most often those employing unskilled or semiskilled workers, believe that a list of shop rules is essential. These must be as comprehensive as possible.	Legally, a list is deemed to be complete, and once it's published, anything not on the list would not be considered legally limiting on the employee. So don't commit yourself to publishing a list unless you feel you must, and don't make any violation of a rule an absolute cause for dismissal—or you may have to fire a good employee for a one-time infringement of the rules. Be sure rules are nondiscriminatory.
Discussing complaints and grievances	There should be some basis for appeal in the event an employee feels a supervisor's policies are unjust. All union contracts cover this procedure.	Don't have an "open door" policy allowing employees to bypass supervisors. Encourage them to talk things over with supervisors first.
Solicitation or distribution of literature	If you don't want employees selling merchandise or circulating petitions during working hours, specify that you will not allow the distribution of any literature, petitions, or surveys or the sale of any merchandise, raffle tickets, etc.	Don't impose this rule after a union has won the right to an election.

Policy Item	What it should say	Problems to avoid
Additional items for your employee handbook	Reporting absence Annual bonus Purchase of company merchandise Dress code Safety rules Aptitude and ability tests Service awards Relocation expense Outside employment Exit interviews Noncompetition agreement Hiring of ex-felons, handicapped Wages during a transfer Fines and penalties Accepting gifts Annual party or outing Use of company equipment Good housekeeping Rehiring former employees Use of telephones How pay is computed Employee gift fund	Athletic activities Retirement First aid Preemployment credit investigation Confidentiality agreement Repayment of loans Expense reimbursement Referring applicants Coffee breaks Parking lot rules Fire drills Change of address, phone, etc. Bonding of employees Role of the personnel dept. Polygraph examinations Attending seminars/ meetings Conflict of interest Access to personnel file Proof of citizenship Security checks Overtime pay for supervisors Bond purchases Check cashing

HOW TO
GET MORE
FROM YOUR
EMPLOYEES

If you want to get more out of your employees, reward them." This simple principle is at the heart of Edward J. Feeney's program for improving employee productivity. Since founding his consulting firm, Edward J. Feeney Associates, in 1973, Feeney has specialized in applying behavior modification techniques to business. During 1981, he and his staff of twenty full-time consultants will have worked with more than 100 companies studying performance and recommending ways to improve it. As a result of implementing his suggestions, Feeney claims, his clients average a 200 percent to 600 percent return on the investment in his services during the first year.

Feeney believes his techniques have universal applicability. He has worked with all types of firms—manufacturing, service, and retail. At least half of his clients gross below $50 million a year; about a fourth gross below $25 million.

Last month *Inc.* contributor Carol Rose met with Feeney in his Redding, Connecticut, office to find out more about his methods.

INC: Don't most employers already reward their employees in one form or another?

FEENEY: If you think about it, people are actually rewarded for *low* performance every day. Take overtime. The worker who gets more done has less opportunity to work extra hours. The slow worker is rewarded with overtime. Or look at the way budgets are commonly decided. Often budgets are based on the previous year's expenditures. A department head who went $50,000 over budget is likely to get a $50,000 increase for the next year. But a manager who brought his department in at $50,000 under budget isn't given any extra money, even though he's more likely to spend it wisely.

INC: Are there methods of motivating employees that are ineffectual?

FEENEY: Managers should never review past bad performance with their employees. Criticism just doesn't work. Everyone reacts adversely to it, resists it. Employees get defensive, badmouth the company, sulk, and show low rates of productivity.

Group incentives aren't particularly effective either. The rewards are often too minuscule to matter to the individual employee. And rewards distributed to everyone, such as flexitime, profit-sharing, or bonuses don't work, because the worker gets the reward regardless of performance. Merit or even salary increases are also less useful than you'd think, because they're added permanently. We recommend managers deal with what they want their employees to do in the present and near-future. And that the reward be a consequence of the employee meeting that expectation.

INC: So what have you found most effective?

FEENEY: Money. I firmly believe money is the single most powerful reinforcer. It's a myth held by some management people that money *isn't* a strong reinforcer. What makes money so powerful is the multitude of reinforcers you can buy with it. And the reward doesn't have to be a lot either. We've found that small amounts of cash, given very often, are among the most potent incentives we've tried. In my own office I used money very successfully to get my secretary to do the billing—a task she hated—on time every month. She had asked for a raise. Instead I said I'd give her an extra $25 every month if she got the billing out accurately and on time. The first month she missed the deadline, and I withheld the $25. She complained, but the next month and for 44 consecutive months, she got it out on time.

INC: Is money cost-effective though?

FEENEY: It really is. Companies that balk at giving bonuses are often penny-wise and pound-foolish. Take a $5-million company that's experiencing waste that amounts to $100,000 annually. If the workers could cut this in half, the company would be saving $50,000 a year. The company can give 40 percent of that back to the workers and still save $30,000. Since a typical company of $5 million may be earning only $200,000 on the bottom line, it would increase its profits by 15 percent.

INC: There must be instances where money doesn't work.

FEENEY: Sure. We worked with one firm that employed an independently wealthy woman as a telephone reservations agent. The company wanted to fire her for wasting time and failing to meet production standards, but its hands were tied because of a labor contract. We tried getting some clue to what might motivate her and learned she had a lot of ideas about how the company should be run. So we tailored an incentive program just for her. Whenever she hit the target for making reservations, she got fifteen minutes with the manager to discuss her ideas. She became a very useful employee.

Rewards like this—I call them activity-related rewards—can be extremely effective. Employees will generally indicate the kind of reinforcers that will work for them. Listen to what they ask for, what they complain about. They may ask for time off, special equipment, additional training, or increased responsibility. They may complain about taking inventory, sweeping the floors, or putting labels on products. Whenever you have the choice, give your employees what they want when they exhibit the desired behavior.

INC: What about just praising the employee for a job well done?

FEENEY: Praise can be extremely potent. The trouble is, it's difficult to administer on schedule. And to be effective, reinforcers must be regular. Still, it should be used whenever possible—and in conjunction with monetary and activity-related rewards. A company president in particular can use praise very effectively.

Simply put, people perform better with praise. It's especially effective in the beginning stages of productivity programs—in helping staffs build up to certain levels or training them in specific techniques.

INC: You've pointed out that employees are often rewarded for poor performance. How do you tell, in terms of profits, what's effective behavior and what isn't?

FEENEY: First you need to define which areas would produce the highest profits if human performance were improved. For instance, we discovered the cost of labor for a typewriter-ribbon manufacturer was only 10 percent of the total product cost. But material was close to 50 percent and there was quite a bit of waste. We set up a system that allowed employees to measure for themselves how much they were wasting and put in an incentive for reducing waste. As a result the company's after-tax earnings rose from about 2 percent of sales to 6 percent.

Next, decide by what standards you want to measure employees. Observe workers on the job and compare the behavior of those who perform well with those who don't. Try to quantify jobs to see their dollar value. Every task can be quantified—everyone eventually generates an output. Look at numbers of letters filed or typed, data entered into a computer, speed in processing paperwork. You can isolate the elements in any given task and give them dollar values.

INC: Do you have a systematic way for training employees in effective behavior?

FEENEY: We set up a performance measurement and feedback system before suggesting appropriate incentives. We usually develop a feedback chart listing very specific behavior. We made a chart for an airline, for example, listing items departure gate agents could check off. They'd note after each interaction whether or not they did such things as make gate announcements or call each passenger by name—things we'd already concluded were effective.

Ideally employees should monitor their own performance. They'll catch mistakes faster and get immediate feedback when they're doing well. You're showing them you trust them, too. Self-monitoring also reminds them constantly of the standards they're working against. It's important that the monitoring occur as soon as possible after the transaction—or even while it's progressing. Delayed feedback isn't very effective.

INC: So after you've analyzed performance, developed standards, and set up a workable feedback system, you're ready to develop incentives.

FEENEY: Exactly. Once you know precisely what you want, reward it. Here's a typical case. Not long ago a furniture manufacturer with a chain of independent dealers called us in to look at declining sales. We looked at the figures and identified the top salespeople. These people sold five to six times more than others, but if we asked them why they did so well, they couldn't really say. One salesman said it was in his blood—he came from a family of super salespeople. Since we couldn't give the others transfusions, we had to watch what they did.

By observing the leaders, we learned their behavior really did differ—they'd come right out and ask for the order, make more home visits, get the customer's name right away, and so on. Once we knew what worked, we made up a checklist and asked the employees to monitor themselves.

We saw, too, that when it came to any kind of incentive system, management was actually giving disincentives for good performance. For instance, the average ticket from a sale made in the home was $2,200 compared to $568 from a sale made in the store. But the salespeople had to pay their own mileage for home visits. And commission wasn't paid until the furniture was actually delivered. Hardly incentives for making home visits. We recommended the company pay mileage and change the way commissions were paid. We suggested salespeople be paid a portion of their commission immediately after making the sale; the percentage they'd get would be directly proportional to the percentage of the down payment. As a result of these changes, overall sales increased dramatically. Down payments shot up from 12 percent of the sale to 40 percent or 50 percent, and home visits increased by 4.5 percent.

INC: When and how you give rewards seems important.

FEENEY: Scheduling is one of the most important aspects of any incentive system. It's crucial to give the reward frequently and consistently. Initially, to reach the performance level you want, you should reinforce almost every time the desired behavior occurs. Even if the person tries and fails, you should reinforce the effort. You want him to keep trying. You also reward any improvement, however slight. Then once the productivity level has been reached, you gradually reduce the frequency. When the desired behavior has been achieved, you can cut down still more. This keeps employees from taking the rewards for granted or from feeling overcontrolled. It also saves the company time and money. However, it's necessary to continue a definite schedule of rewards, keeping them frequent enough to maintain the productivity level. Aim for an interval between reinforcers that's as large as possible without adversely affecting performance.

INC: I imagine the schedule of reinforcement would depend on the kind of behavior you want.

FEENEY: Yes. A reinforcement schedule can be either fixed or variable. To maintain performance at a uniform level, I always suggest reinforcing on a random schedule. Give your employees the incentive twelve times a year, but don't tell them when they'll be getting it. This avoids a feverish, deadline burst of activity followed by a slump.

Situations in which a uniform level of performance is required include places where work flows from one department to another and should flow consistently. Or where you're looking for regularity. For example, a quality-control inspector should do a consistent number of checks per hour. There's no advantage in his doing 1,000 as opposed to 10. What's important is that he base his data on a regular number of inspections.

If, on the other hand, you want performance peaks and valleys, reinforce predictably on a fixed time schedule. Arrange the reinforcement to coincide with your peak activity period.

Where you need to maintain performance at a consistently high level—for example routine jobs where speed is important—you should tie reinforcement directly to performance rather than to a time schedule. Reinforcing after a fixed and fairly small number of positive responses by an employee gives him or her maximum incentive to maintain high levels of performance. A cash bonus in small amounts is the perfect reinforcer in this situation, because it's positive and can be used with great frequency.

Companies whose production schedules tend to be heavier at the end of the week or month could also benefit from fixed reinforcement schedules.

INC: So, in a nutshell, your message is to reward the worker for good performance.

FEENEY: Absolutely. Quantify the dollar value of human performance, set up a system for developing and maintaining this desired performance, then reward it consistently. People like to be rewarded. They just do not resist getting gifts, recognition, money, or preference in job assignments. They like it and want more of it. And they'll work harder to get it.

INCENTIVES
CAN BE
BAD FOR
BUSINESS

Whether they know it or not, most executives are Skinnerians. It was Harvard psychologist B. F. Skinner who popularized the theory of positive reinforcement, which holds that presenting a reward after a desired behavior will make that behavior more likely to occur in the future. To our pets we say, "Good dog!" and offer a biscuit. To our employees we say, "Good job!" and offer a performance bonus.

It seems to make sense. But research has been accumulating that shows tangible rewards as well as praise can actually lower the level of performance, particularly in jobs requiring creativity. Study after study has shown that intrinsic interest in a task—the sense that something is worth doing for its own sake—typically declines when someone is given an external reason for doing it.

Author and sociologist Philip Slater put it starkly in his book *Wealth Addiction:* "Getting people to chase money . . . produces nothing except people chasing money. Using money as a motivator leads to a progressive degradation in the quality of everything produced."

The problem is not with money per se, which most of us find desirable. Rather, it is the fact that waving dollar bills in front of people leads them to think of themselves as doing work *only* for the reward. Performance tends to suffer as a result.

In one study, Teresa M. Amabile, associate professor of psychology at Brandeis University, asked seventy-two creative writers to write some poetry. She gave one group of subjects a list of extrinsic reasons for writing, such as impressing teachers and making money, and asked them to think about their own writing with respect to those reasons. She showed others a list of intrinsic reasons: the enjoyment of playing with words, for example, and satisfaction from self-expression. A third group was not given any list. All were then asked to do more writing.

The results were clear. Those given the extrinsic reasons not only

17

wrote less creatively than the others, as judged by twelve independent poets, but the quality of their work dropped significantly after this brief exposure to the extrinsic reasons.

This effect, according to other studies, is by no means limited to poets. When young tutors were promised free movie tickets for teaching well, they took longer to communicate ideas, got frustrated more easily, and did a poorer job in the end than those who got nothing. In another study, a group of subjects who contracted in advance for a reward made less creative collages and told less inventive stories. Students who were offered a reward for participating in still another experiment not only did more poorly at a creative task, but also failed to memorize as well as the subjects who received no reward.

What's going on here? The experts offer three explanations for such findings, and all of them have important implications for managers.

First, rewards encourage people to focus narrowly on a task, to do it as quickly as possible, and to take few risks. "If they feel, 'This is something I have to get through to get the prize,' they're going to be less creative," says Amabile. The more emphasis placed on the reward, the more inclined someone will be to do the minimum necessary to get it. And that means lower-quality work.

The very fact of turning a task into a means for attaining something else changes the way that task is perceived, as a clever series of experiments by Mark R. Lepper, a professor of psychology at Stanford University, demonstrated. He told a group of children that they could not engage in one activity they liked until they took part in another. Although they had enjoyed both activities equally, the children came to dislike the task that was a prerequisite for the other.

Second, extrinsic rewards can erode intrinsic interest. People who come to see themselves as working for money or approval find their tasks less pleasurable and therefore do not do them as well. "Money may work to 'buy off' one's intrinsic motivation for an activity," says Edward L. Deci, a professor of psychology at the University of Rochester and a leading authority on the subject.

What's true of money is also true of competition, which, contrary to myth, is nearly always counterproductive (see "No Contest," Managing People, November 1987). Deci put eighty subjects to work on a spatial-relations puzzle, and he asked some to solve it more quickly than those sitting next to them. Then each of the subjects sat alone—but secretly observed—in a room that contained a similar puzzle. It turned out that those who had been competing spent less time working on the task voluntarily—and later told Deci they found it less interesting—compared with those who didn't have to compete. The external prod of winning a contest, like that of a bonus, makes a task seem less enjoyable in its own right. Not surprisingly, what's seen as less enjoyable is usually done less well.

But there is a third reason why the use of external motivators can backfire. People come to see themselves as being controlled by a reward. They feel less autonomous, and this often interferes with performance. There's no shortage of data showing that a feeling of freedom trans-

HOW SMALL COMPANIES ALLOCATE BONUSES TO EXECUTIVES*

Discretionary	58%
Achievement of sales goals	24%
Achievement of profit goals	30%
Percentage of sales	8%
Percentage of profits	28%
Return on equity/assets/sales	8%

* Total exceeds 100% because of multiple responses.
  Source: 1987 *Inc.* Executive Compensation Survey

lates into happier and more productive employees. In 1983–84, Amabile and Stan Gryskiewicz, of the Center for Creative Leadership, in Greensboro, North Carolina, interviewed 120 research-and-development scientists, asking each to describe one event from their work experience that exemplified high creativity and one that reflected low creativity. The factor they mentioned most often, by far, was freedom or its absence. Receiving a clear overall direction on a project is useful, the scientists said, but they worked best when they could decide for themselves how to accomplish those goals.

Rewards are often offered in a controlling way, and to that extent, says Deci's colleague Richard Ryan, they stifle productivity. He emphasizes the enormous difference between saying, "I'm giving you this reward because I recognize the value of your work," and "You're getting this reward because you've lived up to my standards." Likewise for verbal feedback: the question isn't whether you give enough of it, or even how positive it is. What matters is how controlling the person perceives it to be.

This point was made in a study conducted by Deci, Ryan, and James Connell. From questionnaires completed by several hundred workers in a corporation that manufactured business machines, they found that those who worked for controlling managers were less satisfied with their jobs and more concerned with pay and benefits. The attitude seemed to be, "If you're going to control me, I'm going to be alienated, and what I'm going to focus on is money." In a related laboratory study, Ryan found that when subjects were praised, told in effect, "Good, you're doing as you should," instead of simply letting them know how well they had done, motivation was low.

Does all this mean that employees should be paid less or ignored when they do good work? Definitely not. Is it an argument for scrapping incentive plans? Probably not. What the research indicates is that all incentive systems—along with verbal feedback—should be guided by two clear principles. Higher-quality work, particularly on jobs requiring creative thinking, is more likely to occur when a person focuses on the challenge of the task itself, rather than on some external motivator, and feels a sense of self-determination, as opposed to feeling controlled by means of praise or reward.

Practically speaking, this means that incentives announced in advance are more likely to undermine performance than are unexpected bonuses that recognize an outstanding job after the fact. Particularly deadly are incentive programs run as contests in which some teams (or individuals) will not receive bonuses no matter how well they perform. Managers need to consider the impact of any incentive payment on the workers who *don't* receive it—another hidden cost of rewards.

Provided these conditions are met—and everyone feels the system for awarding bonuses is fair—incentives may not be harmful. But a supportive workplace, one in which workers are allowed autonomy and are not only informed about company goals but help determine them, may not even need incentive systems.

The larger point is that innovation cannot be forced but only allowed to happen. You can help create the conditions that allow it by playing down the significance of rewards and playing up what employees find appealing about the task itself. Effective supervisors take care of their subordinates' financial needs but don't make a big deal about money and its relationship to performance. Instead, they concentrate on the most powerful motivator that exists: the intrinsic interest people have in solving problems. People are most interested when their curiosity is aroused—when discrepancies exist between what they thought was true and what they've just encountered—and when they are challenged by a task that's neither so difficult as to be overwhelming nor so simple as to be boring.

What's more, employees should be matched with the kind of work that they find interesting. "In hiring we almost never look at intrinsic motivation," Amabile observes of most organizations. Yet having someone work on the sort of problem to which he or she is naturally attracted is likely to produce better results than using some artificial means to boost performance.

Of course, some tasks are universally regarded as dull. In these cases, the idea is to get people to internalize the importance of doing them—to transform external reasons into internal incentive. Deci and his colleagues have recently turned their attention to this problem. Their findings suggest that a manager should acknowledge that the task is boring, explain why it needs to be done, and try to maximize a feeling of autonomy.

In another experiment, Deci and graduate student Haleh Eghrari had ninety subjects press a computer-keyboard space bar every time a dot of light appeared on the screen, a task most found uninteresting. The researchers admitted to one group that the activity wasn't much fun, but they explained that it could be useful for learning about concentration. These individuals were praised for their performance afterward. A second group was told that they "should attend to [the task] very carefully . . . since it will be for your own good." Later they were informed that they had done well "as [they] should." The third group was given only instructions without explanation.

As with the competition study, each subject was then left alone in a room and given the option of continuing to play with the computer once the experiment was over. Those in the first group chose to do this more often

president of Procter & Gamble Co., said that the chief challenge of big business was to shape its policies so that each worker would feel he was a vital part of his company with a chance to share in its success. P&G's landmark profit-distribution plan divided profits between the company and its workers in the same proportion that labor bore the total cost. If wages were 50 percent of costs, the workers' bonuses would be a whopping one-half of profits. Sadly, P&G's example was not widely emulated, and today only 15 percent of the U.S. work force participates in such a profit-distribution or gain-sharing plan. A paltry 10 percent own stock in their companies, despite the generous ESOP incentives available since 1974.

The significance of this appalling record was suggested by a survey that Daniel Yankelovich conducted in the early 1980s. U.S. and Japanese workers were asked to agree or disagree with the statement, "I have an inner need to do the best I can, regardless of pay." The U.S. workers, maligned by so many (especially their managers), outscored the Japanese. Then the two groups were asked a much more practical question: who did they think would benefit most from an increase in worker productivity? This time, the tables were turned. Some 93 percent of Japanese workers thought that they would be the prime beneficiaries, while only 9 percent of the Americans felt that way. In other words, Japanese workers believe that increased productivity is a matter of self-interest—and the facts support them.

So Kohn may be right about the pitfalls of incentive systems, but he's dead wrong in suggesting that bad incentive systems are a major problem for American business. The far greater—and more commonplace—sin is to ignore the worker's incremental contribution altogether.

Competition is still the spice of life. The ancient philosopher's line is that the world would have no beauty without contrasting ugliness. For better or (sometimes certainly) for worse, comparison—which is to say, competition—is the chief motivator for individuals and groups, whether it takes place in teen beauty pageants, among Nobel-level scientists, or on the shop floor.

Now competition can go too far. I agree with Kohn that competition may cause a worker to focus excessively on speed and what the guy next to him is doing, thereby losing sight of the intrinsic value (that is, quality) of the task at hand. I have seen the disastrous consequences of basing incentive pay on work group competition—especially when workers are not trained adequately, and when the company does not provide the time, the place, and the tools to work creatively on individual and team improvement.

On the other hand, I have also seen group competition work wonders in a plant, under the right conditions. Look at New United Motor Manufacturing Inc. (NUMMI), the extraordinary joint venture between General Motors and Toyota. Its predecessor, a GM plant, was at the bottom of the heap in terms of productivity, quality, absenteeism, and numerous other performance indicators. Now, the 2,500-person operation scores at the top. The dramatic turn-around is mainly a result of employee involvement. Every worker is trained in at least a half-dozen jobs; each person must be good enough to train his or her colleagues; fellow hourly workers are team leaders; and the company provides all the training, tools, time, and space required for problem solving. Competition among teams is sky high, on the job and off, but meticulous preparation came first.

But, group competition aside, I think Kohn is focusing on a secondary issue here. We face enormous business problems today, and they were not caused by too much competition. Rather they reflect the broad deterioration of the national economy—a consequence of the virtual absence of competition from World War II until about 1965. During that period, almost all of our major industries became tidy oligopolies, in no shape to compete with anyone.

Kohn decries the ill effects of copying, and too much distraction with competition. I submit that it is far worse to ignore the competitive reality, and to refuse to copy at all. Consider the Ford Taurus, one of the biggest American product successes in decades. For years, Ford had systematically ignored or denigrated Japanese automobiles and, to some extent, European ones as well. In developing the Taurus, however, it did a complete about-face, purchasing hundreds of vehicles from around the globe. Following a copy-and-exceed strategy, Ford set out to best those vehicles on hundreds of features, from the inner workings of the engine to the ease of gas-cap removability. That is, of course, precisely the strategy for which we once scorned the Japanese. Ironically, it is the same strategy with which the Americans (and then the Germans) surpassed the British in years gone by. The process may not be as creative as Kohn would like, and it certainly reflects an obsession with competition. But it works. And its success demonstrates once again that we have far more to fear from too little than from too much competition.

Let me just add a personal note in conclusion. Many years ago, I was a Ph.D. student of management, and I read with pleasure almost every word of psychologist L. Edward Deci, whom Kohn so reveres. Intrinsic motivation and autonomy have been major, if not dominant, themes in all three of my books. And I acknowledge that the astonishing success of enterprises such as NUMMI are testimony to the importance of intrinsic motivation and self-control. For drawing attention to those issues, Alfie Kohn deserves two full and hearty cheers.

But I must withhold cheer number three, for I feel that, overall, Kohn is addressing matters of secondary concern. Excessive emphasis on incentives and competition is simply not a wide-spread problem in American business. What we need is a lot *more* positive reinforcement, and a lot less of the negative kind, throughout the corporate landscape. And far from cautioning companies about the dangers of incentives, we should be applauding those that offer their employees a bigger piece of the action. Likewise, we should welcome competition, whatever its source. We have competitive pressure to thank for the positive things that are happening in large companies these days, including the new willingness to copy from the best. Better that than the practices of inward-looking companies and workers, closed to ideas that were Not Invented Here. They are the ones who have made such a bungle of American economic performance world-wide over the past twenty years.

Life ain't simple, as that *New Yorker* cartoon suggested, and neither is business. Kohn has much to say that is thoughtful and wise, and that ought to be heeded. But let's not ignore the forest for the trees.

—TOM PETERS

THE
AUTHOR
REPLIES

—and refuses to back down

When Tom Peters argues that the problem in the real world is too little positive reinforcement rather than too much, he is doing two things at once. He is describing what's going on, and he is prescribing what needs to be done instead. I have no quarrel with the first. But the cartoon phrase "Oh, if only it were so simple . . ." seems more appropriate to Peters's prescription—that we should just crank up the positive reinforcement— than to my review of the hidden problems with this tactic.

I do not dispute his argument that praise is better than punishment. Likewise, I say "amen" to his call for more goodies to find their way to workers instead of executives. The research shows quite clearly, however, that—when people feel controlled by praise, or when they come to think of themselves as working for extrinsic rewards—quality is likely to suffer. Peters's suggestion that we simply base those rewards on quality rather than quantity will not solve the problem. It may well be true that we have the capability to "keep score on quality," but it is clearly untrue that "the sheer act of keeping score will provide a positive stimulant to improvement."

The problem is not just that an artificial incentive for doing a job well is a less effective motivator than intrinsic interest in the job. It's that the incentive can actually do substantial damage by eroding that interest. And the more a task involves creativity, the more a manager must take care in handing out bonuses and praise. All else being equal, concentrating on the score is probably an *obstacle* to improved performance in the long run, at least for tasks more complicated than licking envelopes.

Up to this point in the discussion, though, my differences with Peters are probably more a matter of emphasis than of substance. I agree that workers ought to be recognized more for their efforts, and he agrees that rewards can stifle innovation. But we part company, and I think Peters parts company with the data as well, on the question of competition. As I tried to show in an earlier column ("No Contest," November 1987), the best amount of competition in a company—or anywhere else, for that matter— is none at all.

Even though it's well supported by the evidence, this fact flies in the face of everything we were raised to believe. It's hard to accept the painful truth that we are all made losers by the race to win, that excellence has nothing to do with beating others, that any win/lose arrangement not only is psychologically destructive and ruinous to relationships, but also inherently counterproductive.

A close reading of Peters's examples shows that the wonderful results he cites were not really a result of competition at all. Is social comparison or learning by observing useful? In moderation, yes. But benefiting from others' example isn't at all the same thing as trying to defeat them. Does the Toyota–General Motors collaboration seem to be successful? If so, it's because of the employee involvement Peters describes. I'd be willing to bet that the workers (and their productivity) are thriving in *spite* of the additional element of group competition, not because of it.

It baffles me that someone with Tom Peters's expertise would help perpetuate the myth that "we have far more to fear from too little than from too much competition." What we have to fear is too little attention to quality, and competition is to quality as sugar is to teeth. Its effect on self-esteem is similar.

The research to back this up (which I review in my book, *No Contest: The Case Against Competition*) is so persuasive that I'd say the single most damaging mistake a company can make in devising an incentive plan is to set it up competitively. If a bonus is to be made available to employees, any individual (or, better yet, any team) that reaches a certain level of performance should receive that bonus. A contest sets us against one another, so that my success makes yours less likely. In reality, we have a great deal to fear from too much competition, and any amount is too much.

—ALFIE KOHN

THE
"OWNERSHIP"
FACTOR

Lots of his competitors assume that they understand what Dave Liniger is doing with Re/Max International Inc., his internationally franchised real estate business. Their assumptions, however, in many cases mislead them.

Likewise others outside of real estate have concluded that what they think this transplanted Hoosier is doing in his business wouldn't work in their own. They ought to think again.

Liniger has built his company around a compensation system that appears to attract the best the industry breeds into his business—and to hold them there. Sixteen thousand Re/Max agents are, as Liniger likes to say, in business for themselves but not by themselves. Few have any financial incentive to leave Re/Max to set up a competing firm.

The skeptics' premature dismissal isn't hard to understand. The Re/Max compensation concept *sounds* terribly simple: the agent who handles the sale of a property keeps the commission—all of it. He doesn't split it 50–50, or even 80–20, with the owner of the real estate agency. He just keeps it—and pays the expenses incurred.

"Oh," says a competing broker whom I asked about Re/Max, "you mean rent-a-desk? They never work."

Right, they don't—at least not for long or very well. Liniger borrowed his idea from a rent-a-desk agency that he once worked for. It's still around but hasn't grown substantially. Between a rent-a-desk operation's owner and his agents there's no support, no encouragement, and no soul to an association that is strictly contractual.

So how come Re/Max is doing so well? Why, with only 22 of the 5,000 real estate agents operating in Orlando, did one of the Re/Max agencies there account for 3 percent of the transactions completed during February? Or how come in the Denver market and in parts of Canada, where it's been established the longest, Re/Max handles 20 percent and more of the residential housing sales? And how come last year Re/Max, which wasn't even doing business yet in New York City and had only a toehold in other

Northeast markets, accounted for 287,500 completed residential real estate transactions, behind only Century 21 Real Estate Corp.'s 700,000 and Coldwell, Banker & Co.'s 313,850?

Maybe people don't appreciate what Liniger is really doing because the concept, while it is a radical departure from the way most service businesses compensate their employees, is too simple—misleadingly so. But given the numbers he has produced, it seems odd to argue, as many conventional brokers do, that Liniger's compensation plan just doesn't work. Re/Max International sure *looks* like a success. You'd think the doubters would at least wonder why.

Since Liniger opened the first office in Denver in 1973, Re/Max has grown, as of February, to 14,909 sales associates working from 1,017 franchised offices in the United States and Canada. By Liniger's count, Re/Max agents participated in residential real estate transactions worth $24.4 billion last year, a 55 percent increase over 1985. Liniger and his wife, Gail, own 97 percent of the Denver-based franchisor, Re/Max International. Its gross revenues, which depend more on the number of agents in the Re/Max system than on the value of the commissions they generate, exceeded $7 million last year, by *Inc.*'s estimate. Liniger will say only that they continue to grow 40 percent to 50 percent annually. He claims the company has shown a profit each year save one since 1977.

When you ask Liniger, chubby and scrubbed-faced at forty-one, what makes the company work, he sits you down at the end of a long, polished wooden table in his commodious conference room, dims the indirect lighting, and presses a single button. A curtain slides open and nine computer-controlled rear-screen projectors silently throw to the wall a mosaic of images and graphics that fade into one another, overlap, grow large, disappear, reappear again. Re/Max, the wall would have you believe, is the corporate hot-air balloon fleet, a slogan ("Above the Crowd"), conventions, advertising support, franchisee services, referral networks, relocation programs, training, seminars, and awards banquets.

Very impressive, and the wall doesn't lie. Re/Max is all those things today—just like other real estate franchises that distinguish themselves by the color of their blazers or the design of their signs. But those things can't account for Re/Max's growth, because ten or twelve years ago, when the growth was just beginning, the company had none of them. All Liniger had in his kit back then was a compensation concept. After the slide show, when he talks without the fancy packaging, you find that that's what he's still selling today.

His market? Not the real estate buying-and-selling public, but the brokers and agents who service them. "We're in the real estate salespeople business," says Liniger. The distinction is an important one.

To appreciate the appeal—to broker and agent alike—of the Re/Max system, you need to spend a minute with the microeconomics of the real estate business.

In a typical residential sales office, agents, or sales associates, work on commission. Actually, they work on partial commission. When an agent generates a commission in a transaction, she or he keeps roughly half of it. The other half belongs to the house—the broker who owns the agency.

How much does a sales associate take home? The National Association of Realtors (NAR) doesn't calculate an average annual gross income figure for agents, but the Washington, D.C.–based trade association does publish extensive survey-generated data. Using the NAR numbers for 1985 (the most recent survey), you can figure that the average (full-time equivalent) agent's share of the commissions she generated that year was $14,475.

The other half of the commissions went to her employer, who, after expenses, earned an average of $58,543 in 1985. That figure includes the firm's entire net income and the employer's own salary but none of the commissions income he might have generated himself.

So, according to the NAR survey, the average real estate agent is probably shopping with food stamps, and her boss, while doing considerably better, is in no danger of achieving a perch on the *Forbes* 400.

Some sales associates, however, earn a great deal more than the average. Verna Parfeniuk, for instance, took home $160,000 last year, which was extraordinary even for Parfeniuk, the top producer in the Winnipeg, Manitoba, agency where she had worked for fourteen years. More fortunate than most agents, Parfeniuk enjoyed a 60–40 commission split. But it still galls her that she had to hand $4 of every $10 she generated in commissions over to her agency—even after she had more than covered the expenses that the agency had incurred on her behalf. What were those expenses?

The NAR survey found that each agent a broker-owner employs costs, on average, $12,618 annually in expenses (which includes the broker's own salary). But Parfeniuk handed her boss $80,000 last year. "I got tired of giving so much of my [commissions] to the broker," she says. After all, he didn't spend very much more to support her aggressive and effective selling than he spent on other agents generating half or less of her commission volume.

If agents such as Verna Parfeniuk are bringing four, five, or more times the average commission income into an agency, other agents must be contributing far less. Hotshots like her, in other words, not only carry their own shares of the expense and profit burden, but they must subsidize the schmoozing of the less-than-average agent and the training of the newcomer as well. About 80 percent of new sales associates don't renew their licenses after the first year. "There were always so many new people," Parfeniuk says, "and after fourteen years I decided to do something for myself."

The something she did was jump over to Re/Max, where sales associates keep 100 percent (or, in some offices, 95 percent) of their commission income. If she had been there the year before, instead of earning $160,000 on a 60–40 split, she'd have kept $240,000.

But she would have had to pay the expenses that the broker had picked up for her. OK, let's say she pays what NAR figures it costs a broker to keep an agent employed, $12,618. She still nets $227,382, which is substantially

RE/MAX REDUX

How 100-percent commissions work in other service businesses

Opportunities for applying Re/Max's compensation concept abound. Other service businesses have tried it, if only on a small scale.

For instance, ten years ago, in her first job as a travel agent, Lesli Gordon started at a salary of $125 a week. Last year, however, she pocketed $85,000—every cent of the commissions she had earned minus her share of overhead expenses and a small monthly fee paid to the agency owner.

"People should get paid if they do the business," she says.

Gordon is a rogue in the travel industry. Most agents still work on salary, although a few take a percentage—usually about half—of the commissions they earn for their agencies. Gordon was on a 70–30 split for a while—70 percent to the agency owner, 30 percent to herself.

The problem with the travel-agency business, according to Gordon, is the same one that Dave Liniger spotted in real estate. "Agency owners," she says, "are always having to bring in new agents who aren't up to speed. So there's never enough money to pay the top people what they're worth."

Gordon's solution, as well, resembles Liniger's. With her owner's consent, she created a separate branch around the corner from Omni Travel's principal Cambridge, Massachusetts, location. Then she recruited partners, now numbering eight, mostly from outside the agency, to work with her. "I didn't want the doctors' wives," she says, "the Junior League types who were doing it for fun. I wanted people who were living on their salaries. They're the ones that need the money."

One partner, a top performer, was bringing $11,000 a month in commission into his former agency and drawing a salary of $375 a week. "He was getting screwed," says Gordon. Last year, their second full year in business, the nine partners in Gordon's breakaway office accounted for more than 40 percent of Omni's business, earning more than $600,000 in commission on some $6 million in sales.

In addition to the monthly fees, they also pay the agency owner for such services as bookkeeping and accounting, covering much of Omni's overhead. But Gordon's success and the agency's owner's apparent reluctance to embrace the 100 percent commission concept throughout the agency mean that Omni tentatively has a tiger by the tail. The high earning potential of the rogue group around the corner could lure the better performers out of Omni's conventional agency office, leaving it with just new hires and the Junior League types.

Further, Omni's hold on the tiger's tail is tenuous at best. The nine full-commission partners don't own the business in the sense that they could sell it. "But we could pick up and walk away with it," Gordon says.

"Of course, salon owners don't like the rent-a-booth concept," says Don Rollfing, co-owner with Sandee Ricklefs of The Hair Cartel Inc., in Denver, which rents 18 booths to experienced, independent hairdressers. He charges each $130 a week. Other salon owners don't like the concept, according to Rollfing, because they don't make as much money at it.

At least they think they wouldn't.

If Rollfing were running a traditional 50–50 shop, his expenses would be much the same as they are now, and he'd probably be grossing at least $250 a week for each hairdresser he employed. But he doubts that he'd be able to keep all 18 booths filled—and certainly not with good employees. The young ones just out of school don't know anything, he says, and the good ones are hard to find. His turnover in five years of owning The Hair Cartel, he claims, is less than a dozen.

The rent-a-booth salon is easier to manage, Rollfing says, because the hairdressers working there are, by necessity, more experienced and more self-disciplined than those in a conventional shop.

When their chairs are all rented—which is most of the time—Rollfing and Ricklefs collect $2,340 a week. Each of them also cuts their own customers' hair, earning slightly more than $1,000 a week on average. Pooled, that all comes to $225,680 in gross revenues. They could make it more by opening another salon, but Rollfing points out that he and his partner deliberately work only four days a week. "Money," he says, "is not the most important thing to me. I like to smell the roses."

---

more than the dollars she actually took home. Or, say her expenses are twice—even five times—the average. She *still* takes home more.

In the dollar department, the high-performance sales associate clearly comes out ahead when she can bank all (or substantially all) of her commission income net of expenses. Re/Max, with an average of 12,000 agents on board last year, claims that it generated commissions of $816 million—meaning that the average Re/Max agent grossed $68,000 before expenses and management fees, or about $53,600 net of those items. That's a lot more than the $14,475 that the average agent took home.

It would be fair to say, then, that one reason Re/Max works is that Re/Max agents earn more.

But what about the broker? What does the 100-percent commission concept do for him when his agents appear to be getting all the money?

"Oh," says Mike Stefonick, a Re/Max broker-owner in Blue Bell, Pennsylvania, since 1978, "it solved all my problems." *All* his problems?

In exchange for their keeping the total commission, Re/Max agents pay their brokers monthly fees and expenses. These vary among offices. Typically, however, they include the following:

• Their pro rata share of common office expenses, that is, basic telephone service, rent, secretarial help, utilities, and insurance. Associates, however, control these costs. They and the broker-owners decide by vote whether to buy a new office computer, replace the carpet, or hire a second receptionist. These costs can run between $500 and $1,000 or more per month.

• All of their personal expenses, which includes long-distance calls and special advertising or marketing costs;

• A monthly $50 joint-advertising fee, most of which is spent at the regional level for high-dollar-cost programs such as TV and billboards; and

• A management fee, usually $300 to $600 a month, negotiated annually and fixed by contract.

And how does that solve all of Stefonick's problems? First, he says, if you own a conventional real estate office, everyone gets paid before you do. "Here, I have no overhead." The agents, he says, pay all of it in their shared expense fees.

"In a conventional office, if my top performer takes a two-month vacation," he says, "my cash flow suffers." Re/Max agents must pay their bills whether they're having a good month or a bad one, so the Re/Max broker's cash flow is more predictable. Stefonick says he doesn't have to leave money in the till to pay his expenses, because the cash rolls in every month.

And most of the monthly management fee each sales associate pays, Stefonick points out, is pure net profit to him, just like a salary.

"So," he boasts, without any embarrassment, "I operate for free out of an office with a guaranteed profit and get to keep everything [in commissions] I make."

If, as Re/Max claims, it had 14,909 agents working from 1,017 offices in February of this year, then each office had, on average, fifteen agents. The average agent pays his broker a monthly management fee of $400, about 20 percent of which the agent passes on to the Re/Max regional office. In turn, about $20 of this goes to company headquarters. The typical Re/Max broker-owner can expect a gross income—before his own commissions, if any—of $4,800 per month, or $57,600 annually. That looks all right compared with the National Association of Realtors survey finding of $58,543 for the average (non-Re/Max) broker, but it's not exciting.

This calculation, however, penalizes Re/Max for its high growth rate. Many Re/Max offices, only recently opened, haven't yet recruited their full complement of agents. You get a better idea of the average broker's earnings by looking just at Re/Max offices that have been open for at least two years. These, on average, contain twenty-eight agents, giving the broker a more respectable income of $107,520 after regional fees and before his own commissions.

Then not only are Re/Max agents banking more than their peers in conventional agencies, but Re/Max brokers are making more, too. How can this be?

Re/Max commission rates on property sales are no higher than any other real estate company's, and Re/Max agents handle the same kinds of property sales—high end and low end—as other agents. Where in the world is the money coming from? The explanation lies in the fact that they just handle more of them.

According to the 1985 NAR survey, the average agent collected commission income on fifteen transactions that year. Re/Max claims that its average agent, on the other hand, was involved with twenty-four transactions in 1986. The average Re/Max agent, in other words, handled 60 percent more deals than his conventional-agency peer.

That difference would explain why there is so much more revenue for Re/Max brokers and agents to split. Of course, it doesn't explain how the agents were able to generate all those transactions. Could it be that Re/Max sales associates are, on average, better producers than the typical real estate agent?

Re/Max agents handle more sales and generate more commissions, founder Liniger suggests, because they have, on average, four more years' experience than the typical agent. They tend to be the best performers in any area. They *have* to be, he says, or they couldn't survive at Re/Max.

When an agent signs on with a Re/Max broker, she or he immediately confronts a monthly nut that can run from $1,200 to $2,000 or more in management fees and expenses. Not many trainees or part-timers will willingly assume an obligation that large. There are no spots in a Re/Max office for part-time agents, neophytes, sluggards, or anyone else who can't generate enough commission income to meet expenses. Consequently, Re/Max brokers, as a rule, won't hire—indeed, *can't* hire—any but veteran, high-producing agents. These are the only ones who can afford to work in a Re/Max office. And consequently, Re/Max brokers and their agents are governed by a relationship that is subtly but profoundly different from the relationship between a conventional broker and his agents.

"The broker's job," says Re/Max vice-president Bob Fisher, "is to make sure his agents stay with him by making them as happy as possible. That's why we say we're in the sales-associate business."

By contrast, a Century 21 broker with a conventional office says that his job as broker-owner is to be a motivator and a teacher. "People come to me with no knowledge, no investment, and I train them. . . . I give them all my leads, all my expertise." And he hopes that, with his help, they become good agents. The commission they share with him will, eventually, return his investment and then some. "What I'm about," says the broker, who doesn't want his name used, "is creating leaders."

His problem, though, you'll remember, is that eight out of ten agent recruits don't stay beyond a year. Consequently, much of his teaching—and his office overhead—is lavished on short-term assets that are really liabilities—trainees who don't yet pay their own way. And then, when he *does* create a leader, the idea of who needs whom in this relationship gets turned on its head. Good, experienced agents don't need teaching. What they need is motivation and office support, but half of their commission income is a heavy price to pay for that. To protect his investment and his cash flow, this particular Century 21 broker requires new agents to sign a noncompete agreement. And noncompete agreements do not happy agents make.

The Re/Max broker, on the other hand, can think of his agents as clients, not investments. They come to him trained and experienced, and what they want is good support—which they're willing to pay for with their management fees. To the extent that the broker provides it—in the form of well-managed office services, a pleasant working environment, and exposure to equally professional colleagues—he'll retain his client base.

San Crandall, an experienced sales associate, joined a new Boston-area Re/Max office last year. She likes it. "You're not working with people who don't know what they're doing," she says, "so you can turn something over to a colleague and not have to worry about it. . . . We have a manager who's there to fix any problems that come up. We get good feelings from the broker at the top. When we have office meetings we're always telling one another, you did a great job on this one or that one.

"It's really like being in business for yourself without having to be on your own. The person who wouldn't come into this environment is a person who doesn't feel confident, who is not in control."

* * *

Re/Max International, the company that Liniger started in Denver in 1973, is no longer in the real estate business per se. Now, it's strictly a franchisor producing products and services—training programs, awards banquets, corporate relocation, a referral network, advertising research, publications, and the like—that it can give or peddle to its broker-franchisees.

Like most franchisors, when Re/Max was young it depended on growth—the revenue generated by franchise sales—to survive. No more. Last year, according to Liniger, just 15 percent of its revenues came from franchise sales or renewals, a proportion that Liniger expects will continue to shrink.

In fact, Re/Max International could stop growing tomorrow—never sign up another agent or sell another franchise—and still survive quite well. That's partly because Liniger has kept the company private: its level of profitability matters only to him and the Internal Revenue Service. And partly it's because the company is financially structured—from international headquarters to individual brokerage—to live off its operating income.

The bulk of the franchisor's annual cash flow comes from the $250 annual dues each sales associate remits to the Denver headquarters, plus an override of about $20 per associate per month from each broker. With an average of 12,000 agents on board last year, Re/Max International should have grossed from dues and overrides alone nearly $6 million. That is, as Liniger points out, a steady income stream, not directly tied to the amount of commission income that Re/Max agents can generate. If Re/Max agents have a good year, they pay no more, but in a bad year they pay no less. Thus Re/Max International, like its broker-franchisees, thrives to the extent that it manages to satisfy, and retain, its agent-customers.

In 1973, the company consisted of a few understaffed Denver-area offices, each with a broker-manager. It was not the immediate success Liniger had fantasized. "I assumed," he says, "that every good agent would want to work for me. They didn't." The best of the agents he hoped to attract weren't interested in moving, no matter how much money he promised, from established firms to what might have been a fly-by-night. In the first month he interviewed 204 potential sales associates. Four agreed to join him.

Competing conventional brokers badmouthed the concept. When Stacy Burton left a conventional Atlanta agency to join Re/Max, his wife began getting anonymous phone calls at home. "I wouldn't say they were threatening," says Burton, "but they wouldn't leave their names, and they'd tell her, 'He's crazy,' and 'He'd better watch what he's doing.' It only egged me on."

Thinking at first that he could build a system of company-owned agencies, Liniger had opened eight offices by the end of the first year but recruited only twenty-one agents. Losses accumulated, generating several hundred thousand dollars of short-term, mostly trade, debt to suppliers and advertising media. A group of investors that he had counted on for capital pulled out when its suburban real estate development ventures failed, victims of the 1973 OPEC oil embargo. It took him another full year to find twenty-one more agents, and more than three years before the roster topped 100.

In 1975, Liniger abandoned the company-owned office strategy and sold his first franchise to expand beyond Denver. But growth was still slow. He was making a mistake, Liniger finally realized. "I was targeting the wrong people." He'd been trying to persuade brokers with existing agencies to convert to Re/Max and getting very few sales. Eventually he figured out why. "They'd have to fire 80 percent of their agents, all but the top performers, to get the concept to work," he says, "and they weren't willing to do that." So Liniger shifted his focus to wooing other brokers' sales managers and top agents—people ready to go out on their own. The results were dramatically better, and those kinds of people are still buying Re/Max franchises today.

Tenacity has its rewards. Early this year Re/Max moved into New York, the last major state to approve its franchise documents. It's already the number-two agency in Canada. What next? "All we want is half of the top 20 percent of the real estate agents in the United States," Liniger says. That would be roughly 78,000 sales associates (and another 12,000 in Canada), which doesn't seem a completely outrageous goal. Century 21, with 75,000 full-time U.S. associates, is currently number one.

With success comes challenge, from inside or out. In what ways is Re/Max vulnerable? At least three threats exist: the real estate market could take a dive; the competition could outmaneuver Liniger; or he could grow smug.

What if the market collapses and residential sales fall off by, say, a third?

Falling commission revenues would hit sales associates in their pockets, but how badly? The average non-Re/Max agent, who takes home only $14,475 now, would be living—if you could call it that—on just $9,650. On the other hand, two-thirds of the average Re/Max agent's $68,000 annual gross revenue is still $45,000. If her expenses hold at $1,200 a month, the agent has $31,000 to get by on. If she took her $45,000 in commissions to a 50–50 agency where the broker covers expenses, she'd take home only $22,500—no reason to leave Re/Max.

And logic suggests that it might not even come to that. If it's true that Re/Max agents are more experienced and better producers than the typical agent, they ought to outperform the market in a downturn. In the early 1980s, when mortgage rates topped 15 percent and residential sales declined, Liniger says the Re/Max market share per associate actually *increased.*

Up the line, Re/Max brokers and the franchisor itself are cushioned, but not isolated, from market shrinkage, since their revenues depend not on commissions but on the flat fees that agents pay. Only to the extent that in a market downturn agents either don't pay their bills or leave the company does Re/Max or the brokerages suffer. During the 1981–83 real estate recession, Liniger says, they didn't write off any agents' management fees, but they sometimes stretched collection. And would a Re/Max agent want to leave?

Say the market really took a hit, falling by half. The Re/Max agent who stayed on would pay the same fees but generate just $34,000 in commission to cover them. Her net: $19,600. What if she moved to a 50–50 agency where expenses were covered by the broker? She gives half her $34,000 in commission to the broker and keeps $17,000—still no reason to leave Re/Max.

OK, so the market threat doesn't seem substantial. What about competition? From whom? Conventional agencies can never beat Re/Max in agent compensation. Suppose a sales associate in a conventional agency keeps half of the first $100,000 in commissions she generates and 80 percent of the excess. If she brought $200,000 into the agency, she would net $130,000—$50,000 plus $80,000. Not bad. But the Re/Max agent would keep $185,600 net of expenses, quite a bit better. Besides, the conventional broker can't afford to be too generous with his top agents, because it's their commissions that subsidize the agency's recruiting and training.

A large conventional-agency organization could always convert itself to the Re/Max format, but that hardly seems likely. It would have to shed too many people. And as for a start-up modeled on his own plan, Liniger says that could happen, but Re/Max enjoys a tremendous lead.

And that leaves smugness, the third threat. Take your market for granted, succumb to the arrogance of success, or mistreat the people you sell to, and you'll be supplanted no matter how clever your concept. So far, Liniger talks like a man who respects that truism.

"You have to be careful," he says, "of getting hardening of the attitudes, of thinking that yours is the only way. This year Gail and I went to the Re/Max Colorado state convention like we always do, but we decided not to stay. We'd been to so many, you know. We were driving home that night, and I thought, 'No, we can't do this.' I told Gail that somewhere there's another Dave and Gail, and they're out talking to their operating people while we're going home to sit on our butts. That's how companies fail. So the next day we drove back and rented a hotel room. . . . We're not to the point that we know it all yet."

—TOM RICHMAN

UP FROM
DRUDGERY

Diedre Moire Corp. is not without its imperfections. Typical for its age, the seven-year-old company relies far too much on the talents and energy of its founder, who, in the course of a quarter hour one Monday morning: repaired a laser printer, debated with New Jersey Bell over underused WATS lines, manned a switchboard during the operator's unexplained absence, and interrupted a meeting to take a message that the office refrigerator was broken.

So what? As he and his firm mature, Stephen Reuning will probably learn to be more executive and less handyman. For now, what's more interesting than Diedre Moire's rough edges is the shape Reuning has given it. He's experimenting with an organizational innovation that, if successful, could make the company a significant force in a service industry—employee recruiting—that is full of tiny firms that tend to stay small.

But it's not just in employee recruiting that Reuning's experiment is potentially useful. The East Brunswick, New Jersey, firm could be a model for other businesses in which the selling of a service and its delivery are closely linked. Insurance and travel agencies, for instance, or financial planning firms, spring to mind. They are all businesses in which the employee who performs or delivers the service or product also sells. His or her performance is easily quantified.

The overarching effect of such a system for service industry employees is that while most firms can provide only a job, albeit a well-paying job, Diedre Moire (mo-RAY) offers a career. Consequently, people who at practically any other recruiting firm would have burned out and left tend instead to remain at Diedre Moire and move up within the organization. Reuning believes that lower turnover will enable him to expand the company by building on the capital that accumulates in the employees he has already trained and nurtured.

A new idea? Not at all. But it's an apparently unique adaptation of a powerful old idea to a new use. Others in the industry say they've not seen it tried before.

* * *

40

Reuning, 31, is a college dropout who devours ideas like a kid eating popcorn. He's read every self-help, sales management, and motivational book on the shelves and listened to the audiotapes, too. Heavily sales oriented, Reuning nonetheless pursues eclectic interests. "Most young, single guys go home on the weekend and party. Steve, on the other hand," recalls a former business partner, "would go home and build a television set and in the process teach himself electronics." More recently, when he needed a computer programmer, Reuning learned programming himself from books. Spanish and basic German, too. And how to structure his business so that it wouldn't peak out prematurely like other companies in the employee-recruiting field.

Reuning left Rutgers University at Newark after a year because, he says, it was too slow. "I could have learned in three weeks what they spent a year teaching me." After two other jobs, he answered an ad and was hired in 1979 by Richard Southern, who operated a small recruiting firm in New Jersey. This company, like Diedre Moire today, occupied a middle spot in the spectrum of recruiting firms. On one end are the high-volume employment agencies whose fees are paid by the job applicants they place in, for the most part, clerical and line jobs. On the other end are high-priced executive recruiters who work on retainer for the company seeking to fill senior positions.

Diedre Moire makes its money by filling technical and line-management positions. It, too, is paid by the company doing the hiring—usually 30 percent of the annual salary that goes with the job. But unlike retained search firms, such personnel consultants as Diedre Moire work on contingency—no match, no money. And they rarely work on exclusive contracts, which means they're competing with other firms on both sides of the deal: for clients with jobs to fill and for candidates qualified (and willing) to fill them. Each deal means closing at least two sales. "When you sell a product," says Michael Randazza, who works for Reuning, "you put it in a box and it goes out the door. In this business, you've got to talk the suit into the suit bag."

Recruiters at Diedre Moire work at small desks in crowded offices. The din of dozens of simultaneous telephone pitches is punctuated frequently by impatient intercom messages—"Mike Randazza to your desk. Mike to your desk." When a consultant is having a problem closing either part of a sale, he—most Diedre Moire consultants are men—may switch the call to a speakerphone so that his manager or colleagues can coach him. It adds to the cacophony. On the walls are charts and pushpins in various colors to track activity. Every morning brings a fresh start, a blank sheet to fill before the day ends. Typically in the industry, recruiters burn out in a few years; the average recruiter holds his job for 33.7 months.

The problem, Reuning saw after working in the business with Southern, is that good people have no place to go in a two-tiered company in which the owner manages and everyone else sells. Poor performers become discouraged and leave. Good performers leave, too, often to start their own firms. It's their only escape, the only way they can stay in the business but get off the phone.

That's what Reuning did. He had learned the business quickly while working for Southern, and in 1980 he opened R.M.S. Systems Inc., his own recruiting firm, with Southern as a shareholder. There was nothing remarkable about the firm. It was a clone of the business he was leaving. And eventually its growth stalled, too. Reuning decided to find a solution to the growth problem.

He might have franchised. The only really large firms in the industry, Snelling & Snelling Inc. and Dunhill Personnel System Inc., grew by franchising their operations in hundreds of locations. But franchising doesn't pretend to solve the root problem behind slow growth—burnout. It simply multiplies revenues by multiplying locations; each franchise of these larger firms tends to be much smaller than the typical independent recruiting firm.

Reuning did what he always does when he doesn't know what to do. He turned to books. He pulled back from the business, giving it just enough time to keep it going, and spent six months studying and talking to people. There had to be a way, he thought, to interrupt the vicious cycle that continually stripped firms like his of their best recruiters, who would themselves become competitors only to spawn yet another generation of ambitious deserters.

He called nearby Rutgers and other university business schools. He devoured the books they suggested. No one book held the answer he was seeking, but together they helped him formulate a strategic concept. It had its roots in three very different companies—Procter & Gamble, First Jersey Securities (now owned by Sherwood Capital Inc.), and Mary Kay Cosmetics.

From P&G, Reuning took the notion of internal competition—that no existing company product (or service) should enjoy exclusive call on a company's capital or exclusive rights to one of the company's markets. If product managers within P&G can compete for the same diaper buyer, selling groups within Diedre Moire can compete for the same clients. Intergroup rivalry, he figured, would stimulate performance.

From First Jersey Securities he took to heart lessons about training and motivating salespeople. Notwithstanding the company's problems with federal regulators, says Reuning, its sales force was very good. "First Jersey had pumped-up salespeople who were gung-ho First Jersey. Bob [Brennan, the director] was a showman." Brennan built great company loyalty and esprit into his salespeople, says Reuning. They weren't just individuals working for their own gain. They understood that when First Jersey made money, they all made money.

Reuning wanted that attitude to inform his own organization. Today Reuning's employees and managers testify that it does, partly because Diedre Moire provides its salespeople with opportunity to expand with the business. And partly because Reuning does play the showman, always hyping the company and dramatizing the role that the individual plays within it.

From Mary Kay, however, came Reuning's radical innovation. He took the cosmetic company's multilevel marketing scheme and transformed it into multilevel management. Mary Kay uses the pyramid sales structure because, besides selling product, it motivates salespeople to recruit and train other salespeople. The motivation is straightforward: senior sales reps share in the commissions earned by those they recruit. Mary Kay uses the pyramid sales system to build a large, active outside sales force. Reuning uses the principles of the same system to build a stable, self-managing *inside* sales organization. It's an intriguing adaptation.

In 1982, when he had finished his six-month sabbatical and was ready to put his new strategy in place, Reuning changed his company's name. R.M.S. Systems became Diedre Moire Corp., a name Reuning says sounds nothing like an agency. (Diedre and Moire were the first two proper nouns in a novel, *The Seventh Moon of Saturn*, that Reuning had seen on an employee's desk.) But the new company was much more than R.M.S. with a different name.

Conceptually, multilevel management is simple. Employees at Diedre Moire advance through four levels of sales and management responsibility, their potential compensation and their management responsibilities growing at each level. Promotion depends largely but not exclusively on an individual's ability to sustain certain sales levels for a prescribed time. And the option of whether to advance always rests with the employee. When he or she satisfies the promotion requirements, the decision to move up or stay put, permanently or for the time being, belongs exclusively to him or her. At the highest of the four management levels, the individual becomes Reuning's partner—the 50 percent owner of a branch office. If it weren't for that possibility, say several of the highest-earning employees, they wouldn't stay at the company.

Here's how multilevel management at Diedre Moire is supposed to work.

You come aboard as a consultant, a worker bee in the business, earning a 30-percent commission on the client fees you generate. At Diedre Moire, if you're reasonably good, you can expect to make $30,000 or more per year. Jim Busch, a Diedre Moire consultant, made about $40,000 in 1987.

Let's say that you are as good as Busch. When you get to the point where your fees average $7,400 per month for six consecutive months (that's $26,640 per year income to you), you qualify for a promotion—to group leader. Group leaders hire and train their own consultants, and they collect a 7-percent override on those consultants' commissions. Further, once you're a group leader, if one of your consultants becomes a group leader himself, you continue to collect an override on his sales *and* on the sales of all the consultants in his group as well. The override—up to 3-percent—depends on the subgroup's production level. Now, you're in the chips—earning $40,000 or more per year. Lance Hilfman, a group leader, projected his earnings at $60,000 last year. But you can do better still.

To get to the third level, floor leader, you must have at least five consultants working for you. Their output must average $7,400 per month or more for three consecutive months. Moreover, two of them must themselves be group leaders, each supervising at least two consultants. Now, you earn the same commissions and overrides as a group leader—plus a 1-percent commission on the sales of any subgroup headed by a floor leader that you hired and trained. Michael Randazza, a senior floor manager, collected close to $80,000 in commission and overrides last year.

Sound complicated? It isn't, really. Besides, you don't need to conquer the numbers to grasp the idea.

There's still one additional level, the fourth, remaining in Reuning's system. He calls it office manager-partner. To qualify, a floor leader must have eight consultants working in his or her personal group, oversee two subgroups of at least four consultants each, and have had one of his or her group leaders advance to floor leader. When that happens, Reuning wants to make you his partner and give you an office of your own to run. You may take half of your consultants with you.

Diedre Moire will finance the office start-up costs and own all the expansion venture's stock, which you'll begin to purchase with your profits until you hold 50-percent of the shares. Five years after Reuning initiated the concept, there still are no office manager-partners at Diedre Moire, a surprise and disappointment to the founder. "Maybe they're making too much money as floor leaders to make the extra effort," he theorizes. He is not, however, discouraged.

That is how the system is supposed to work. Here's why Reuning thinks it will.

First, and most obviously, multilevel management allows employees to build equity in the business without diluting Reuning's own ownership or control. Reuning gives up only half of the additional business that an office manager-partner builds, and anyway he gets paid for that half. But even before employees get to that fourth rung on the management hierarchy, they acquire equity of another sort. They "own" part of the earnings of the employees they have recruited. "Most companies don't give people a piece of the action. Here," says Reuning, "if you go for it, you can have it."

Second, and more significantly, it puts employees in control of their own incomes and rates of advancement by removing the usual subjective points of evaluation. Promotions depend exclusively on employees' measurable production—and on whether and when they want to advance. "Eighty percent of the people in a group, if you ask them," says Reuning, "would put themselves in the top 20 percent of the group. So if you don't promote them, you're going to have a problem. With a numerical system, it's up to the employee to rationalize his failure to advance. 'Maybe I didn't want to work that hard this year,' he might say, 'but I know I could if I wanted to.' He can also say, 'I won't be ready until I'm thirty.' If he does, he's not looked down upon."

Reuning wanted a system that would say to a person, "This is your company, not mine. I'm going to give you leadership and facilities. I'm going to make sure the systems are here. How far you go is up to you."

Did he get such a system? And does it work?

"I got the standard you-can-go-as-far-as-you-want routine when I came," says group leader Hilfman, twenty-nine, who has been with the company for three years. His complaint is that when he arrived, there was opportunity but no training to help him seize it. "Any salesperson could be a group leader," he says, and people without training—including himself—often made poor group leaders.

Here was a problem that Reuning hadn't fully anticipated. It may have removed unfair subjective barriers to advancement, but the multilevel-management system also incorporated two assumptions that turned out not to be entirely valid. One was that good salespeople would necessarily make good sales *managers*. Not true, at least not all of the time.

Group leaders at Diedre Moire are expected to train junior consultants in effective selling techniques. How do you get inside a company to find the individual who's ready to make a move? How do you get to the hiring decision maker? Group leaders also must help new consultants learn to pace their days. Too much time spent on candidate searches and not enough on finding slots to fill may boost production this week but leave a consultant with no jobs to offer in weeks ahead. Effective closing techniques? Effective interviewing techniques? It's the manager's responsibility to pass them on—and to see that paperwork gets done and that the company's database is constantly updated.

People who are untrained as managers probably won't perform these duties well. Promoting untrained people to group leader, says Steve's younger brother Gregory Reuning, 30, often meant that the performance of their groups suffered. Gregory himself joined the company as a consultant and has advanced to floor leader.

The second assumption implicit in Reuning's original plan was that anyone who qualified for advancement would want to advance. There was, according to consultant Jim Busch, pressure on people to move up before they were necessarily ready—resulting, again, in managers not yet capable of managing.

The fallacy of both assumptions became apparent when people like Hilfman, who was terrific at sales but not so terrific at managing people, were promoted to group leader. Hilfman's group didn't perform well. He has had several consultants work for him but fail to blossom until they were moved to someone else's care.

Extensive and pervasive management training appears to have solved one problem. Reuning inaugurated a daily training meeting, attendance mandatory and participation spirited, running from 8:15 until 9:00. People attend off-site seminars, and the impressive library of audiotapes and books gets heavy use. The absence of training, apparently, is no longer an issue, and neither is pressure to advance.

"My strength," says Busch, 29, "is that I'm an excellent salesman. My weakness is that I'm not well organized." He has been eligible to be a group leader for months, but he's held himself back. "I get management tapes, management training. They encourage me to take stuff home. . . . Taking on somebody [as a group leader] now would not be a service to them, because I'm not organized enough to be able to help them. Soon, though, I should be able to manage it."

The multilevel-management system has another attractive characteristic: the effects of bad management, whether from inexperience or inability, are locally contained. A poor manager can affect the performance only of the people in his own group. A single managerial misfit cannot poison the rest of the organization. Nor is there any conceivable way that he will be promoted and given broader responsibility.

Other system problems?

Jay Earl earned $37,000 as a group leader in 1986 and expected to do much, much better in '87 but didn't. It's the turnover rate, he complains. In a fifteen-month period, Earl had to hire ten consultants to end up with three. "The turnover takes away some of the incentive to be a manager," he says.

But Reuning points to the same attrition rate, and instead of seeing a problem sees progress. "If I want to add one person now," he says, "I have to hire three. But I used to have to hire ten." In his opinion, shared widely, the turnover rate will continue to come down as the training produces better managers. "People won't be quitting because they think their managers are incompetent," Gregory Reuning says.

They would be quitting if the multilevel-management system weren't in place.

"The system? That's exactly why I came to the company," says Busch.

If he weren't managing three other people, says Earl, he wouldn't be here, "because I'd be burned out being a recruiter on my own. Besides the override incentive, managing gives you a break from the daily grind of working the phone."

Reuning, by and large, is pleased. Multilevel management clearly gives the company advantages in recruiting and retention, but it doesn't pressure the company's margins. The total commission Diedre Moire pays on fees produced comes to a maximum of 41 percent (30 percent to the consultant, 7 percent to the group leader, as much as another 4 percent to those whose consultants have started subgroups). Diedre Moire also offers a benefits package worth 23 percent of compensation. In contrast, other recruiting firms may pay straight commissions of 30 percent or more with some benefits or 50 percent commission with no benefits, both without the opportunity to move up in the managerial hierarchy.

The failure of the system to produce an office manager-partner probably will be remedied soon. Michael Randazza, at thirty-four a veteran floor leader, qualifies for the move. In 1986 he earned $79,000. "Why haven't I become a partner yet? I enjoy going home. If I had a company, I'd live there. I'm a single man with other interests." But Gregory Reuning expects to be running his own office in the next year; he's now a floor leader earning $60,000. And Jay Earl expects to be a partner, too, though he doesn't know when. "If he didn't offer that option, I'd have been gone a long time ago."

Diedre Moire, with its unique shape, is already larger by sales and number of employees after just five years than the majority of firms in its industry. It employs forty-five people, including support staff, nearly four times the work force of the typical firm. Reuning projects 1987–1988 sales at $3.6 million, up 47 percent from the year before. Net income, he says, should be about 10 percent.

Its organizational structure does impose some limits on Diedre Moire's *rate* of growth. Reuning says it's constrained mostly by the rate at which the company can train managers—a process that takes a minimum of six to eighteen months. "If I had $1 billion in capital," he adds, "I couldn't grow any faster than I am." Still, he expects the number of operating employees—consultants and managers—to double to sixty or more within the next twelve months and to double again the following year. The nice thing, he says, is that beyond expanding his support services, he doesn't have to plan for 120. Given the multilevel management system, the growth just happens—so long, that is, as the company's market, which is closely related to the business cycle, holds up. A recession would hurt, but Reuning is working on diversification tactics.

Expansion through franchising would allow faster growth. But Reuning believes that franchising would cost him control of service quality and that the multilevel-management system is not easily replicated by a franchisee who hasn't been bred within the system.

Multilevel management is Reuning's attempt at changing—and, he hopes, improving—the performance of an organization by altering its *structure*. He didn't set out simply to do a better job of running a company with the aim of achieving superior results. Diedre Moire is organically different from the conventional recruiting firm. The people employed there work within a different motivational framework intended to produce a different set of responses.

Reuning is ready to apply multilevel management to a new data-entry department. Reuning will calculate an average cost per entry—say, 75¢. Then he'll pay the clerk a salary, but at the end of the month he'll multiply the clerk's entries by .75. If that product is greater than the salary, the clerk gets the difference as a bonus.

Clerks who consistently meet production goals will, over time, become supervisors, earning an override on the production of people under them. The idea here, as in sales, is not to create a chain of command. Supervisors aren't bosses so much as they are mentors. "The idea," Reuning says, "is to have someone with wisdom working next to you and to give that person an incentive to see you succeed."

A big advantage to multilevel management, as practiced at Diedre Moire, seems to be that it makes personal and company goals congruent. "Here," says Hilfman, "my professional growth is in my hands. The same for the money I make. I don't know anywhere else I could say that."

—TOM RICHMAN

WHY WORK?

A company's goals are necessarily organizational: growth, profitability, market share. But goals have to be accomplished by people, and people have their own objectives. Hence the fundamental and age-old problem of management is how to motivate employees to do what the company needs done.

Traditionally, motivation has been a matter of carrots and sticks. Authoritarian-minded managers prefer the latter: supervise employees closely, reprimand or dismiss them if they screw up. Progressive-minded managers like the former, relying on "positive reinforcements" such as bonus systems and awards. Despite their differences, both groups have one big trait in common, which is that they treat people like jackasses. Move in the right direction and you'll get your carrot. Act up and you'll get a whack on the rump.

So long as jobs were simple and American corporations unchallenged, this approach to motivation won managers' hearts and minds by default. Today it's coming under attack, not least in the pages of this magazine (see "Incentives Can Be Bad for Business," January, and the follow-up exchange between Tom Peters and Alfie Kohn, April). As Michael Maccoby observes in *Why Work: Leading the New Generation* (Simon & Schuster, 1988), there's a reason for this. The current global marketplace is not only more competitive, it's qualitatively different from what preceded it, and the differences have dramatic implications for the problem of motivation.

Think about the connections. Today, customers expect high-quality, customized goods—which means that employees must pay extraordinary attention to detail. Customers also expect extensive personal service, which means that employees must respond to their needs with courtesy and intelligence. As information is more widely diffused throughout business organizations, employees are expected to work smart as well as hard. What Maccoby calls the "technoservice" economy, in short, is redefining many people's jobs. Workers who once just loaded trucks or processed papers now are expected to make judgments, solve problems, develop productive relationships with customers and colleagues—in other words, to work like thinking human beings.

Right here is where motivational systems appropriate to jackasses begin to break down. Traditional punishments and rewards can get people to show up for work and do what they have to do to look good in the boss's eyes. But what companies need today is employees who want their performance to *be* good, not just look good. For that, conventional approaches to motivation are usually too blunt. No amount of supervision, for instance, can force an employee to smile at a customer and be helpful when the boss isn't looking. And no bonus system yet invented can reward someone who sees a little problem in the mail room, solves it on the spot, and never tells anyone that the problem even came up.

Nearly all traditional motivation systems, moreover, are founded on the principle of treating everyone the same. Such systems may elicit similar behaviors—they do in donkeys—but they can't elicit similar attitudes. A reprimand may turn around one employee and only anger another. A bonus may be received gratefully or cynically, and may cause as much resentment as inspiration among those who didn't get it. Yet what a company needs in the modern economy is productive attitudes, not just productive actions. In this sense, motivational systems based on external rewards and punishments are fundamentally out of date.

What's the alternative? According to Michael Maccoby, it's to de-emphasize external motivations—carrots and sticks—and instead to understand people's internal motivations—their drives, interests, and values.

Now this is a squishy notion, no doubt about it. *Understand employees' motivations?* (I hear you say.) *Suppose they're motivated to go fishing?* Bear with me. Nearly everyone wants something from work in addition to a weekly paycheck. Feelings of accomplishment or security. Opportunities to meet new people or learn new skills. Nor are people stupid; they know that what they want at work has to be compatible with business objectives. If they can further their own goals while meeting the company's, however, no manager need worry about motivation. They'll drive themselves.

What's most interesting about Maccoby's book is its investigation of people's work goals. A psychoanalyst and cultural anthropologist as well as a much-sought-after business consultant, the author has spent more than a decade interviewing and surveying managers and employees at every level. *Why Work* assembles the wide variety of responses that he got into half a dozen character types. "Experts" get their satisfaction mainly from the work itself—doing a craftsmanlike job, for example. "Helpers" get theirs mainly from working with—and finding ways to assist—other people. "Self-developers" view work mostly as a means to develop their own skills, knowledge, and competencies. There are other types, too—but you get the idea.

Because people bring different personalities and aspirations to the workplace, they react differently to managerial attempts at motivation. Experts, for example, typically treasure their independence and therefore resent managers who try to cajole or coach them into higher productivity ("A good supervisor should be seen and not heard," said one). So a good motivational tool is to give them as much freedom as possible. Self-developers, seeking to learn, usually welcome a more collaborative relationship with senior managers. ("I like supervisors who will work with you in a give-and-take relationship.") Experts may view a bonus as appropriate recognition of a job well done. Self-developers are more likely to view bonuses as manipulative, particularly if the whole bonus system is perceived as unfair or arbitrary.

What's a manager to do? One step, obviously, is to get to know your employees—not so that you can put them into Maccoby's admittedly stereotyped pigeonholes, but so you can understand what they're looking for from work. Another is to mistrust across-the-board incentive systems, which necessarily assume that everyone will react to carrots and sticks in similar ways.

Where possible, motivation should come from the job itself and from how it helps the company, rather than from external punishments or rewards. About half of Maccoby's respondents, for instance, view themselves as experts, saying that their prime sense of satisfaction comes from a job well done. Suppose their responsibility was not just the task at hand but figuring out how they could do it better? Manufacturing workers could investigate more efficient production scheduling, better tools and equipment, or more training. Customer-service employees might decide they needed more information—and would have to figure out how to get it. Just such a notion, of course, is behind the many employee-participation and employee-involvement schemes that both large and small companies have been implementing over the past several years. "Participation is a way of asking the worker, 'How can you do your job better?'" says one expert on the subject.

Self-developers, says Maccoby, make up about a fifth of the work force and are typically concentrated among younger workers. In some ways this group presents managers with their thorniest motivational problems. Self-developers value money, but only as "part of the total reward package they would like to negotiate." They value advancement, but only if career doesn't interfere too much with family or personal life. What they seek from work is not only a chance to learn but a chance to contribute—which means they need to understand how their jobs tie in with the company's objectives. For the self-developers on your staff, maybe the best thing you can do is offer them regular chances to learn new tasks, all the while showering them with information about where the company is headed and how each new job helps it get there.

From one viewpoint, Maccoby's message is stark. The old methods of motivation don't work anymore. New methods will have to begin with people's own goals—and people's goals differ. From another viewpoint, however, the message reveals an advantage small companies enjoy over their larger competitors. Most big companies feel they have to treat employees as interchangeable parts, relying on well-defined incentive systems to get them working together. Small-company managers, by contrast, don't need grandiose across-the-board policies; they can more easily tailor their motivational tools to individual interests. Growing companies in particular are constantly creating new and challenging jobs, which makes it easier to match corporate goals with individual ones.

In an economy in which success depends more and more on people pulling together—as human beings, not as donkeys—that's a powerful competitive edge.

—JOHN CASE

SHOW AND TELL

If you're one of those chief executive officers who gives only lip service to the idea of keeping your employees informed about how your company is doing, you could be making a big mistake. Years ago I found out quite by accident that because I kept the people who worked for me in the dark, they tried to guess what was going on. They guessed wrong, and they guessed negatively.

My new company was growing quickly, and my five managers and I were putting in some pretty long hours together. As time went on, I began to pick up on some innuendos that bothered me. Although it masqueraded as a joke, the gist of the message I was getting was this: we're doing the work, while you're getting most of the credit and all of the money.

At first I was only annoyed, but the more I thought about it, the more irritated I became. So I did the right thing, but for the wrong reason. I called the managers together to let off some steam. First, I asked them to write down what they thought the company's profits were and how much they thought I personally was drawing out. I was amazed when I gathered up and read the papers. Everyone had guessed much too high.

Still somewhat upset, I then passed out copies of our financial statement and went over it item by item. I made it very clear how much money we needed to bring in just to finance our growth. And as far as I was concerned, if the company were going to make it, they'd have to work even harder. Now it was their turn to be amazed. They'd been assuming all along that the higher our earnings, the fatter my personal bank account was getting.

Once they saw the whole picture, they started asking questions, and I could see they were genuinely interested in how the company was doing. I told them that from then on we'd have regular management meetings. I would answer any of their questions and would distribute and review our monthly financial statements, a practice I've continued ever since, in good times and bad.

The word "epiphanic" means having an intuitive grasp of reality through learning something simple and striking, and the great management truth I learned that day had just such a quality. Its implications went far beyond sharing the company's financial statements. As time went on, my managers became almost as interested in all facets of the company as I was. This was not only healthy for the company, which was growing too fast for me to keep on top of everything, but my job became much more satisfying as people took on more responsibilities and became less dependent on me. All this did not, of course, happen overnight. But subtle changes occurred almost immediately.

To my surprise—and delight—the more light I shed on the company, the more information I got back in return. In our management meetings and on a casual basis, people were losing their inhibitions about speaking up, and I was getting some very useful feedback. It seemed to confirm the old law of physics that for every action there is an opposite and equal reaction. Gradually, many of the burdens of running the business began to shift from me to my managers, and they seemed to welcome it.

Since I'd fallen into this new arrangement by accident, I wasn't quite sure just what was happening. In an effort to find out, I invited one of the managers out to lunch a few months later. As we talked, I told him that I had noticed a new enthusiasm in his attitude toward the company and his work, and I wondered what had caused the change. He didn't hesitate for a second. When I started passing out copies of the financial statements and explaining them, he said, it was as if someone were explaining the game of hockey to him and showing him how to keep score. He felt he could now tell when we were winning the game, when we were behind, and what needed to be done to keep going forward. He said he felt more comfortable knowing what was going on even if it didn't always affect his own job. If he knew what the problems were and could help out in solving them, it made him feel better. His previous employer had told employees only the good news. When they weren't getting any news, they assumed it was bad, and they were usually right.

This was a revelation to me. As an inexperienced manager, I had assumed that if the company were ever in real trouble and I opened up to my people about it, I'd run the risk of the good ones leaving when I needed them most. But this manager was telling me the opposite would happen, and he was right. I've found since that almost without exception employees who are kept posted, and feel as if they have a stake in the business, work even harder when all is not going well. While we were waiting for the lunch check, my young manager said one more thing that has stuck with me ever since. "If I had to tell you in one sentence why I am motivated by my job," he said, slightly embarrassed, "it is because when I know what is going on, and how I fit into the overall picture, it makes me feel important."

I believed then, and I believe now, that the strongest motivation a person can have is a sense of self-fulfillment. But only a few jobs in my company—or in any other organization—are really that self-fulfilling, and these are usually held by people at the top who already are highly motivated. What this manager told me years ago has proven to be true: employees who have a sense of importance about their role are highly motivated workers, and an easy way to develop that sense of importance is to tell them what is going on in the company and where their work fits in.

For many years, it's been my policy to answer any questions my people have about the business, and there have been very few times when I've thought it was in the best interest of the company not to be completely open. When that does happen, I say that I can't give an answer then, but will when I can. Although they may be curious, and may speculate, they know from working with me that I will always keep my word.

The question for a CEO, I've come to realize, is not whether you owe it to your employees to keep them abreast of company affairs. That's irrelevant. Forget what you owe your employees. Focus instead on your own interests and those of your company. If my experience is any guide, you'll discover that the more open you are, the more responsibility your people will take on. And the more committed they'll feel to you and your organization.

I started one of my companies twenty-nine years ago, and almost half of the people who are now with that organization have been with me more than fifteen years. If I had to give the main reason why they have stayed with me through thick and thin, it would be that I have made it a point not to keep them in the dark.

—EVERETT T. SUTERS

THE
TURNED-OFF
WORKER:
WHY
JOHN
AND
MARY
WON'T
WORK

Harold Brown, in his early thirties, repairs office copy machines for a major manufacturer. He's known as one of the best in the branch office where he's worked for four years. He visits his office once a week, for an hour or two; otherwise, he's out on the road. Not always working, however. Harold's good enough to fix most machines in minutes instead of hours. That means he has plenty of time to spare for coffee stops, long lunches, picking up his children at school. Harold calls that "working smart, instead of just working hard."

Twenty-seven-year-old Carol Kerr is ten months into her second job since leaving college, as director of advertising and promotion for a West Coast computer company. Her boss is delighted with her work; he's already given her two raises because he's worried that someone else in their competitive industry will steal her away. He has reason to worry. Carol is currently job-hunting.

Larry Tate has been a medical technologist all of his working life and he's now almost fifty. He's proud of performing tests that help physicians diagnose and treat their patients. There was a time when his supervisor knew he could count on Larry for the tough jobs, like middle-of-the-night emergencies. Now his boss thinks Larry is slowing down; maybe it's his age. Larry does his job, but nothing extra—no more late hours or rush tests.

Maria Caly, in her late twenties, is a kiln operator at a small dishware manufacturer in the Northwest. Talk to her over a beer after work and she'll tell you how difficult the dishmaking process can be: glazing errors, for example, can ruin an entire batch of dishes worth several thousand dollars. That's a big sum for a small company, a mom-and-pop operation that employs fewer than twenty people. Maria has some ideas on how to cut down on errors but she hasn't talked to the owners. "Why bother?" she asks.

What's the matter with Harold? And Carol and Larry and Maria? Why aren't they more committed to their jobs and their companies?

These are questions asked not only by bosses, but also by social scientists who monitor worker attitudes and performance. They say both factors have seriously deteriorated over the past ten years.

The signs are everywhere. People like Harold, Carol, Larry, and Maria (not their real names) can be found in virtually every company. Some, like Carol, talk of job-hopping. Others stay in their jobs but find ways to stay out of their offices and factories as much as possible; the administrative assistant who consistently arrives half an hour late and leaves fifteen minutes early, the young textile worker who says he'll only come to work four days out of every five as long as he can cover his bills on four days' pay.

Others are physically present, but admit they have little energy or enthusiasm for their work. Some perform their own tasks adequately, sometimes even superlatively, but refuse additional responsibility, even though it would mean more money or status: the twenty-two-year-old shift worker who avoids overtime or night work, the machinist who turns down a promotion to foreman.

Not even supervisors and managers are immune. They usually have a greater personal stake in their jobs and companies; their attitudes toward work should, therefore, be more favorable. Data collected from more than 150 companies over the past twenty-five years supported that assumption until last year. Then, for the first time, researchers Michael Cooper and Peter Gelfond reported a significant increase in managerial discontent. Cooper, who heads employee-attitude research for Philadelphia-based Hay Associates, describes these managers: "This is the fellow who plans a vacation for a week he knows he'll be asked to do extra duty, because a special project is due; or who politely refuses to cancel a weekly tennis match in order to have dinner with a customer."

Discontented workers can no longer be explained away as "the young guys who just don't know how to work" or "the old guys who don't have the horses to do the job anymore," or accepted as "just the price of doing business."

The price has gone too high in terms of declining performance within companies. In polls done recently by the Gallup Organization for the U.S. Chamber of Commerce, 83 percent of business leaders and 53 percent of workers at all levels agreed that worker attitudes are an important factor in declining U.S. productivity. That decline puts the United States near the bottom of the heap in terms of annual growth in gross national product per employed worker: 0.1 percent between 1973 and 1979, compared to Japan's 3.4 percent and Germany's 3.2 percent.

Are such figures tolling the death of the American work ethic? Is work itself and the concept of doing work well simply less important to most Americans than it once was?

The statistics say the answer is no. Columbia University economist Eli Ginzberg estimates that 24 million Americans, not currently counted as unemployed, want paying jobs and would take them if they were available. These include the young people and retired workers who want to move into the work force in unprecedented numbers.

The desire to work isn't limited to those who are not currently holding jobs. Seven out of ten working Americans say they would want to work even if they had enough money to retire immediately, according to a major survey done by the University of Michigan for the U.S. Department of Labor. They say they work to avoid boredom, to achieve personal satisfaction. One woman who is approaching retirement with apprehension puts it this way: "Work's the gas that makes me go. I don't know what I'll do without it."

Nor has there been any decline in the desire to do a good job at work. The most recent survey on worker attitudes, sponsored by the U.S. Chamber of Commerce, found that almost nine out of ten workers say it is important to them to work hard on their jobs and do their best. A majority also believe that it's possible to change worker attitudes and abilities, and thus improve a company's performance. The sample was representative of all American workers over eighteen: business owners and managers, professionals, tradesmen, clerical/office workers, salespeople, service workers, and laborers. Why aren't those attitudes reflected in the way people work?

Harold Brown says he started working smart rather than hard when his boss was demoted so that a friend of the new national service manager could take over the position. To Harold, the message was loud and clear: In this company, what's important is not what you do, but who you know. He can't leave immediately because he has two kids and a wife whose career is blossoming. So he does his job, draws his pay, and waits for the chance to move on.

Carol Kerr would rather not move on. She loved her job for the first three months, even though she and her assistant were putting in long hours to clean up the mess left by her predecessor. Then she overheard her boss tell her assistant that too much hard work could be threatening to other people in the department. Carol felt demoralized and stopped working extra hours. No one noticed; in fact she got two raises after that. She's confused and disgusted and says almost everyone else in the company is, too. "Nobody knows what's expected of him or her; nobody gets rewarded for anything in particular; and morale is horrible." The company blames its high turnover rate on a competitive job market.

At first Larry Tate didn't mind coming back to the lab at night to run emergency tests. Sometimes he even stopped at another lab on his way in to pick up test supplies because his supervisor hadn't ordered what he'd requested. He started minding after the last of a series of emergencies, one that kept him in the lab all night. He walked out past the doctor who had ordered the tests; the doctor said nothing. No one had ever said anything, but somehow this was the last straw. "All I wanted was a pat on the back, somebody who'd acknowledge that I was a valuable person. If no one else thinks my job is important—not important enough to make sure I have supplies, and to say thanks once in a while—why should I?"

One of Maria Caly's coworkers stayed after hours for a year to solve a glazing problem that was leaving dishes watermarked. The owners wouldn't accept his solution, until he tested it—also on his own time. When it worked, they gave him a pat on the head, says Maria, almost as if he were a child who'd stumbled onto something by accident. "They treat us like kids who work to buy soda and candy, not like adults who know more about making dishes than they do. What would make me work harder? A little respect, somebody asking my opinion."

It is tempting to dismiss these stories as saying nothing new: to say that the problems are inevitable ones in any work situation, that the companies represent that minority which will always be poorly run.

It is dangerous to do so. Workers do *not* dismiss them. The American worker expects more from his work than ever before because of social, economic, and demographic shifts that have been particularly dramatic during the 1970s (see box, below). Disappointment and frustration are the result. Job satisfaction among *all* categories of American workers declined significantly between 1973 and 1977, according to surveys by the University of Michigan's Institute for Social Research.

THE WORK FORCE: A NEW DIVERSITY

In 1950, the typical American worker was a white male, aged twenty-five to forty-four, who worked at a blue-collar job to support a wife and family.

In 1980, there was no typical American worker. Jobholders were almost as likely to be female as male; to be young as to be old. Less than 15 percent fit the description of the so-called traditional worker: a married male wage earner whose wife does not work.

That radical shift in the composition of the American work force resulted from equally radical changes in social values and economic conditions during the last three decades. It, in turn, has created new social values that affect the workplace—and will continue to do so throughout the 1980s.

The 1950s worker was scarred by the Depression and World War II. He saw self-denial and hard work as the road to the security, stability, and material well-being he longed for. The economy, fueled by the postwar demand for goods and services, rewarded him by doubling his disposable income during the next decade.

Yet the 1960s worker was less certain of the worth of financial rewards. Prosperity had not brought him or the nation the contentment he sought. Another war fueled social unrest and economic uncertainty. His children resisted simple obedience to authority and carried that resistance with them from classrooms into companies. They were better educated than ever before; the average worker now had almost one full year of training after high school. More of them were women, too, as females under thirty-five moved into the labor force at unprecedented rates.

By the 1970s, the American worker was turning from an ethic of obligation to others—his family, his employer, his country—that he had felt so strongly in the fifties. He stopped believing that self-sacrifice automatically paid off and turned instead to an ethic of duty to oneself first. So did his wife and the wives of his coworkers as they moved into jobs in large numbers: Nearly half of all married women were working by the end of the decade.

The two key changes within the work force that evolved during the sixties and seventies—more women, more educated workers—will make their clearest mark on the workplace of the eighties.

Most female workers will be strongly work-oriented, anxious for job success; at the same time, many will ask for personal satisfaction from work, as well as greater flexibility at work to accommodate their roles as wives and mothers. Their husbands may become less work-oriented since they are no longer the sole support of their families, and may also put a premium on job flexibility and more leisure time.

More and more working people will have training after high school and will come from middle-class families. They will care less about jobs that simply pay the bills, more about work they feel is self-fulfilling. They are apt to be frustrated by work they feel does not use their skills.

A third change will complicate these two. Because of the low birthrate of the sixties, the number of younger workers will drop. This fact and the aging of the baby boom generation will result in an overabundance of the prime-age work force—people aged twenty-five to forty-four who are usually trying to move up a career ladder. There will be fierce competition for promotions and great frustration for those who fail to attain them. As a result, some of these workers are likely to put more emphasis on traditional rewards—security, earnings, benefits, promotion, and retirement.

Throughout the eighties then, the mark of the work force will be diversity: in the types of workers, in the attitudes and values they bring to work, and in the benefits they seek.

Daniel Yankelovich, president of the survey research firm Yankelovich, Skelly and White Inc., sums up the so-called worker problem: "Changes in the composition of the work force and the values that Americans bring to the workplace have generated a new work contract—a new interpretation of the unwritten rules that determine what people expect to receive from their jobs, and what they expect to give to them. These values and beliefs are so markedly different from the traditional outlook, that they promise to transform the character of work in America in the eighties."

When workers bring one unspoken contract to the workplace, and management brings another, the result is frustration for both. Worker frustration leads to one of two behaviors, says Michael Cooper, who diagnoses employee problems and plans change programs for client companies of Hay Associates. "The first reaction is to fight, as with strikes. If that fails, or if the informal organization tells you it's not even worth trying, then the next step is to withdraw."

For the worker who is mobile and has marketable skills, that means seeking another job. For the overwhelming majority of working people, however, it means withdrawing not physically, but mentally and emotionally. The result is a passive workplace: quiet, minimally productive, and often marked by high rates of absenteeism.

Such withdrawal is precisely what workers like Harold, Carol, Larry, and Maria—and others who are stockbrokers, sanitation workers, managers, mechanics, and secretaries—described to researchers from the Public Agenda Foundation. Carol Greenwald, Judith Golub, and John Doble have just completed the first phase of an ambitious project to find out what would make working people work harder and more enthusiastically. The Foundation is a non-profit group founded by Daniel Yankelovich and former secretary of state Cyrus Vance, and supported by grants from corporations and nonprofit foundations. Its aim is to find ways to give average Americans an opportunity to define problems as they see them, and then communicate those findings to both corporate and national leaders.

Project director Carol Greenwald sums up their findings thus far: "Many people have disassociated themselves from their *workplace*, although not from work. They do so because they believe extra effort goes unnoticed and unrewarded."

The rewards they want are not only the traditional ones of money, security, and a comfortable workplace. Those have lost much of their power to motivate. That does *not* mean they are unimportant. But workers view a decent salary and workplace more as rights than as rewards that inspire extraordinary effort or enthusiasm.

In concrete terms, the unwritten contract that exists in workers' minds asks for new answers to two closely related questions: What does my job require me to do? And, what is my reward for doing that job well?

Their own answers indicate that they are motivated to work hard when:

Their tasks are interesting, varied, and involve some challenge, learning, and responsibility.

"Day after day, hour after hour, century after century, I'm glued to this switchboard. Why can't I do regular calls one day, long distance the next, and maybe international the third? It would be more interesting and I'd be learning something new. I get reprimanded if I'm curt with customers, but it's hard to be nice when you're bored to death."

Operator, telephone company

They have enough information, support, and authority to get the job done.

"I'm really embarrassed when a customer wants to cash a check for more than $50 and I have to ask him to wait ten or fifteen minutes while I get it okayed by my manager. That means sending a courier to our office at the other end of the airport, and these people are running to catch planes. It's the worst part of my job."

Teller, airport branch office

"I worked at a convenience food store, in a neighborhood with a lot of elderly people. Little old ladies came in and had to carry items one by one to the counter because we didn't supply baskets. I asked our district manager for baskets and for some grocery items that we didn't normally carry that these people kept requesting. I think I really could have improved business if I'd gotten them. After five months of asking, I got fed up and left."

Clerk, food store

They help make decisions that affect their jobs because bosses recognize that they know their jobs best.

"My company was remodeling our lab and they asked us to submit ideas for changes. A group of us got together on our lunch hours, talked over a lot of ideas, and settled on the one we thought was most important: a sloping floor that would make cleanup easier. Our work can be really messy and some days it takes as much as two hours to clean up. One of the guys had some drafting training, so we even drew up a real plan. We submitted it and never heard a thing. When the remodeling was done, we got fancy windows but no sloping floor. No one asked whether fancy windows were important to us."

Chemist, food testing lab

"I've been in this office for twelve years and I've watched quite a few managers come and go. They came in, they each set up a new system, and the new system never worked that well. Two years ago a Japanese company bought us. What a difference! Everyone was asked about what worked best. Some ideas were rejected, but at least they asked."

File clerk, fish processing firm

They understand how their own work fits into the larger picture.

"We get these jobs from clients and each of us does a piece: the secretary gets one, I get another, the project manager gets another. We never understand what the whole project is about, what it is we're really doing for the client. Why can't we all sit down together at the beginning and hear about the whole thing?"

Technician, data processing company

They see rewards linked to performance, and understand how employees can advance.

"I thought my pay was super when I started. Then last month a guy comes in right out of school and gets as much as I do after a year. Now I've been working a lot of weekends because my supervisor knows I'll get the job done right. So what's going on? Maybe they see this as a testing period and there's a promotion at the end of it. But nobody tells me that. So I sit here wondering why in the devil that new guy's getting the same treatment as I am."

Systems analyst, computer firm

WHAT THE EXPERTS SAY

"Changing Employee Values: Deepening Discontent?", Cooper et al., *Harvard Business Review,* Jan.–Feb. 1979. (Reprint available for $3 from Reprint Service, *Harvard Business Review,* Boston, MA 02163.)

"Early Warning Signals: Growing Discontent Among Managers," Cooper et al., *Business,* Georgia State University, Atlanta, Jan.–Feb. 1980. (Reprinted in *The Best of Business,* Fall 1980.)

Both articles are based on an analysis of data collected over the past twenty-five years from company clients of Opinion Resource Corp., in Princeton, New Jersey. They are among the few reports that compare employee and managerial attitudes, and how they've changed.

"Thank God, it's Monday," James O'Toole, *The Wilson Quarterly,* Winter 1980. O'Toole argues that the best evidence of new attitudes among American workers comes from companies, not from academic studies. He looks at worker behavior via five case examples. (Reprinted in *The Best of Business,* Fall 1980.)

"The New Psychological Contracts at Work," Daniel Yankelovich, *Psychology Today,* May 1978. Yankelovich is probably the most respected analyst of worker attitudes. Here he describes his theory of the New Breed worker values that "will transform the character of work in the '80s." (Reprint no. 41073 available for $2 from *Psychology Today* Reprints, P.O. Box 278, Pratt Station, Brooklyn, NY 11205.)

"Workers' Attitudes Toward Productivity," Chamber of Commerce of the U.S., 1980. The most up-to-date data on worker attitudes, gathered by The Gallup Organization and presented in an easy-to-read format. (Single copies available for $8 from the Chamber of Commerce of the U.S., 1615 H St. NW, Washington, DC 20062.)

"Work Innovations in the U.S.," Richard E. Walton, *Harvard Business Review,* July–Aug. 1979. Walton, a specialist in organizational behavior, gives basic questions for managers to answer before they attempt to change the content and structure of jobs within a company. (Reprint available for $3 from Reprint Service, *Harvard Business Review,* Boston, MA 02163.)

"Human Resources and Demographics," November 1980. One of ten sections of a special House-Senate study on economic change, this pamphlet analyzes data on fertility, population trends, labor force characteristics, and the U.S. employment structure. (Available free from Joint Economic Committee, G-133, Dirksen Senate Office Building, Washington, DC 20510.)

"Employment Projections for the 1980s." A compilation of articles from the Labor Department's *Monthly Labor Review,* plus supporting tables that project the U.S. economy to 1990. Included is a section on expected changes in the size and composition of the labor force. (BLS Bulletin 2030—Stock No. 029-001-02312-0—available for $4 from any regional Bureau of Labor Statistics office, or from the Superintendent of Documents, U.S. Government Printing Office, Washington, DC 20402.)

Theory Z: How American Business Can Meet the Japanese Challenge, William G. Ouchi (Reading, MA: Addison-Wesley, 1981.)

"You sure don't get ahead on merit in this company. Last year I decided to try an experiment. I did a half-baked job: read the newspaper every morning and misplaced forms, which slowed down processing. At the end of the year, I got the same raise as everybody else. And it was the best I'd ever gotten because the company made a lot of money last year. Why should I work hard if nobody cares?"

Clerk, insurance company

They are treated as individuals, personally important to the company.

"I've been here for five years. After the first two, I was ready to leave. Nothing I did seemed particularly important to anybody, and I felt like just another office machine. Maybe I showed it, because my boss came to me and told me he really appreciated my work, really wanted me to stay. That made a big difference."

Secretary, steamship agency

When couched in phrases like participation and power, the new contracts workers bring to their offices and factories seem threatening and disruptive. When translated into the words of real people like these, they seem almost embarrassingly sensible—embarrassing because they exist in so few workplaces. As Daniel Yankelovich notes, "It is astonishing how little it takes for most people to feel wanted, needed, challenged, useful in their jobs."

And that is just what today's workers must feel if they are to be as productive as they and their employers would like. The companies whose stories follow are reaping the benefits of those more productive workers, because they've learned to ask "What's the matter with Mary's job?" instead of "What's the matter with Mary?"

—SHARON FREDERICK

WHEN WORKERS AND COMPANIES BOTH WIN: FOUR STORIES

S. Bent Brothers:
Giving youth a reason to stay

A year and a half ago, S. Bent Brothers faced a potentially crippling labor condition, attrition through aging. The $13-million company, based in Gardner, Massachusetts, manufactures Early American chairs in a process that combines craft with industry. Many of the 315 jobs at Bent demand a high level of skill, and most are held by workers in their late fifties and early sixties.

Bent had few promotable workers to take over these slots as older employees retired. Younger people who joined the company simply weren't interested in learning the necessary skills, and few of them stayed long enough to do so.

"Before we could teach them the skills, we had to find a way to keep them here," says Bill Bellofatto, the company's vice-president of manufacturing. Bellofatto gambled that he could do just that by making younger workers feel more involved with the company, through a quality circle program.

Quality circles have been standard in Japan since the 1960s and are credited with playing a leading role in that nation's high productivity. A circle is a group of workers, usually from the same area or department, who volunteer to meet on a weekly basis to identify, study, and suggest solutions for workplace problems. Proposals are approved by a management steering committee. As preparation for a circle, workers are trained in how to collect data, work in a group, and present conclusions in a formal meeting.

Program costs vary, based on whether training is done by outside consultants or company personnel. Bent has done its own training, starting in 1979, so its main investment is time taken from production. In one instance, circle members working on a conveyor decided to give up a half hour of their lunch break, rather than shut down the operation for a full hour.

After just over a year of active circle operation, Bent's results are promising. Turnover rates of 30 percent and absenteeism of 10 percent to 15 percent have dropped to almost nothing in those departments with circles. "It's a little amazing to see younger people starting to think of themselves as permanent employees and to really look for opportunities to get involved," says Bellofatto.

Charlene Blouin, twenty-six, echoes Bellofatto's enthusiasm. Blouin has already been through two project presentations, acting as a group spokesperson on one. She has become so involved with the process and the people that she recently turned down a transfer to a higher-paying job in another department. "I'm learning a lot that I didn't know about the work," she says. "And the people in my group are great."

The learning process that Blouin mentions is often an added benefit of a quality circle. By giving younger workers a chance to work closely on a shared project with older ones, circle groups function as informal training sessions.

Quality circles have also had a very positive effect on older workers, says Bellofatto. George Taavitsaisen, sixty-two, has worked at Bent for twenty years, first on the production line and now as a receiver in the shipping department. He knows how hard it can be to change old ways of doing things.

He remembers the apprehension he felt as his circle group prepared to make its first project presentation. Neither he nor any of the other workers involved in the presentation that day expected to get very far with their suggestion. They wanted the heat turned down in the company's light storage area, where the 110-degree temperature that was maintained to prevent warping made work almost unbearable. The group had done extensive research on the reaction of wood at different temperatures and moisture levels. They were convinced that the company's preventive measures were excessive. Their report convinced management, too.

Taavitsaisen was pleasantly surprised. "Many times we feel that management isn't really interested in hearing about our problems. And many times the older worker doesn't come out in the open with these feelings, at least not like the young ones who up and leave and probably lodge a strong complaint on the way out the door. But, just because you don't hear about things doesn't mean they aren't there."

ALZA Corp.:
Holding on to people in Silicon Valley

ALZA is a pharmaceutical research firm located in Palo Alto, the heart of California's Silicon Valley. The region has become synonymous with the booming electronics industry—and with the phenomenon of the transient worker, a phenomenon it spawned. Companies compete fiercely to hire and hold both technical and support people in the face of an estimated turnover rate of 60 percent.

In a situation this competitive, a good salary is a given and workers look for something more than dollar inducements. At ALZA, the something extra is flexibility. Evidence that the policy pays off, says human resource director Harold Fethe, is a turnover rate among ALZA's 329 employees that consistently remains well below the area average.

When Rita Williams starts her workday at ALZA, the sun is already casting late-afternoon shadows across the expanse of lawn that workers refer to as "the backyard." It is 4:00 P.M. and, having finished her classes at a local junior college, Williams will spend the next four hours processing text for research reports and proposals.

Williams has not always been a part-time staffer. For five of her seven years with ALZA, she worked a full daytime schedule as a secretary. Then, at the age of twenty-seven, she decided to go back to school.

"I just woke up at my desk one day and realized that I didn't want to be a secretary all my life," she says. When Williams announced her decision, the company's response was to offer her the option of continuing to work, but in another department where the hours could be arranged to accommodate her class schedule.

"Our flexibility avoided a big loss: not only of a skilled employee but also the time and money spent in finding a new one," says Harold Fethe.

This sort of helpful accommodation is common. ALZA's policy is to offer as much freedom as possible to all of its workers, within the bounds of operational efficiency. Full-time employees work any eight hours starting between 7:00 A.M. and 10:00 A.M., unless the nature of the work performed in a particular department demands that everyone be present at the same time. If it does, employees vote on their common start and quit times.

"Our employees tend to be very independent people with minds of their own," says Fethe. "They do their best work without rigid structure and supervision. In order to attract and keep that type of person, you have to set up a system that rewards responsible autonomy."

Williams agrees. "If you provide people with a comfortable, flexible environment, they work better. People here aren't afraid of hard work, but they don't believe in making it into a difficult, puritanical experience either. After all, work is something like two-thirds of your life. Why shouldn't it be enjoyable?"

Hope's Windows Inc.:
Surviving with the workers' help

Hope's Windows was experiencing a downturn in one of its key markets during 1977. Job orders had fallen off so badly in the pressed metal division that the company was forced to idle twenty-three out of thirty-five workers. The problem was not the economy but a hitch in the estimating process that left Hope's consistently coming in with too-high bids.

The company, located in Jamestown, New York, is a custom manufacturer of steel and aluminum windows. Thus, contract bids are the chief source of orders and the company's $12.5 million in annual revenues.

To solve the problem, Hope's management went directly to the people who make the windows. "After all, they're the ones who know the work and who know, better than anyone else, how long it's apt to take," says personnel director Richard Ahlstrom, a thirty-year employee of Hope's.

The result? A bidding committee made up of managers and production workers that was so successful it has become a permanent fixture, helping to fine tune bids so that the company wins 80 percent of the press metal work it seeks.

"Whenever the sales department gets something complicated—and some of those architects can really design strange ones—we try to tear the thing down and build it in our minds, so we can tell them how long the job is likely to take," explains thirty-five-year-old Dale Mansfield, a hollow-metal layout man who serves on the committee.

The bidding committee is one example of an overall labor–management strategy adopted in 1974 by Hope's Windows. The basic idea was simple: Ask workers to tackle specific company problems by volunteering to serve on small temporary committees. Committee members report their recommendations to a steering committee made up of both management representatives and representatives of the company's four unions. The same steering committee isolates problems and sets up committees.

The only real cost of the committees is in production time lost during meetings. The company's investment has paid off tenfold, both in strict financial terms and in terms of workers' attitudes, says Ahlstrom. "People work best when they feel part of things, when they're listened to." If changes suggested by a committee are solely for the workers' benefit, they are jointly funded through company and union contributions.

Dale Mansfield, who's been at Hope's for ten years, agrees. "In a lot of companies the managers act like they're too good to be speaking to a 'nobody.' Here they listen to people like me. No manager can do every job or understand every job. So how can he always know what needs to be done? I don't think managers are relinquishing anything by asking us what we think. We're just providing the information; management still has to make the decisions. But, with their ideas and our ideas, maybe we can come up with something that will really help the company."

Rimrock Co.:
Real caring is a benefit

It's an easy commute from Rimrock Co. in Columbus, Ohio, to four or five other, larger companies that offer more money for comparable work. With seventy-five employees and annual sales under $10 million, Rimrock simply can't compete with the likes of General Electric for the skilled workers it needs to manufacture automated die-casting equipment.

"Most guys could make 15 percent to 20 percent more, some of them 40 percent more, somewhere else," says thirty-five-year-old machinist John Baumler. "But the way people are treated here keeps an awful lot of us from leaving. It's not like some places I've worked where they look at you like you're a fixture or tool that can be replaced. Here I have the feeling I can help make this place the way I want it."

The main reason is what Rimrock calls a human resources board or HRB. Baumler is one of eight worker representatives elected biannually by coworkers to hear grievances, handle safety and benefit questions, set pay ranges (though not actual wages), and generally solve workplace problems.

Rimrock cofounder and chief operating officer Charles Steigerwald is the first to admit that the HRB was conceived as an alternative to unionization. "To say that we didn't make changes to keep out the unions would be less than honest," he says. What's more important, both Steigerwald and Baumler agree, is how management treats the board. "The HRB is only as good or bad as management will let it be," says Baumler. "If it fails, it's because of the way management tries to use it." If Rimrock's board were nothing more than a union shield, it would never have lasted, he says. There's really no significant cost to the company, adds Steigerwald; the only expense is a small fee paid to the consultant who helps run monthly HRB meetings.

Steigerwald says Rimrock's people "are really the only thing we've got that makes us any different from the next guy." So, he reasons, it pays to keep them happy. There are no time clocks at Rimrock, nor are there standard break times. Free coffee is available; workers help themselves whenever they like. All factory personnel work four ten-hour days, rather than a five-day week. Some can moonlight for extra money; others use the time to maintain their own small farms.

Baumler calls such flexibility "outstanding," whether it's in terms of his schedule or his job itself. "I used to work the assembly line at Ford, hanging bumpers. It was the same machine, the same job, even the same part, day after day. You'd get up in the morning and there wasn't anything to look forward to." Rimrock can't afford job specialization, one of the key reasons it resisted unionization, and that's fine with workers like Baumler. His job designation is all-around A class machinist and he's particularly proud of the "all-around."

To Baumler, the most important thing Rimrock offers is what he calls respect: "Finding out what someone is good at and building up that capability rather than running down his weak points. Nowadays nobody is willing to take time to talk with people, explain things to them. It's 'do it now and do it my way', without any regard for the fact that it's a lot easier to work *with* someone than *for* someone."

GETTING TO
KNOW YOU

How many times have you driven home at night with a gnawing feeling in the pit of your stomach because one of your key people is disgruntled for who-knows-what reason? And who among us hasn't spent endless hours fixing people's bruised egos or injured psyches after a harmless offhand remark has festered and done its damage?

Over the past twelve years, I have tried many different approaches to keeping people enthusiastic and energized by their work—and not in my office for repairs. About a year ago, a friend who is the chief executive officer of a rapidly growing company introduced me to a technique that I've found remarkably successful. It involves nothing more than formally structuring time so that you and other members of your team can discover what makes one another tick. It's amazing how one person's seemingly trivial actions can have such profoundly negative effects on someone else. Equally amazing is how people change their behavior once they're aware of one another's hot buttons.

To illustrate both the problem and the technique, I'm going to use a couple of real examples from my friend's company.

The Symptoms

Linda, the controller, left work depressed, demotivated, and upset. She had worked until past 3:00 A.M. three nights running, polishing up the company's forecasts—and the CEO had dressed her down for being a day late with the reports. Sure, she could have warned him that her analysis was a day behind, but he must have known how profoundly she cares about the company and how much she worries about meeting cash-flow projections. The next morning she dragged herself out of bed and drove to the office with a leaden feeling, turning over in her mind her letter of resignation.

How many times have you seen these mornings-after? The problem is, you usually don't know what happened or why. All you know is that one of your employees seems down. And you hope whatever is bugging him or her will go away.

67

Bob sat stony-faced by the telephone, glaring at his watch. It was ten minutes past three o'clock. The CEO had said he would call back at three. Bob had been at the company four months as executive vice-president, and everything had been going well. Now, he was uneasy. Wasn't his work any good? He had thought that he could trust the CEO. Now, he wasn't sure. After all, when you say three o'clock, that's three o'clock. When the phone rang shortly after four, Bob answered it in an icy, flat tone. He had a hard time discussing the major contract he was negotiating. He was furious and disappointed.

Again, how often have you been puzzled by a response? You haven't a clue as to what provoked it, and you get a twinge of anxiety, guilt, or anger depending on how the rest of the day has gone.

The Cure

Most people, if asked, will freely tell you what propels them to new heights of achievement and what turns them into listless, enervated drones. And most people, if they know what moves and what slows their fellow workers, will make the effort to treat them with care. The trick is to make sure the exchange takes place. Here's what I've found works best.

Gather together a small group—it could be your managers, your board, or a work team, but should be no more than ten people—for a meeting away from the office. Make sure that you take enough time for people to relax and let their hair down a bit. Provide refreshments, but require no advance work, no handouts, and no flip charts. You'll want people to volunteer—maybe you'll even go first—to answer the following questions with complete candor.

• Why do you work here? What do you get out of your work? What are your aspirations?
• What are the behaviors, actions, or circumstances that make you motivated, energized, and happy with your work?
• What are the things that people do that dampen your enthusiasm, that make you angry or depressed?

When faced with these questions, both Linda and Bob were frank.
Linda: "You know, for me it's very simple. I love this company. I think what it's doing is great, I think the people who work here are committed and really terrific to work with. That's why I work here. Nothing fancy or heavy about it. You want to know what turns me off—takes the wind out of my sails and leaves me dead in the water? Just doubt whether I care, or don't recognize how committed I am. When you chew me out for being late with something and imply I don't take my job seriously, I'm finished. I don't function for days after something like that. I can't give you something that isn't right. It might have serious consequences for the company I love. But if I get just an inkling that I'm appreciated, I'll work all night and still be smiling the next day."

From then on, everybody understood the key to keeping Linda on an even keel. When she was late, instead of doubting her commitment, the CEO made sure she knew how important getting a particular job done was to the company's success. And he found that a little praise went a long way.

Bob: "I came to work here because of the culture of this company. We respect people. Our business is built on respect for the individual and on trust. Trust is the fundamental ingredient. I can't work with someone I don't trust. Trust is built up over time and derives from countless little actions—like doing things you say you are going to do. For example, if I say that I am going to give you a report on Wednesday afternoon, then you'd better believe I'm going to deliver. Otherwise how can you trust me? And if I say I am going to call you at ten o'clock, then I'd better not call at eleven. So if you want to spook me, just don't meet a commitment. I'll get quiet and detached for a couple of days. I suppose I should be more mature about these things and confront people at the time, but I don't."

Once Bob's quirk was acknowledged, it took little effort to work around it. People knew they shouldn't promise to call him back at a precise time. A couple of people even began to give themselves an extra day to get jobs done for Bob, and then turned them in early.

There's nothing more common in business than seeing committed, competent men and women being turned off and demotivated because of misunderstandings. In my experience, a small amount of time invested in learning about the people you work with yields impressive dividends.

—JAMES E. BERNSTEIN, M.D.

SEVEN GROUND RULES

To be effective, small-group sessions should stick to the following format

Meetings should be held off site, away from the office or plant.
Allow at least a half day for a session.
So that the effort will be taken seriously, the chief executive and senior managers should be present.
Include no more than 10 people at a time.
No minutes should be kept.
There should be no advance preparation.
It's up to the CEO to set a mood of candor, to see that the discussion doesn't get personal, and to assure employees that there are no personal risks involved.

PERSONNEL DEVELOPMENT: BE SURE YOU CHOOSE THE RIGHT INCENTIVES

Does it make more sense to reward employees for work they're already doing—by giving them added fringe benefits—or to provide bonus incentives for greater productivity? To answer that question properly, management must first consider the difference between satisfaction and motivation, and decide which is more appropriate to the company's goals.

Satisfaction is a feeling; motivation is an influence. A "satisfier" makes an employee feel better than he would without it—but it does not necessarily change his actions. Regular pay, fringe benefits, and other constant forms of compensation are in this category.

A motivator, on the other hand, is something that influences an employee's decisions—an incentive to select a course of action. To get results, an incentive must offer rewards for specific achievement that the recipient can in fact influence. And if the rewards are monetary, experience shows that they must (1) be amounts large enough to be felt by the recipient, and (2) have a clear, understandable connection with specific goals.

The most costly "incentive" plan is one that provides rewards on a more or less random basis, unrelated to actual performance. A company that proceeds this way may limit its compensation expenses—but it is unlikely to see any return on the investment. Conversely, a compensation scheme that offers large rewards for specific achievements may require a greater cash outlay and enrich individual employees—and yet be a good value for the company.

The cases cited here show how two companies analyzed their needs and came up with different answers to the incentive-vs.-benefit question.

Henry Towne runs an $8-million paper supply company that has a stranglehold on a ten-town market. Towne Paper's market position goes back to 1904, when Henry's father founded the firm. Since then, every restaurant, hospital, school, and factory in the area has known that it could rely on Towne Paper for on-time delivery of any order.

The key managers and sales staff at Towne Paper are on salary. They earn good incomes, operate company cars, and enjoy excellent vacation, profit-sharing, and medical insurance plans. Henry Towne's direct compensation in 1978 was just over $100,000. The firm's two top managers, for warehouse operations and sales, earned $38,000 and $52,000, respectively. Towne Paper's twelve salesmen received salaries ranging from $18,000 to $34,000 last year.

The company's sales volume is growing at about 9 percent a year, keeping pace with the regional economy. Towne Paper is so well entrenched that no other paper distributors appear interested in trying to capture a share of its market.

Late last year, Henry began to think about establishing an incentive compensation plan for his two key managers and sales force. When he compared his business strategy with his compensation ideas, he began to put "incentive" in perspective.

Towne Paper is committed to maintaining its well-established customer relationships. The firm doesn't need a powerhouse pool of executive talent or a sales organization handpicked to penetrate a market it already monopolizes. At best, an incentive program would only create new expenditures and drain profits. At worst, the incentives could stimulate actions by the managers and salesmen that could actually hurt the company's customer relationships.

Only poor service will stop customers from buying their paper and maintenance supplies from Towne Paper. Giving the salesmen an incentive to jack up short-term sales with their long-term accounts might only tempt them to oversell or overstock their customers.

Henry Towne abandoned the idea of establishing an incentive plan. Even a lackluster program would have cost at least $40,000 to implement. Instead, Henry spent $10,000 to set up a first-class, company-paid dental insurance plan for all of his fifty employees. As it turns out, the warehouse manager and four of the salesmen each has a child in need of orthodontic care. At close to $2,000 a crack, they had been putting it off. Henry found a dental plan that will cover virtually all expenses—to his employees' great satisfaction.

In contrast, consider Technology Products, Inc. (TPI), a company committed to major growth. TPI's business is flourishing, but its market is limited. Sales have reached about $3 million a year, and the firm's two founder-managers are earning $60,000-plus salaries and excellent benefits. More important, TPI has 20 percent ($600,000) in pretax profits. The company has plans for expansion based on development of a line of engineered products for a new and larger market.

One of the most important steps in launching TPI's new program was the recruitment of a top product development manager to lead the engineering effort.

The salary survey statistics in TPI's industry indicated that the product engineer should earn no more than $35,000 or $40,000 a year. But, since

TPI is banking heavily on its product engineering program, management decided to make the chief technical executive the third-highest-paid position in the company. It may be unusual to pay a product development person an incentive based on performance. But in TPI's case, a compensation plan based on the sales and profit performance of the new line promises to be a very effective way to achieve the company's goals.

TPI attracted one of the best product development engineers in its industry, with a compensation package that includes a $40,000 salary plus performance incentives. The package provides income opportunities of $55,000 and $65,000 in the first two years. That depends on the new line achieving its objectives of 20 percent ($160,000) in pretax profit on sales of $800,000 the first year and 20 percent ($400,000) in pretax profit on $2 million in sales the second year.

The incentive plan is encouraging design of a product that not only will sell in the expanded market but can be made at a cost that will generate growth and greater profits for TPI.

—RICHARD J. BRONSTEIN

ZANE TANKEL WROTE HIS OWN RULES FOR MANAGING PEOPLE

I once worked for an insurance company," says forty-year-old Zane Tankel, president of Collier Graphic Services in New York City. "That outfit would ring a bell at the beginning and end of coffee breaks and lunch, with a final bell at the end of the day. We all counted the minutes to the next bell. It was like being in prison."

As a recent graduate of The Wharton School of Business at the University of Pennsylvania, Tankel knew all the textbook reasons for a strong organization. But the insurance company began his real-world education in how to create structure without stifling people. That lesson has helped him take Collier, a printing and engraving company, from near-bankruptcy in 1963 to $17 million in sales this year.

Tankel's management style is an unorthodox blend of textbook rules and people sense:

Forget what you want; figure out what the guy working for you wants.

Tankel says his earliest lesson in management came during college, where he majored in sociology and did volunteer social work at a Philadelphia crime-prevention bureau.

"I worked with teenage offenders, and I saw that they got into trouble for very different reasons: some guys because it got them respect from buddies, others because they were hyper, some because they were just plain bad.

"People are motivated in different ways in their work behavior, too. Rules don't make them work; you've got to win over the individual. If I don't have that pressman downstairs *wanting* to work for me, he'll mentally put in his own work rules and do just so much.

"Typical incentive programs just widen the gap between good employees and marginal ones. The good ones get better and the marginal ones stay marginal. Personally, I believe the ideal is to *elevate* marginal employees to the same level as the top employees. You do that by knowing them. A guy's incentive to work isn't what *I* think ought to be an incentive:

it's what *he* thinks it is. Maybe it's because he likes me, or because he just takes a lot of pride in his craft.

"I always try to project myself into the other guy, to figure out what he wants, and I ask my managers to do the same."

Make the union your partner.

Collier started as a letterpress engraver back in 1932. By the time Tankel took over, the printing industry was moving away from letterpress and toward the newer, less costly offset process. "In 1969 one of our major clients was planning to switch to offset," says Tankel. "At the time, we had no offset capabilities, and the changeover cost was beyond our means. But the client guaranteed us a $400,000 chunk of business if we'd figure out a way to do it. With that kind of money at stake, I *had* to do something."

Tankel figured he might be able to find an offset company that would accept the $400,000 commitment as equity, but where and how would he find it? There was one source of reliable information: the union. They knew who had the skilled people and who was meeting their payroll. "The union also had a vested interest in the success of both companies," says Tankel. "The union collects dues from employed people, not the unemployed."

The plan worked, with the union suggesting a company and putting Collier in the offset business. It had a fringe benefit, too. Tankel's overture to the union went a long way toward gaining the confidence of his union employees. "The men really rallied around me. They would punch out and then stay to look over a job, try to catch errors that weren't their immediate responsibility. They were going way beyond what they'd ever done before.

"And every time they responded that way, I felt—and still do—that I should do a little more for them. That doesn't mean you get so caught up in boosting morale that you lose sight of the bottom line. Everyone here knows that he's here to earn money and the company's here to earn money, too.

"My philosophy is simple: A happy employee is a more productive employee so, selfishly, I want my employees to be happy."

Be grateful when employees show up for work.

Sometimes it pays to show appreciation when people simply do what's expected of them, says Tankel. During a transit strike, for example, many of Collier's employees had to struggle to get to work. When the strike was over, Tankel handed out desk sets and plaques to the stalwarts who had showed up regularly.

"At the time, a couple of my managers didn't think we needed the extra $3,500 expense. But they changed their minds; the effect on the people was great."

Then there was the time Tankel gave a case of wine to everyone who came in during a blackout, and another case of wine to those who trudged through a blizzard to get to work. "I appreciate loyalty," he says, "and I always try to let everyone know it."

Fire some of your best performers.

Collier's top salesman in 1969 was also Tankel's top pain in the neck. "He'd come in and completely disrupt the place with complaints, ranting and raving about jobs that weren't done right. It wasn't worth spending hours each day soothing hurt feelings and undoing the damage, so I fired him," says Tankel.

"The place was calmer, although a lot of people thought I was crazy for firing our top salesman. But we did all right, and the experience confirmed my belief that the price of a disruptive person is much higher than that of a nice guy who maybe doesn't sell as much."

While Tankel isn't afraid of drastic measures, he's also quick to try to salvage a good employee who's temporarily off the beam. One of his managers had developed a hot temper with clients, and Tankel saw the attitude spreading. In all other respects, the man was a credit to the company.

"I had some strong things to say to him," says Tankel, "but I needed to catch him in a receptive mood. One Friday, after hours and just after an employee party, I stepped into his office.

" 'You're not handling clients properly when you lose your temper,' I said. 'Maybe you know how far to go, but your people may not. They're starting to think it's all right to yell at clients, and I don't think that's good for the company. I'm sure if you think about it, you'll agree.'

"I planned the timing and the words carefully, and it worked. We had few problems after that."

Let employees know about secret management plans.

"If an employee doesn't have enough background information," says Tankel, "he will always misinterpret a management move. He may see the decision as a threat, or an insult, or as something stupid." That rarely happens at Collier, because of what are called "mini-meetings," quarterly gatherings of all personnel in each department, where company matters are discussed. The meetings are staggered so that one takes place somewhere at Collier every other week.

"I make sure I have an agenda; meetings are not just some crazy attempt to make people pals with one another. We use them to keep plant people abreast of management moves. There are times when we think, 'Well, we certainly can't let anyone in on *that* piece of information.' But once we discuss it, we often change our minds and put it on the agenda. We haven't been sorry yet."

Tankel's belief in openness paid off last year when the company decided to purchase a computer-automated prepress system for making four-color, plate-ready film. The system, called CAS 2000, was bought to replace many operations that had previously been done manually. Tankel knew that employees at Collier could view this development as a threat to job security.

"We launched a campaign to sell the idea to our employees," said Tankel. "We sent a personal letter, signed by me, to every employee explaining how good the system would be for our future growth together.

"Then, I invited the system's manufacturer to our Christmas party, and asked him to give everyone the complete audiovisual sales pitch. Afterward, there were many questions. I tried to show everyone that this was *not* a labor-saving move—it was a productivity-raising system."

Then the company newsletter came out with a complete description of the system and more assurances of job security. "Collier has one major ingredient within the company that will set the CAS 2000 apart from any industry system—our people," said the newsletter.

As the CAS 2000 was being installed, the union grievance committee requested a meeting with Tankel. "How many people will this new system replace?" they asked.

"None," replied Tankel.

"Will the union be able to pick the operators?"

"Absolutely not."

"Why not?" they demanded.

"My signature is on the financing papers," said Tankel. "If the union wants to sign the notes, then it can take part in those decisions."

The meeting went on for two hours. When it was over, the union was satisfied that the CAS 2000 was good for the company and its employees, and that no jobs would be lost. "We showed respect for the union," says Tankel. "That, plus our willingness to tell all about our plans for the new system, resulted in a very smooth transition to the CAS 2000."

Think big in hiring new people, but don't sack old-timers.

Tankel began building a management team a year after he took over Collier; it was finally in place by 1977. "It's like building a new plant," he says. "You hire people more skilled than you need at the time so you can grow, just the way you build a bigger building and grow into it."

Hiring wasn't easy at the beginning because of Collier's small size and weak finances. "The people I wanted told me that I couldn't afford them and didn't need them," he recalls. But he kept trying to find the kind of people he wanted for three key spots: vice-president of operations, of finance, and of sales and marketing.

Tankel snared a big-company financial man by using him first as a consultant, both to show him what Collier's small-company environment could offer and also to see how he got along with the man then handling the money, "a guy who'd been with me since the days when we wondered every Thursday where we'd get the payroll for Friday.

"I wasn't going to throw the old out in order to bring in the new. When you start doing that, everyone down to your janitor starts getting worried. A guy's work begins to look like just a job, not a career where he feels loyalty to a company because he's got somewhere to go within it."

The tactic worked. Tankel got his vice-president, who gradually assimilated finance functions. The more professional approach to finance brought a computer, and Tankel's former accountant took over as head of data processing.

Tankel attributes Collier's growth during the past few years to his willingness to spend as much as necessary to get the right personnel. In the years ahead, he plans to build on that team and on the company structure now in place, while also holding on to the feeling that Collier is a people-sensitive organization.

Tankel's goal? "Oh, I wouldn't mind being at $100 million within five years or so," he says, grinning.

—NORMAN SCHREIBER

CREATIVE PEOPLE
CAN MEET DEADLINES

Managing highly creative people is a tough job. Whether you're dealing with a computer programmer, an engineer, or a copywriter, effective management requires allowing the employee the freedom to make mistakes. It also means setting and enforcing deadlines and giving recognition that counts.

The hardest thing for the manager of a smaller company to learn when dealing with creative people is not to overmanage them. "You build creative muscle the same way you build real muscle," says Tom Connellan, author of *How to Grow People into Self Starters*. "You add weights one at a time. But if you keep running in and lifting the weights for your staff, they're never going to build any creative muscle."

The overbearing manager typically gives double messages. He says, "Take risks," but really means, "Don't make mistakes." Or he says, "Be creative," but means, "Don't surprise me." If employees aren't making mistakes or surprising you, chances are they're insecure, afraid of failing, and aren't pushing themselves to their creative limits.

Michael Corboy, president of TOCOM Inc., a Dallas manufacturer of two-way cable television equipment, has found that it works to manage over the coffee machine and in other informal settings where he can ask questions and offer encouragement to his engineers. "My role is to nurture my staff's ideas, while keeping them out of blind alleys," says Corboy.

These coffee break sessions supplement formal monthly reviews when Corboy checks the progress of his engineers toward the goals they have already agreed on. "Good people want to be measured, but not every day," says Corboy.

Because of the way creative people work, deadlines are critical for almost any project. "Most creative people are used to fighting deadlines," says Andrew Crawford, president of Ascott Corp., a textile printing company in Ann Arbor, Michigan. "But they do their best work as the deadline becomes imminent, and they'll never get anything done if you don't set one."

Sidney Green, president of Terra Tek, a cluster of seven high-technology companies in Salt Lake City, uses benchmarks to monitor research and development projects. Recently, one company received a contract to develop a mechanical system for measuring rock properties. When Green asked his project manager to put together a schedule that included benchmarks, Green got dates for completion of the design, machining of parts, assembly, debugging, and shipping. "I checked the dates to make sure they were reasonable," says Green, "and periodically we would sit down to see if they were being met."

Green explains that one of the keys to using benchmarks effectively is to use terms that the creative person responsible can understand. "If we have a scientist who doesn't like to be bothered with budgets," he says, "we'll set benchmarks related to technical accomplishments and then have someone else translate them into financial data."

In monitoring the progress of a project, Green insists that meeting periodically with employees is the only way to know how the project is going. "Creative people by nature will be creative in answering you on how they are doing. They'll say 'everything is great' but neglect to tell you they're 50 percent over budget. They don't perceive that as a problem."

Leo L. Beranek, former chief executive officer of several companies, says managing a creative department requires separation of business and creative functions. At Bolt Beranek and Newman Inc., a Cambridge, Massachusetts, research and development firm specializing in computer technology and sound, Beranek instituted a dual-management system under which the creative and financial managers within a department report to different bosses.

While the technical manager oversees the creative part of the project, the business manager attempts to find ways to save money and to eliminate bottlenecks. If the technical group fails to keep on schedule or within the budget, the business manager sees that the problem is brought to the attention of top management. Says Beranek: "Creative people like the system because they can do their jobs better with less attention to red tape and financial matters, while meeting their goals on time and within budget."

Problems that threaten schedules frequently arise in the creative process; to resolve these before they seriously affect the project's budget, management must maintain frequent personal contact with employees. During a monthly review meeting on a software development program, Ray Cotten, CEO of Camsco Inc., in Richardson, Texas, saw that the project was beginning to run behind schedule, so he called a meeting of all those involved.

The meeting revealed a serious breakdown in communications between the marketing department and the systems designers. The key designer on the project had become frustrated when he learned that those in marketing assumed the package would include features that he had not been told about at the outset. Instead of talking to management, the designer had become depressed and worked harder to solve a problem he couldn't realistically handle alone.

When Cotten made it clear he would get additional support to solve the problem, the designer was greatly relieved. "Often, programmers get so used to working in a problem environment," says Cotten, "backing off and going at a problem again and again, that they can't separate the ordinary problem from the extraordinary one until it's too late."

Besides regular monitoring and support, recognition is critical. One of the tools Michael Corboy of TOCOM uses is memos, circulated around the company, commenting on an individual's good work. And, when the trade press picks up on a new development at TOCOM, Corboy makes certain that the engineers involved in the work get special mention. Finally, he uses company picnics and Christmas parties to let spouses know how well their mates are doing.

"Creative individuals work for people, not companies," says Andrew Crawford, Ascott's president. He claims the best way to recognize the achievements of an employee is by doing unexpected things. Crawford will give his designer time off, or the opportunity to work on a project the designer has been pushing for. "If you give them something they weren't expecting, they think 'The boss cares about me.'" Crawford keeps his reward system informal, and he doesn't promise things ahead of time.

Another CEO cautions against taking credit for the work of your creative staff. "It's awfully tempting in a small company where the CEO is the focal point to take credit for everything. Don't steal your people's thunder."

—DAVID DELONG

THE EMPLOYEE WHO IS
NO LONGER USEFUL

Warren joined Diemakers Inc. shortly after it was started in 1960. There was only one person working with him when the company gave him the title of die-casting supervisor. But, in the next ten years, Diemakers grew from forty to 150 employees, and Warren's staff swelled to six.

Warren was a proud man who worked hard for the firm, and he was only a few years away from retirement. But as his responsibilities grew, Warren had trouble keeping up. Employees began taking their problems to the department's strongest manager, the second-in-command.

"We had a situation that outgrew the individual and we should have dealt with it directly," says George Spalding, president of the Monroe City, Missouri, die-casting company. Instead, Diemakers' management never confronted the supervisor about his limitations. Warren's feelings of frustration and failure mounted until he finally retired.

Warren's predicament illustrates one of the toughest management situations: handling the loyal employee whose skills have not kept pace with those required by a growing organization.

Too often, as in Warren's case, the employee is left in the job even though he can no longer handle it. This takes an emotional toll on the employee, reduces the company's effectiveness, and sends a message to other employees that management's claims about rewards for performance are hypocritical.

Why do so many entrepreneurs and managers fail to confront these problems? The most common excuse is that other problems of running the company are more important. "When you're trying to stay on top of a growing company, you tend to ignore this kind of problem, especially if the employee is at a low level in the organization," says Diemakers' Spalding. "But you can't overlook it because disgruntled people at any level can cause havoc in a company."

The other reason, of course, is the unwillingness to face the pain even if, in the long run, it might make things easier for all concerned. "Don't kid yourself," said one chief executive. "Confronting a loyal employee about his limited capability makes for a very bad day. But if you can't address these situations, you're in the wrong job yourself. Most chief executives who don't take action think they're being good guys. The truth is you're a lousy guy for doing that."

Says John P. Imlay, chairman and chief executive officer of MSA, an Atlanta-based financial software company, "You've got to focus on the 100, not the 1. You must make decisions in the best interests of the company—all the employees—and explain to the individual how your decision will be best for him in the long run."

In handling this problem, the question always arises: what do you owe a loyal employee?

"Most of all, you owe him the right not to be kept in suspense," says Thomas Connellan, a management consultant from Ann Arbor, Michigan. "An employee can face bad news better than he can face uncertainty."

Not only does a loyal employee deserve to be kept fully informed of his future with the company, but you also owe him a sincere attempt at resolving his problem. Assess his skills and look at potential openings in the company that he might fill on a permanent basis. (Temporary assignments only postpone the inevitable.)

If an employee has been with the company for a long time, he may have special skills or knowledge about the firm that would prove valuable in a staff position or a job with limited responsibility. Be honest, though, and don't transfer someone to another department unless you sincerely think he can do the job.

One high-technology firm found its operations manager couldn't handle the job, so it transferred him to the marketing department where he became an overpaid marketing administrator. When that didn't work out, he was transferred to a sales job. Finally, it became clear he couldn't sell, and the company gave the employee 2,000 shares of stock (as a way of saying "thank you") and fired him.

But transfers don't have to fail if they are done realistically, says Dave Tomlinson, president of Amwest, a Salt Lake City–based hardware distributorship. When Amwest expanded to a multibranch operation, Tomlinson's credit manager became frustrated. Instead of firing him, Tomlinson put him in charge of credit record keeping, a job that paid less but was better suited to his capabilities.

The key is to keep titles and compensation in line with the job being done. Nothing undermines company morale faster than management's claims that it pays for performance, when everyone can see it's making exceptions.

Another alternative is to find the employee a position with a company in a growth stage similar to yours when he joined your firm. An employee who was valuable to you once is probably still valuable, if he works in the right setting.

As much as a manager may hate to fire someone, the fact is you don't owe anyone a job he can't handle, even if that means leaving a position temporarily unfilled. "It's safer to leave a job vacant than to fill it with someone who's not capable of handling it," said one chief executive. "If it's vacant, the rest of us make sure the important things don't fall between the cracks."

If you hesitate at the unpleasant task of dealing with an incompetent employee, ask yourself, "How fair am I being to everyone else in the company?" You know the answer to that.

—DAVID DELONG

consider holding back any *voluntary* lump-sum termination payment, life insurance assignment, or the like until he's performed his obligations. In addition, make sure the employee turns in his credit cards, box of samples, or other property or papers he's had in connection with his job.

Make every effort, though, to keep the parting amicable. After all, under circumstances neither of you may foresee now, you and your ex-employee may end up doing business with each other.

Arbitrary or hasty dismissals can damage morale and productivity. In a small company, the effects can spread through the entire organization. On the other hand, procrastination can diminish the efforts and commitment of other workers.

There is no one correct way to hand someone his walking papers. "Firing is a wrenching experience," says Arnold Silverman, executive vice-president of Dymo Industries, a West Coast small-firm conglomerate. "Few people do it well; none ever do it in time."

When is "in time"? That's hard to say. There's a fine line between haste and procrastination. By firing an employee the moment the idea grips you, you risk throwing away a potentially valuable worker. "If the firing isn't for bad performance, malfeasance, or demonstrable incompetence, it's better to salvage what you've got than go through the ordeal of firing and finding a replacement," says John M. Considine, president of Dunhill of Lexington, Kentucky, a recognized specialist in employee terminations.

If the situation can't be salvaged, postponing the inevitable confrontation only heightens the tension and bitterness of a dismissal. A manager can turn to no one for answers to the question: have I given him enough chances to turn things around? However, the following advice from executives who have faced the firing dilemma may be helpful.

First, if you're a manager, ask yourself who's really at fault for the employee's poor performance. Perhaps it's due to things over which the employee has little or no control—insufficient resources, a poorly defined job assignment, or lack of support or communication from the top.

If the employee is at fault, he should have fair warning, unless malfeasance is involved. Tell him what's expected of him. Give him goals and a deadline for reaching them. Remind him that continued failure means farewell. "It's much better to get things out in the open early and be blunt about it," says Dymo's Silverman. "I've seen guys actually come alive after facing the problem."

If an employee doesn't come alive, he may elect to resign. Robert M. Wald, head of a human resources firm in Los Angeles, points out that "everyone knows whether he's performing and whether he has the confidence of his superior. Those who know that they are in over their heads may make the move themselves to avoid the agony of a close examination."

If an employee's performance is analyzed, fully document the process. This forces you to write down exactly what constitutes poor performance. Thus, any misunderstandings can be identified and aired before the matter goes beyond the point of no return. If the employee later must be fired, written records will provide an objective reference—essential should the case come to court.

Record only information that's relevant to the firing, and make it timely. Timeliness is imperative. Marc J. Lane, a lawyer and author of the *Legal Handbook for Small Business*, tells of an executive who lied about his medical history when he joined a company. Two years later, this deliberate omission was used as grounds for his dismissal. When he sued, the court ruled that his medical history was no longer relevant, and could not be used against him.

Outside consultants can be useful to help you define poor performance. Business peers and company directors can also help. But beware of using consultants in employee dismissals, especially in actual showdowns. Other key employees may perceive this reliance on outsiders as "gutless" management.

Avoid giving a raise or an artificially favorable efficiency report to an employee who is even remotely a candidate for the chopping block. Either move could jeopardize a company's defense in court: a jury may not understand how a company can fire a worker who has just received a pay increase.

If the employee has failed in his performance evaluation, and dismissal is inevitable, don't stall for time. "The sooner it's done," says Jack Harris, president of Acrian, a West Coast electronics producer, "the less ill feeling and trepidation on the part of the employee, and the better new problems are contained."

In the "please step into my office" session, get to the point immediately. Be objective and honest. Resist lecturing the employee about flaws in his character or competence—or risk the same lecture coming right back at you. Conduct this session with sensitivity and compassion. Limit the meeting to the facts supporting the case. Here's where a written history helps.

Don't use this time to criticize, debate, or defend. Emphasize the strengths or talents of the individual. In explaining why the firing is necessary, stress that the job *performance*—not the individual—was the cause of it.

An articulate explanation of what happened and why it happened is as important to the manager as it is to the employee. The fired employee is less likely to repeat mistakes. The manager's sense of guilt is lessened when he can see a logic and legitimacy to his actions. "Nobody has ever left me who didn't know precisely why things didn't work out," declares Ken Fisher, president of Prime Computer, Framingham, Massachusetts. "It isn't important that they agree, but that they understand why it happened."

Be prepared for shock and surprise: it's a common reaction even when the employee has been aware of his performance problems. Don't be caught off guard by the employee, or the session might turn into a shouting match.

Don't be stingy in making severance arrangements. It just doesn't pay. Many small-company executives have equity positions, so walk-around cash isn't always the principal concern. Provide a departing employee with assistance, not so much in money (though three to six months' severance pay is the norm) as in moral and professional support.

Assistance can include lending him an office and the services of a secretary while looking for another position; supplying references (tell him what you're going to say, to allay apprehension, but don't exaggerate his abilities or he might end up with another position he can't handle); and setting up interviews for possible job openings. You might want to pay for the services of a professional personnel firm that specializes in executive "outplacement." Most of all, try to understand that although he didn't work out for you and your company, he may fit in very well somewhere else.

When firings get sticky, some of these rules are thrown out the window. At Prime Computer, for instance, an executive suspected of having a drinking problem had to be fired, but there was great concern among the directors that the executive might crack under the strain. "You make the decision to fire, sure," says Prime's Fisher, "but the fear is that you're going to destroy the man—his psyche, his ego, his belief in himself." In such awkward situations, Fisher says, "anything goes. You have to do whatever it takes. Not telling the truth is permissible if that's what it takes to put the pieces together and send him out the door whole."

In some firms, firings are executed with the precision and secrecy of a gangland murder. In these companies, without warning, employees are dismissed late in the afternoon on Fridays. Because farewells among employees can be awkward, or worse, the exit interview extends beyond work hours. Then, under the watchful eye of a supervisor, the fired employee goes to his office to clean out his desk. He is then escorted to the lobby and shown the door. Any further contact with the company is restricted to the personnel office.

The Friday-guillotine method involves certain risks. The sudden disappearance of a fellow worker can destroy corporate loyalty and build insecurity in the work force. Morale and productivity might suffer as a result.

There are two critical points about firing to be remembered. First, as disagreeable a task as firing may be, your procrastination only lets wounds fester. If firing is the only alternative, do it promptly.

Second, if firing is warranted, then do it. It's one thing to transfer an employee to a job he can handle; it's entirely another to relocate an employee within a company merely to avoid the agony of the termination process. "It may seem an act of kindness," says Don Conaway, president of Checon Corp., a $5-million-a-year maker of electrical contacts in Attleboro, Massachusetts, "but what you end up with is deadwood or an alienated employee spreading venom throughout the plant."

Employees are quick to realize when someone is being carried on the payroll. By not firing, you may accumulate a group of inefficient workers—frustrated and resentful employees who are a threat to company morale and to productivity.

If you handle it well, a firing can be the start of something better, not only for the company, but also for the out-of-place employee. Too often, it's simply "the end of a chapter"; no one learns and no one benefits. Although there are no hard-and-fast guidelines, the wise and sensitive manager can cut his company's losses. With luck, a firing can turn out to be the best thing that ever happened to an employee headed for a new position. "You have to believe you're doing the guy a favor or it tears you up," says William Anderson, president of Matrix, a plastics component maker in Rhode Island. "I feel that if I'm open and honest from the start, the burden is on the employee and he can't shift it back on me."

—JOHN R. HALBROOKS

PART

II

LEADERSHIP

PREFACE

So-called natural leaders are rather a mixed bunch. Some may lure hard work out of their employees the way a masseur works the kinks out of a quarterback's neck at halftime. The employees feel that they are out there on the line, and their CEO or supervisor is right out there with them, supporting their efforts with skill and a certain amount of humility. And then there are leaders whose style is at the other extreme—outwardly demanding and terse—and also very effective. Managers of this ilk are sometimes initially feared, but given the right environment, can be revered by loyal employees who come to view the boss as the patriarch of the clan.

Most people in leadership positions, though, find themselves somewhere in between the patient coach and the autocrat. Understanding leadership style—when and how it is effective and how it can be improved—is crucial for all types of leaders.

We'll begin, in "Manual for the New Management," by recalling one of the seminal books on running a company. Peter F. Drucker's *The Practice of Management* may be three decades old, but it still contains, in its chapters on managing people, the principles of effective leadership. First, says Drucker, demand the best performance from your employees. Second, pile on information; workers should know enough about the company to guide their own performance. Third, encourage workers to develop a managerial vision. An employee should see the company "as if he were a manager responsible, through his performance, for its success and survival."

Easier said than done, you reply; let's see Drucker go out and try it himself. Well, one management expert who did was Allan Kennedy, author of *Corporate Cultures* and founder of Selkirk Associates, Inc., a software company. Committed to building a culture that stressed openness, decentralization, and democratic decisions, Kennedy struggled day by day to bring these principles alive. In "That's Easy for You to Say," we get an inside look at his successes and failures.

Leadership is power, and how one perceives power is likely to influence how one behaves as a leader. In "Power in the Pecking Order," psychologists Eugene Raudsepp and Joseph Yeager make ten statements about power and ask for your response. The explanations that follow will help you understand both your own attitude toward power politics, and the difference between constructive uses of power and destructive abuses.

One very constructive use of power is the emphasis in your company on human compassion. These days, top management is finding that compassion maintains morale, and high morale is a key to attaining company goals. "Should You Manage with Your Head or with Your Heart" is written by a company president who has found a balance between rational decision-making and sensitivity. No one, including Gary Feldmar himself, thinks that Gary Feldmar is perfect, but his ability to communicate his human qualities while maintaining a strong management role make his employees loyal, and Feldmar a satisfied man.

Few managers can communicate human values while they rush through twelve-hour days. In "Stop Working So Hard: Less Is More," consultant Jack Falvey suggests that holding the reins too tightly can put a choke-hold on your business. Open up your schedule—a day or two a week, or an hour or two a day—to plan for the future and make yourself available to others.

Ultimately, of course, you can't reduce leadership to a handy checklist. Great leaders come in many shapes and sizes, influenced by personality, philosophy, and circumstance. Five articles in this series focus on case studies of individuals who exerted strong leadership under widely different conditions.

Jack Stack, of Springfield Remanufacturing, rescued an ailing manufacturing company in the nation's Rust Belt. In "The Turnaround," we see that Stack's leadership tools were information and ownership. By providing his workers with detailed financial, production, and productivity numbers, Stack gave them the tools to measure and improve their performance. And by making them owners through an employee stock ownership plan, he gave them a stake in the outcome. "Why hire a guy and only use his brain to grind crankshafts?" asks Stack. Here is a manager who values the individual.

Dick Groner slugged it out against the big guys in a business that's as unglamorous as they come. In "Supermarket," we see a manager competing in an industry that has no captive customers or unique products. Groner beats larger competitors by doing what small companies do best, by moving quickly and by relentlessly serving the needs of the customer.

Gordon Segal succeeded in a cutthroat retailing market in which customers are often treated worse than cattle. That's not the case at Crate and Barrel, his retail store featured in "On Display." Success starts with knowledgeable employees and imaginative displays. "This is theater, people," Segal tells his employees, "and you'd better be into it because *you're* the stars!"

Arthur Imperatore brought order and direction to a rough-and-tumble trucking business. Imperatore's philosophy is that his company primarily builds men, and moves freight more or less as a result. If you detect a hint of militarism in his philosophy, you're right on the mark. But Imperatore is no General Patton. In "The Importance of Being Arthur," he talks about "symmetry and harmony in the workplace." He aims to give his employees an enriched life and "greater self-awareness." He believes that every man needs a sense of direction and dignity, and he gives it to them by way of a highly structured, efficiency-driven work environment, replete with polygraph tests and time and motion studies. The result? Imperatore's trucking company is one of the best run in the country.

Bill Gore met high standards of quality in a challenging manufacturing environment. Gore makes, among other things, waterproof materials and plastic-coated wire—both of which call for thorough inspection to maintain quality and safety standards. Yet at W. L. Gore there are no ranks or titles. Newcomers are urged to stroll around and see what they might be interested in doing. Bill Gore's "lattice organization," described in "The Un-Manager," would surely never work in Arthur Imperatore's precise organization. But employees at W. L. Gore are loyal and hardworking, and company sales are healthy.

The final perspective on leadership comes from two provocative interviews from the pages of *Inc.* In "'Good Leaders Aren't Perfect,'" author and social psychologist Michael Maccoby talks about his theories of leadership style. The really good leaders today, Maccoby argues, are those managers who take a hard look at their strengths and weaknesses and realize they cannot be all things to all people. When they come to terms with their own abilities, they will be more effective in dealing with the abilities of others.

In "Face-to-Face: Ronald Heifetz," the emphasis is on the critical distinction between exercising authority and exercising leadership. Exercising authority means righting the ship, maintaining equilibrium; exercising leadership means generating *dis*equilibrium by raising questions that force people to address problems and opinions they'd rather not consider. Using the proper approach at the right time is critical to keeping your company on track as it grows.

How effectively one leads depends, in part, on personality. But a good leader also knows that he can't rely on his charm or his ability to scare people into working hard. These stories are intended to show that leadership style evolves with understanding—of one's self as well as one's business environment. Some managers are "naturals," and others must work hard to hone and mature their style. In either case, however, we can benefit from understanding leadership style and evaluating its effectiveness.

MANUAL FOR
THE NEW
MANAGEMENT

Read *Inc.* for a while and you'll learn about companies that manage people in extraordinary ways. Harry Quadracci's Quad/Graphics Inc., for example, where manufacturing employees work three or four twelve-hour days, often spend part of another day learning or teaching the printing business, and own 40 percent of the company's stock. Or W. L. Gore & Associates Inc., whose founder, the late Bill Gore, called *all* his workers "associates" and trusted them to develop their own job descriptions. Or Springfield Remanufacturing Corp., where chief executive officer Jack Stack expects line employees to bone up on every aspect of the company's performance and propose ideas for improvement. Hit certain targets, Stack promises, and you'll get a bonus.

We're not talking fluff here. All three companies have enviable records, combining growth with healthy profitability. Which raises a nagging question: *Where did these guys get their ideas? Is there some management text they've been following—something the rest of us missed?* Asking the CEOs themselves never has been much help; they read a little of this, a little of that, they'll tell you, and combine the book learning with their own instinctive approaches to management. But pay no attention. There really *is* such a book; it just hasn't been at the top of many executives' reading lists, at least not since the year Joe DiMaggio married Marilyn Monroe. It's by Peter F. Drucker, and it's called *The Practice of Management.*

Practice, originally published in 1954 and now available in a Harper & Row paperback, is a seminal work that probes deeply into an array of tough management topics. What makes it required reading for aspiring Quadraccis and Gores, however, are a few chapters on managing people. It is here that Drucker lays out the principles of a well-managed company. Seeing those principles at work in the best-run businesses more than thirty years later is eerie—as if Drucker wrote a manual for leading-edge management in the 1980s, then traveled backward in time to get it published.

Drucker's first accomplishment is to brush away a few persistent mis-

DRUCKER ON DRUCKER: WHAT'S CHANGED SINCE 1954

It fazed Peter Drucker not a bit to learn we were writing an article on his thirty-four-year-old book The Practice of Management; *when it comes to the fundamental principles of managing people, he informed us, "nothing has changed" in the past three decades. We probed a bit, pointing out (for example) that workers today are typically much better educated than back then; surely the proliferation of undergraduate and advanced degrees (including MBAs) must affect how companies deal with their employees. The response was pure Drucker: if U.S. companies think they're getting educated workers, they're living in a dreamworld.*

"One of the delusions we have in this country is that we can hire educated people. The only industries that function well are the industries that take responsibility for training. The Japanese, you know, assume that when you first come to work you know absolutely nothing. That's the right assumption. And the Germans probably have the best system of apprentice training in the world.

"One of the big challenges ahead is not for business to spend more money on training—it already spends more on training than the school system—but to do a better job. Right now it's a scattergun approach. Exactly how to change it I'll leave to the experts. But if you start with the assumption that it's the job of the employer to train—rather than believe that people come trained—I think it would be better. We'd have apprentice programs, a different approach. School isn't preparation for work and never was."

---

conceptions—as persistent today as when he was writing. If you're like most company owners, you expect "a fair day's labor for a fair day's pay." And you hope—maybe you believe—that your employees are "satisfied" with their jobs. In those two shibboleths, says Drucker, lie most of the typical company's people problems. Satisfied employees? Exactly what you *don't* want; you want people who are frequently *dis*satisfied and thereby driven to improve their performance. As for a fair day's work, etc., the whole concept reeks of doing just what's expected and no more. Your company doesn't need timeservers, it needs workers who "willingly direct [their] efforts to the goals of the enterprise"—who work, in other words, the way you do, looking to see what has to be done and then doing it.

You think such people are born, not made? Wrong, says Drucker; it's up to you to make them. Granted, you do have to hire good people. But that's only a starting point, as anyone who has watched promising hires go sour can attest. Even the best people work up to capacity only if they feel part of a worthwhile enterprise, with their contributions both recognized and valued.

How to create such a feeling? Three ways, says Drucker. First: *Demand high performance.* Not minimum acceptable; not average; high. "Nothing gives [people] more pride of workmanship and accomplishment," he observes, and managers like Harry Quadracci know that it's true. At Quad/Graphics, *Inc.* reported in October 1983, "performance is everything. . . . Quadracci and his managers impress upon their employees a pride of craftsmanship—a respect for the presses, and exacting standards for the work they turn out." Quadracci himself teaches part of the "Introduction to Quad Technologies" course offered by the company's training program. The same high standards, Drucker points out, apply to management as well. If managers can't schedule work properly, if telephone systems don't function, workers get the message: no one really cares.

YOUR TAX DOLLARS AT WORK

Imagine yourself a novice entrepreneur, thinking (as many are) about starting a business in your home. Imagine that you turned to your government—that's right, the Small Business Administration—for advice, ordering *Starting and Managing a Business from Your Home* and *The Business Plan for Homebased Business*.

Well, we did just that, only to find our worst fears about the SBA confirmed. On page 1 of *Starting and Managing* we were told to ask ourselves, "Do I have what it takes to be an entrepreneur?" We had figured we'd find that out by starting a business—but hey, you can't be too careful. So we took a quiz to determine our Entrepreneurial Quotient. Sample question: "In courting the opposite sex, did you tend to go for one person at a time as opposed to playing the field?" Aw, shucks. "Most entrepreneurs preferred one person because to play the field would have taken too much time away from business activities."

In search of more solid information, we turned to *The Business Plan*. Alas, it began not with an explanation of P&L statements but with yet another quiz, this one on evaluating our business idea. We proposed, uh, selling iguanas by mail—then we scored ourselves, 1 to 10, according to the booklet's instructions. My level of interest: 10. Personal strength: 9 (nobody's perfect). Market strength (let's be honest): 2. Total: 21 points out of a possible 30— "probably a winner," according to the SBA's start-up gurus.

Still, we have our doubts. Both about iguanas by mail and about the net worth of these publications.

Second: *Pile on information.* "The worker should be enabled to control, measure, and guide his own performance," writes Drucker. "He should know how he is doing without being told." At Springfield Remanufacturing (*Inc.*, August 1986), workers do. Detailed income statements are distributed and discussed. An electronic message board in the cafeteria flashes a constant stream of performance numbers. In CEO Jack Stack's scheme, the information is a tool that enables workers to come up with improvements—which they do, regularly. "Why hire a guy and only use his brain to grind crankshafts?" asks Stack.

Third: *Encourage the development of a managerial vision.* "The worker will assume responsibility for peak performance only . . . if he sees the enterprise as if he were a manager responsible, through his performance, for its success and survival." A pipe dream? At W. L. Gore, new employees may spend six weeks rotating through different parts of the firm. The result: "You get to see the whole picture. And you see that motivated individuals can get an awful lot accomplished at Gore."

What all this adds up to is a simple message: employees can and should be expected to act like owners, working as if the company depended on their efforts, doing whatever needs to be done. What you have to do is treat them as owners, giving them the tools ordinarily available to owners, such

EXPERTS' CHOICES
THE ART OF SELLING

Q: You want your salespeople to read a book that will help them improve their selling skills. What's the book?

W. R. (MAX) CAREY, president and CEO, Corporate Resource Development Inc., an *Inc.* 500 company specializing in marketing and sales consulting (Atlanta):
"I think the best book right now is *Strategic Selling,* by Robert B. Miller and Stephen E. Heiman (Warner Books, 1985). In the past, everyone learned the tactical side of selling—the 'perfect answer for every response,' the 'hammerlock close,' and so on; then they learned 'dialogue selling,' as pioneered by Xerox and IBM. Today you need to take the next step, figuring out how to position yourself, gain access to the customer, and control the selling process. For example, we're working with a partner to sell a large corporate customer; we have six months of research invested and haven't talked to anybody yet. But when we do it'll be the president, and it'll stick. That kind of approach is what *Strategic Selling* is about."

MIKE CONVEY, vice-president of sales, Black & Decker (U.S.) Inc. (Hunt Valley, Md.):
"Check out *Non-Manipulative Selling,* by Tony Alessandra, Phil Wexler, and Rick Barrera (Prentice-Hall, 1987). To me, selling is more than just getting an order, it's building a relationship with individuals and companies. Too many people hit and run—they make the sale, and never follow up. When you're developing a relationship, by contrast, you're listening to people, determining what their needs are, figuring out how you can meet their needs. That's the opposite of manipulative selling. This book describes how to do it."

EDMOND LAUSIER, assistant professor of marketing, University of Southern California (Los Angeles):
"I'd recommend *Skyrocket Your Sales,* by Raymond A. Slesinski (Pelican Publishing Co., 1986). What I like about the book is its emphasis on nonverbal signals—how people sit, how they speak, how they look at you, and so on. Listening is a big part of selling, and listening includes picking up what's being communicated nonverbally as well as what's said verbally. Nonverbal clues tell you whether what you're saying is interesting to the prospect. They convey whether it will lead to anything, and whether he's telling you what his needs really are. Rather than spending three or four calls trying to figure out what's going on in your customer's business, you learn to pick it up quickly from all the signals."

---

as information. Maybe, indeed, you need to provide them with ownership itself—as Gore, Quadracci, and Stack have done, through extensive employee stock ownership plans.

In the past few years, the managerial approach of these three companies (and others like them) has made news. They have been written up as pioneers. How curious to find that Peter Drucker wrote the book, so many years ago.

—JOHN CASE

THAT'S EASY
FOR
YOU TO SAY

It all began on Labor Day weekend in 1982. Allan A. Kennedy was sitting in a low beach chair on the shore in front of his cottage on Cape Cod. Next to him was his friend and fellow consultant Tony Merlo. As they relaxed there, watching the sailboats drift across Cape Cod Bay, drinking beer, and listening to a Red Sox game on the radio, Kennedy turned to Merlo and, with the majestic eloquence suited to great undertakings, said: "Gee, Tony, you know, we ought to start some kind of business together."

This identical thought has, of course, passed between countless friends ever since the discovery of profit margins. Coming from most people, it would have fallen into the general category of loose talk. But Kennedy was not most people. For one thing, he was a thirteen-year veteran of McKinsey & Co., the management consulting firm, and partner in charge of its Boston office. More to the point, he was the coauthor of a recently published book that offered a startling new perspective on corporate life—one that challenged the whole way people thought about business.

The book was entitled *Corporate Cultures*, a term that was itself new to the language, and it dealt with an aspect of business that, up to then, had been largely ignored. Broadly speaking, that aspect involved the role played by a company's values, symbols, rites, and rituals in determining its overall performance. Citing examples from some of the country's most dynamic companies, Kennedy and co-author Terrence E. Deal showed that these "cultural" factors had a major effect on the attitudes and behavior of a company's employees, and were thus of critical importance to its long-term success.

By any measure, the book was a ground-breaking work, challenging, as it did, the rational, quantitative models of corporate success that were so popular in the 1960s and 1970s. But its impact had as much to do with its timing as its content. Published in June 1982, during a period of economic stagnation—with unemployment at 9.5 percent, the prime over 16 percent, and trade deficits soaring to record levels—*Corporate Cultures* offered a welcome antidote to the doom and gloom that was abroad in the land. Like

In Search of Excellence, which appeared a few months later, it suggested that Japan was not the only nation capable of producing strong, highly motivated companies that could compete effectively in the international arena. America could produce—in fact, was already producing—its own.

What the book did not detail, however, was how corporate cultures were actually constructed. The authors could describe a particular culture and demonstrate its effects, but they offered few clues as to how a company might develop a culture in the first place. So the news that Allan Kennedy was going into business was greeted with more than passing interest among the followers of corporate culture. Here was an opportunity to find out how a living, breathing culture could be created, and the creator would be none other than the man who wrote the book.

After an extensive survey of business opportunities, Kennedy and Merlo decided to develop microcomputer software for sales and marketing management. They felt this was their most promising option, given the anticipated growth of the microcomputer market and their own experience as consultants. Acting on that assessment, they resigned from McKinsey and, in February 1983, formally launched Selkirk Associates Inc. with four of their friends.

Kennedy had lofty ambitions for Selkirk. More than a business, he saw it as a kind of laboratory for his theories. He wanted it to function as a society of professional colleagues committed to building a culture and a company that would stress collaboration, openness, decentralization, democratic decisions, respect, and trust. In this society, each individual would be encouraged to devise his or her own entrepreneurial response to the challenges of the business.

For Kennedy, this was not a long-term goal, something that would evolve naturally in the fullness of time. On the contrary, it was a pressing, immediate concern. Accordingly, he focused all his attention on creating such a culture from the start. "I spent lots of time," he says, "trying to think about what kind of values the company ought to stand for and therefore what kind of behavior I expected from people." These thoughts eventually went into a detailed statement of "core beliefs," which he reviewed and amplified with each new employee. In the same vein, Kennedy and his colleagues chose a "guiding principle," namely, a commitment to "making people more productive." They would pursue this ambition, everyone agreed, "through the products and services we offer" and "in the way we conduct our own affairs."

And, in the beginning at least, Selkirk seemed to be everything Kennedy had hoped for. The company set up shop in Boston, in an office that consisted of a large, rectangular room, with three smaller attachments. Each morning, staff members would pile into the main room and sort themselves out by function—programmers and systems engineers by the windows; administrators in the middle; sales and marketing folk at the other end. In keeping with Kennedy's cultural precepts, there were no private offices or, indeed, any physical demarcations between functions.

It was a familial enterprise, informed with the very qualities Kennedy had laid out in his statement of core beliefs. The work was absorbing, the comradeship inspiring. Most mornings, the staff feasted on doughnuts, which they took to calling "corporate carbos," as a wordplay on "corporate cultures." They began a scrapbook as an impromptu cultural archive. Included among the memorabilia was "The Ravin'," an Edgar Allan Poe takeoff that commemorated Selkirk's first stirrings in earlier temporary headquarters:

> Once upon an April morning,
>   disregarding every warning,
> In a Back Bay storefront,
>   Selkirk software was begun:
> True, it was without a toilet,
>   but that didn't seem to spoil it.

To strengthen their bonds even further, the staff began to experiment with so-called rites, rituals, and ceremonies—all important elements of a corporate culture, according to Kennedy's book. Selkirk's office manager, Linda Sharkey, recalls a day, for example, when the whole company went out to Kennedy's place on Cape Cod to celebrate their common purpose with barbecues on the beach. "The sun was shining, and we were all there together," she says. "It was a beautiful day. That's the way it was. We didn't use the terms among ourselves that Allan uses in the book. With us, corporate culture was more by seeing and doing." Sharkey remembers, too, Friday-afternoon luncheons of pizza or Chinese food, at which everyone in the company had a chance to talk about his or her accomplishments or problems, or simply hang out.

Kennedy was pleased with all this, as well he might be. "We were," he says, "beginning to develop a real culture."

Then the walls went up.

The problem stemmed from the situation in the big room, where the technical people were laboring feverishly to develop Selkirk's first product, while the salespeople were busy preselling it. The former desperately needed peace and quiet to concentrate on their work; the latter were a boisterous lot, fond of crowing whenever a prospect looked encouraging. In fact, the salespeople crowed so often and so loudly that the technicians complained that they were being driven to distraction. Finally, they confronted Kennedy with the problem. Their solution, which Kennedy agreed to, was to erect five-foot-high movable partitions, separating each functional grouping from the others.

In the memory of Selkirk veterans, "the day the walls went up" lives on as a day of infamy. "It was terrible," says Sharkey. "I was embarrassed."

"It was clearly a symbol of divisiveness," says Kennedy.

"I don't know what would have been the right solution," says Reilly Hayes, Selkirk's twenty-three-year-old technical wizard, "but the wall certainly wasn't. It blocked out the windows for the other end of the room. Someone [in marketing] drew a picture of a window and taped it to the wall. The whole thing created a lot of dissension."

Indeed, the erection of the walls touched off a feud between engineering and marketing that eventually grew into "open organizational warfare," according to Kennedy. "I let the wall stand, and a competitive attitude developed where engineering started sniping at marketing. We had two armed camps that didn't trust each other."

As if that weren't bad enough, other problems were beginning to surface. For one thing, the company was obviously overstaffed, having grown from twelve people in June 1983 to twenty-five in January 1984, without any product—or sales—to show for it. "That was a big mistake," says Kennedy. "We clearly ramped up the organization too fast, particularly given the fact that we were financing ourselves. I mean, for a while, we had a burn rate of around $100,000 per month."

Even more serious, however, was the problem that emerged following the release of the company's initial product, Correspondent, in February 1984. Not that there was anything wrong with the product. It was, in fact, a fine piece of software, and it premiered to glowing reviews. Designed as a selling tool, it combined database management, calendar management, word processing, and mail merge—functions that could help customers organize their accounts, track and schedule sales calls and follow-ups, and generate correspondence. And it did all that splendidly.

The problem had to do with the price tag, a whopping $12,000 per unit. The Selkirk team members had come up with this rarefied figure, not out of greed, but out of a commitment to customer service—a goal to which they had pledged themselves as part of their cultural mission. In order to provide such service, they figured, a Selkirk representative might have to spend two or three weeks with each customer, helping to install and customize the product. Trouble was, customers weren't willing to *pay* for that service, not at $12,000 per unit anyway. After a brief flurry of interest, sales dropped off.

"We just blew it," says Kennedy. "We were arrogant about the market. We were trying to tell the market something it wasn't interested in hearing. We took an arbitrary cultural goal and tried to make it into a strategy, rather than saying we're a market-driven company and we've got to find out what the market wants and supply it." Unfortunately, six months went by before Kennedy and his colleagues figured all this out and began to reduce Correspondent's price accordingly.

By then, however, Selkirk's entire sales effort was in shambles, a victim of its commitment to employee autonomy. Sales targets were seldom realized. Indeed, they were scarcely even set. At weekly meetings, salespeople would do little more than review account activity. "If a salesman said each week for three weeks in a row that he expected to close a certain account, and it never happened," says Merlo, "well, we didn't do anything about it. In any other company, he would probably have been put on probation." As it was, each of the participants entered the results of the meeting in a red-and-black ledger book and struck out once again to wander haphazardly through uncharted territory. "The mistake we made," reflects Merlo, "was using real money in a real company to test hypotheses about what sales goals should be."

Finally, in June 1984, Kennedy took action, laying off six people. In July, Correspondent's price was dropped to $4,000 per unit, but sales remained sluggish. In September, Kennedy laid off five more people, bringing the size of the staff back to twelve.

One of those laid off was the chief engineer, a close friend of Kennedy's, but a man whose departure brought an immediate cease-fire between the warring factions. That night, the remaining staff members took down the walls and stacked them neatly in the kitchenette, where they repose to this day. "We felt," says Sharkey, "like we had our little family back together again."

With morale finally rebounding, Selkirk again cut Correspondent's price in the early fall, to $1,500. This time, sales responded, and, in November, the company enjoyed its first month in the black.

But Selkirk was not yet out of the woods. What remained was for Kennedy to figure out the significance of what had happened, and to draw the appropriate conclusions. Clearly, his experiment had not turned out as he had planned. His insistence on a company without walls had led to organizational warfare. His goal of providing extraordinary service had led to a crucial pricing error. His ideal of employee autonomy had led to confusion in the sales force. In the end, he was forced to fire more than half of his staff, slash prices by 87 percent, and start over again. What did it all mean?

Merlo had one answer. "We're talking about an experiment in corporate culture failing because the business environment did not support it," he says. "The notion of corporate culture got in the way of tough-minded business decisions." He also faults the emphasis on autonomy. "I don't think we had the right to be organized the way we were. I think we should have had more discipline."

Kennedy himself soon came around to a similar view. "Look in [the statement of core beliefs] and tell me what you find about the importance of performance, about measuring performance or about the idea that people must be held accountable for their performance," he says. "That stuff should have been there. I'm not discounting the importance of corporate culture, but you have to worry about the business at the same time, or you simply won't have one. Then you obviously won't *need* a culture. Where the two come together, I think, is in the cultural norms for performance, what kind of performance is expected of people. And that's a linkage that wasn't explicit in my mind three years ago. But it is now." He adds that, if the manuscript of *Corporate Cultures* were before him today, he would include a section on performance standards, measurement systems, and accountability sanctions.

On that point, he might get an argument from his co-author, Terrence Deal, a professor at Vanderbilt University and a member of Selkirk's board of directors since its inception. Deal does not disagree about the importance of discipline and performance standards, but he questions the wisdom of trying to impose them from above. The most effective performance standards, he notes, are the ones that employees recognize and accept as the product of their own commitment, and these can emerge only from the employees' experience. "One of the things that we know pretty handsomely," says Deal, "is that it's the informal performance standards that really drive a company."

In fact, Kennedy may have gotten into trouble not by doing too little, but by doing too much. Rather than letting Selkirk's culture evolve organically, he tried to impose a set of predetermined cultural values on the company, thereby retarding the growth of its own informal value system. He pursued culture as an end in itself, ignoring his own caveat, set down in his book, that "the business environment is the single greatest influence in shaping a corporate culture." Instead, he tried to shape the culture in a vacuum, without synchronizing it with the company's business goals.

In so doing, Kennedy reduced corporate culture to a formula, a collection of generic "principles." It was a cardinal error, if not an uncommon one. "There are a lot of people," says Deal, "who take our book literally and try to design a culture much as if they're trying to design an organization chart. My experience across the board has been that, as soon as people make it into a formula, they start making mistakes." By following the "formula," Kennedy wound up imposing his own set of rules on Selkirk—although not enough of them, and not the right kind, he now says. The irony is that a real corporate culture allows a company to manage itself *without* formal rules, and to manage itself better than a company that has them.

Deal makes another point. Kennedy, he observes, might be less concerned with performance today if he had not hired so many friends at the beginning. Friends are nice to have around, but it's often hard to discipline them, or subject them to a company's normal sanctions. Over the long run, Deal says, their presence at Selkirk probably undermined the development of informal performance standards.

Kennedy himself may have played a role in that, too. He estimates that over the past year he has spent only one day a week at Selkirk. The rest of the time he has been on the road as a consultant, using his fees to help finance the company. In all, he has sunk some $1 million of his own money into Selkirk, without which the company might not have survived. But it has come at a price. "Nobody had to pay attention to things like expenses, because there was a perception of an infinite sink of money," Kennedy says.

The danger of that perception finally came home to him last summer, when three of Selkirk's four salespeople elected to take vacations during the same month. The result was that sales for the month all but vanished. Kennedy had had enough. "I told the people here that either you sustain the company as a self-financing entity, or I will let it go under. I'm unwilling to put more money on the table."

And yet, in the end, it was hard to avoid the conclusion that a large part of Selkirk's continuing problem was Allan Kennedy himself—a thought that did not escape him. "I've got a lot to learn about running a business successfully," he says, "about doing it myself, I mean. I think I know everything about management except how to manage. I can give world-class advice on managing, but—when it comes right down to it—I take too long and fall into all the traps that I see with the managers I advise."

Whatever his shortcomings as a manager, there is one thing Kennedy can't be faulted for, and that is lack of courage. Having drawn the inevitable conclusion, he went out looking for someone who could help him do a better job of managing the company. For several months, he negotiated with the former president of a Boston-based high-tech firm, but the two of them were unable to come to terms. Instead, Kennedy has made changes at Selkirk that he hopes will achieve the same effect. In the new structure, Merlo is taking charge of the microcomputer end of the business, while Betsy Meade—a former West Coast sales representative—has responsibility for a new minicomputer version of Correspondent, to be marketed in conjunction with Prime Computer Corp. As for Kennedy, he will concern himself with external company relations, product development strategies, and, of course, corporate culture.

Kennedy is full of optimism these days. He points out that despite its checkered history, Selkirk has emerged with a durable product and an installed base of about 1,000 units. In addition, the company will soon be bolstered with the proceeds from a $250,000 private placement. Meanwhile, he says, some of the company's previous problems have been dealt with, thanks to the introduction of a reliable order-fulfillment process, the decision to put sales reps on a straight commission payment schedule, and the establishment of specific sales targets for at least the next two quarters. "I think we have much more focused responsibility," he says, "and much more tangible measures of success for people in their jobs."

Overall, Kennedy looks on the past three years as a learning experience. "There are times when I think I should charge up most of the zigs and the zags to sheer rank incompetence," he admits. "But then there are other times when I look back and say, 'Nobody's that smart, and you can't do everything right.' In life, you have to be willing to try things. And if something doesn't work, you have to be willing to say, 'Well, that was a dumb idea,' and then try something else." Now, he believes, he has a chance to do just that.

In the meantime, he is in the process of writing another book. He already has a proposal circulating among publishers. In his idle moments, he occasionally amuses himself by inventing titles. One of those titles speaks volumes about where he has been: *Kicking Ass and Taking Names*.

—LUCIEN RHODES

POWER IN THE PECKING ORDER: DO YOU ACT LIKE A TOP CHICKEN?

In 1913, a Danish zoologist named Thorlief Schieldorup-Ebbe discovered that the lowly barnyard chicken lived within a strict organizational structure. Inevitably there was a top chicken who could peck any other chicken in the yard to express its dominance, a second layer of chickens that could peck a third group of still lower-ranked chickens but could not peck the boss chicken, and so on down the hierarchy. He called the phenomenon the pecking order, and the phrase became part of our modern vocabulary.

People form a pecking order just as naturally as chickens, and nowhere is the pecking order more evident than in a modern business organization, where a hierarchy is necessary for productive work. Understanding the uses of power, therefore, is integral to understanding your business, whether it's a two-man shop or a giant conglomerate. Yet many people, bosses and employees alike, prefer not to think of business life in these terms. Ask them how power-oriented they are and they'll modestly reply "not at all." It's not true. We all have attitudes toward power and the exercise of power that determine how well we perform our roles.

Leaders, in particular, need to understand the dynamics of the power in their organizations. Perhaps you've been frustrated when the promised punctual delivery of a crucial result never materialized. Or watched in frustration as a good idea you came up with fizzled out in the hands of your subordinates. Or, worse, had to clean up the mess when an employee made a serious mistake. If these and other common incidents in organizational life give you a serious headache, perhaps you need to examine your attitudes toward power. A fresh look at those attitudes can help you cope and lead better, but perhaps only by changing some of your ways. The abilities that got you to the top, in other words, may not be the same ones required to keep you there.

Broadly speaking, attitudes toward power range from passive to aggressive. The short test opposite will help you measure your own attitudes. There are at least two other ways to use the quiz. Copy the test and ask your subordinates to take it, then discuss why they responded as they did.

A POWER QUIZ

	True	False
1. Keeping the leader happy should take priority over other important work.	☐	☐
2. The need and desire for power is universal.	☐	☐
3. Courtesy is one of the most effective tools for getting things done.	☐	☐
4. Power and politics are the foundations of most organizational results.	☐	☐
5. One of the most important attributes an executive needs is to be fair to subordinates.	☐	☐
6. In a fair organization, the most productive people will succeed and get ahead.	☐	☐
7. It is necessary and effective to criticize subordinates for their mistakes.	☐	☐
8. Packaging the facts and my views to get around people's prejudices would be a distortion of the truth and a sellout of my integrity.	☐	☐
9. Being cordial to people, even if I don't like them, is as important as being good at my job.	☐	☐
10. I shouldn't have to curry favor to get people to cooperate with me or to do the job they are paid to do.	☐	☐

Another revealing method is to put yourself in the shoes of your own key people, answering the questions as you feel they would. A look at their actual answers compared to yours can reveal important things about their views of power and leadership.

Let's examine the answers individually to find out more about your attitudes:

1. Keeping the leader happy should take priority over other important work.

True. Self-serving as it may sound, it's vital for a company to have happy, confident leadership to succeed. Your primary function as a leader is to make decisions. The primary function of your managers is to present you with options. How your people view the decision-making process is important in allowing you to choose between reasonable courses of action and then make your decision stick, without resistance from behind the lines.

Passive individuals often are disappointed when you don't choose the "right" answer to a problem. They may feel you're being arbitrary or that you ignored their point of view. Often this feeling rationalizes their own inability to sell you on their approach. Aggressive individuals, on the other hand, may simply tell you there is only one solution, and that you're wrong if you don't choose it. Neither mind-set leads to effective implementation. Understanding why people disagree with you is important, but after making a decision you can't waste time either apologizing to passive employees or rehashing the battle with aggressive ones. You can't afford wishy-washy agreement or arbitrary nay-saying. But you must realize that your own people can put you in positions where it's impossible not to fall into one trap or the other.

2. The need and desire for power is universal.

True. Philosopher Friedrich Nietzsche saw what he called "the will to power" everywhere he turned, and he concluded that the pursuit of power explained most human behavior. In organizations, power and position are often synonymous, and competition for the top spots is key to achieving results. Pursuing power is therefore a normal and even healthy thing for employees to do. Not everyone can be a leader, however, and an effective boss understands that many employees want to be led. Many passive persons, in fact, deny themselves the pursuit of power and demand leadership; they need it to be comfortable. So a company will only function effectively when its leaders provide clear direction. The boss must be careful not to turn over too much of his decision-making power to aggressive subordinates, since that may lead to losing part of his legitimate right to have the final say. A balance of submissive and aggressive employees is required to keep the organization on an even keel, and effective leaders understand both the need to be led and to channel aggressive behavior into productive channels.

3. Courtesy is one of the most effective tools for getting things done.

True. Courtesy is simply the grease that lubricates any social order. It can be defined as the act of making others feel good or powerful in relationship to their place in the hierarchy. Since the majority of your employees are likely to fall toward the passive end of the scale, it's important to reinforce their self-esteem frequently to keep them most productive. This is true not only for you but also for your managers. Discourteous bumpkins seldom progress far up the organizational ladder, but the boss also has to be alert to phonies, who are usually aggressive people pretending to be passive in your presence. Surprisingly, many bosses are unprepared to cope with a phony or simply ignore his routine discourteous behavior toward others. By ignoring him you simply provide him latitude to carry on the charade, usually to your ultimate chagrin when unhappy subordinates get fed up and quit. Discourtesy isn't all bad, however. Effective leaders use it occasionally to throw a rival off course. As somebody once said, "a gentleman is never unintentionally rude."

4. Power and politics are the foundations of most organizational results.

True. As a species, we fall into pecking orders spontaneously. Someone must be in charge before anything can even be started. Yet many passive people find office politics distasteful. As a consequence, they wind up being manipulated by others who are more aggressive.

The aggressive person's primary motive is to get as much power as possible. He sees people as objects, defers to no one, and tempers his aggression only when forced to do so. The submissive employee, however, often creates a greater problem. According to anthropologist George Maclay, "individuals who have little self-confidence are more strongly driven to fall into a childlike state of dependence and are eager to exchange self-control for control by an outside authority." Such behavior may be flattering to you, but it should be watched carefully since it may mean that those people are not carrying a fair share of the load. "Leaving it to the boss" can result in too much stress for your own good.

5. One of the most important attributes an executive needs is to be fair to subordinates.

False. Being "fair" to a passive person often leads to excessive hand-holding or an inability to make demands on his capacities. Being "fair" to an aggressive, manipulative person can enable him to take over your power and your job. A leader must be in command, must clearly be the person in the pecking order who can peck anyone at will and who is immune to challenges by subordinates. A leader who cannot do this will be perceived as weak, and such weakness will produce rivalries and resentments among subordinates who come to think they are more qualified to handle your power than you are. A "fair" boss is often a wishy-washy boss, like the cartoon character Charlie Brown. Your employees want you to lead, not waffle by trying to be "fair" or a "nice guy." Be firm, yet courteous and considerate, and you'll generate respect and genuine loyalty while keeping hurt feelings to a minimum.

6. In a fair organization, the most productive people will succeed and get ahead.

False. This notion assumes that a person's value can be objectively demonstrated or measured. One of the chronic faults of performance appraisal systems is that they naively assume this objectivity rather than the reality of political judgments. Since bosses must concern themselves with political problems, often the person most adept at solving those problems will be perceived as most valuable and rewarded accordingly. At times these political issues, especially as they relate to the executive team, can obscure other achievements. No matter how objective you try to be, you will always have "fair-haired boys," crown princes, and favorites. It's human nature. Don't try to avoid it, just deal with it so that it doesn't interfere with your larger goals.

7. It is necessary and effective to criticize subordinates for their mistakes.

True. Without feedback your employees will never develop an appreciation for your standards, much less learn from their mistakes. In this case it's the way you hand out criticism that's important. Criticism without courtesy can make a passive person feel "put down" and defensive, leading to lower motivation and interfering with the ability to concentrate on work itself. Overly aggressive criticism can also lead to a desire for revenge. In the passive person's case that usually takes the form of gossip. The aggressive person may disrupt the organization by fighting back overtly.

8. Packaging the facts and my views to get around people's prejudices would be a distortion of the truth and a sellout of my integrity.

False. If a new idea is packaged so that it matches the subjective needs of those affected by it, it stands a good chance of acceptance. Resistance to new ideas frequently stems from a perception of a real or imaginary threat to a person's place in the pecking order. If you expect a new idea to stand on its own merits, be prepared to fail frequently.

Before broadcasting an idea, it makes sense to bounce it off of people further down the hierarchy. Frequently they can see its productive value more clearly than you can because they have less to lose from changes it might produce in the organizational structure. Finding out what the "common man" thinks is worth the effort. It's naively idealistic to think that change ought to be judged on its merits alone; this attitude ignores the powerful signals change transmits to your employees about positioning in the hierarchy.

9. Being cordial to people, even if I don't like them, is as important as being good at the job I do.

True. As a leader and a superior you exercise your power, either consciously or subconsciously, and you come to expect at least nominal deference from those in lower positions. This doesn't mean that your employees have to sell out their values or throw away their pride just to keep you happy—or to keep your top managers happy. Everyone's integrity and pride can be maintained if arguments are carried on constructively, without venom. If your management team has some reluctant members in this area, it's important to help them learn to deal with power pragmatically rather than reactively. They need to develop skills for coping with the facts of power without forcing people into submissiveness against their will. Proper assertive skills can assuage the sense of helplessness many employees feel in the face of power and opposition, and leading your people toward this assertive happy medium will be well worth the effort.

10. *I shouldn't have to curry favor to get people to cooperate with me or to do the job they are paid to do.*

False. If you expect someone to do something because they ought to do it, you will lead a life of righteous indignation or chronic disappointment or both. The simple fact is that there will always be genuine differences of opinion about what should be done. Even when there's agreement on a goal, people will often disagree on its importance. You need to observe your employees closely to learn the things that can serve as incentives for them while helping you achieve your objectives. One of the most important measures of leadership is the ability to persuade people to do things one way in spite of differing opinions.

Power Quiz Answers

1. True 2. True 3. True 4. True 5. False 6. False 7. True 8. False 9. True 10. False

Award yourself one point for each correct answer. You can interpret your score as follows:

If you scored 0 to 3, your view of power may be very naive. People probably take advantage of you frequently. You rationalize or forgive others' offenses, and may cooperate with others even when you disagree strongly with them, just to avoid rocking the boat.

If you scored 8 to 10, you are extremely power-oriented. Chances are that you are abrasive in your use of power and tolerate little or no pressure from others without fighting back. You are likely to turn an ordinary problem into an unnecessary confrontation for the pleasure of winning the point at someone's expense, reflecting your feeling that there are no "win-win" situations, that someone's success always involves another's subordination.

If you scored 4 to 7, you are in the assertive happy medium. You tend to be flexibly cooperative or quietly competitive in your use of power, depending on how you read the situation. You don't mind confrontations, but won't usually provoke them. You treat courtesy as a high art, and tend to receive as much attention as you require in important discussions. You may wear a number of different "masks" rather than always showing the same face to others. This isn't devious; it's using common sense to be effective in different situations.

—EUGENE RAUDSEPP AND JOSEPH YEAGER

SHOULD YOU MANAGE
WITH YOUR HEAD OR
WITH YOUR HEART?

When the son of his sales manager was hurt trying to break up a fight in school, Gary Feldmar sent the youngster a book on bodybuilding and self-defense.

A few weeks after his controller complimented him on a pipe he was smoking, Feldmar had one of his Sasieni Four Dots fitted with a new bit and gave it to him.

The morning after Feldmar hired a new manager, the man's wife received a bouquet of flowers to welcome her to the company.

Unusual management tactics? Perhaps. But then the management styles of the men and women who run small businesses vary as widely as the products they make and the services they provide. Gary Feldmar's style is personal and individual, a mix of what comes naturally and what he's observed in other managers.

A look at Gary Feldmar reveals a manager aware of the delicate balance between reasoned decision-making and sensitivity. He firmly believes that you can be sensitive to people and still be a tough manager.

Gary Feldmar is the forty-one-year-old president and sole owner of Excello Press Inc., a $25-million printing company in Chicago. In the four years since he bought the company his father founded in 1933, Feldmar has doubled sales.

He has done that by transforming Excello from an all-purpose printer to a specialist in direct mail and commercial printing; by investing more than $9 million in new capital equipment; and by revamping a pen-and-ink accounting system and installing a computer.

He has also done it by firing all six of Excello's top managers, replacing them with his own management team, and by adopting a management style clearly his own. His is a curious blend of what he learned while earning degrees in marketing and psychology, during twenty years as a salesman, plus a genuine affection for and interest in people.

Feldmar is an intense competitor. Even now, he sells more printing than any salesman in his company—more than $5 million worth in 1979.

He looks at managing much the way he looks at selling; he woos and wins his managers as he does his customers.

He is just as intense at sport. In 1976, Feldmar was the only amateur to compete in the National Horse Show in Madison Square Garden, the most prestigious jumping event in the country.

John Halbrooks, *Inc.* Associate Editor, recently visited Excello to find out firsthand how Feldmar thinks and why he manages the way he does.

There's an unfortunate macho image attached to the effective business manager: To be good, he must be tough.

In my first ten years of selling printing, I had plenty of opportunities to observe managers in the companies I visited. Obviously, some jobs had errors and I was amazed at how often a manager would call in the person responsible and rip him apart in front of me. I never liked that throbbing-blood-vessels-in-the-head style of management.

I think managers are frightened of being sensitive to people. They're afraid of losing their distance and objectivity. They're afraid of becoming vulnerable.

But that's a little like saying that you don't want to get too close to your wife because she might leave you someday. Or that you don't want to have children because they could be killed in an accident.

My father once told me that you can run a business with your heart or you can run it with your head. Either way is fine, he said, but if you run a company with your heart, you had better be able to afford it.

I like to think that I listen to my heart, but I make decisions with my head.

I believe I am a good judge of other people and a fair judge of my own strengths and weaknesses. I can't think of a more valuable trait in a manager. And I think you can learn to be perceptive. But it means you have to listen.

When you're talking you're not listening, and when you're not listening, you're not learning. I work hard at listening to people. And I start listening the moment I consider someone for a job.

Most managers don't spend enough time making a decision about hiring. You can never be good at delegating unless you hire good people, people you feel comfortable with.

I'm out to hire the best people around. But chemistry is as important as talent. I'm going to be working very closely with this person; he could be Albert Einstein and it wouldn't work unless we get along well. Hiring is like falling in love. How do you know when you're in love? Until I feel in my gut that it's right, I keep talking and listening.

My hiring technique is purposely open-ended. I may have a time limit on interviews but I haven't reached it yet. The courtship of Ron Snyder, our vice-president of sales, lasted seven months. But I got the best.

Recently I interviewed a young man who was everything we wanted in a salesman. We had a deal, but once he gave notice, his company tried to woo him back. Two days later he called to say his boss had made him a sensational new offer, and assured him things would change.

EXCELLO MANAGERS TALK ABOUT THEIR BOSS

Neither Gary Feldmar nor his managers pretend he's perfect. Feldmar himself says he's too competitive, driven, and impulsive. Yet Feldmar's managers respond to his style; below they tell why.

From the beginning, what excited me about joining Excello was Gary Feldmar. He's willing to share both responsibility and power. In every other company where I've worked, I felt my hands were tied. I've had to work through forty other people and endless committees to get an idea across. At Excello I've had a free hand; there's been no resistance from Gary. And that's been terribly exciting.

Pat Carney, General Manager

Gary is one of the best listeners I've ever met. His ego doesn't have to be satisfied by his doing all the talking or by having people agree with him. More than anything else, Gary has an ability to entice you with the future of Excello. What comes across is his love for this company—and his expectation that anyone who joins Excello will share that love.

Ron Snyder, Vice-President of Sales and National Sales Manager

Gary is willing to accept other people's ideas. Department heads meet every Friday to talk over problems, changes, innovations. We kick ideas around for a couple of hours and then Gary joins us. When he comes in, he doesn't knock down what we suggest. He trusts us to have really given some thought to those ideas.

Bill Kepraios, Controller

I always feel that I'm going to get a fair shake with Gary. When I walk into his office, no matter what it's for, I know nothing is prearranged or already decided. I know Gary will listen and agree with me if I'm right. I've never felt that kind of confidence before.

Tom Kostka, Director of Purchasing/Personnel

What sets Gary apart from other managers is what I'd call a presumption of value, almost like a presumption of innocence. He presumes a person's ideas are good until they're proven otherwise. As a result, he really listens to you; he doesn't make you feel as if you're wasting his time. He makes you feel that your ideas could be very important because he believes it himself.

Don Knowles, Assistant to the President

I know companies don't change that rapidly. And I knew he made his decision to stay with his heart rather than his head. Instead of arguing, I sent him a bottle of Dom Perignon. I enclosed a card wishing him success and added that when he realized he'd made a mistake, to please give me a call. Two days later he called and I hired him.

I don't have too many hard-and-fast rules in interviewing. What I won't do is talk salary on the first interview. I try to get the person to tell me about himself. The best way to get a person to talk is to bare your soul to him. I do that; I share my idea of what my strengths and weaknesses are and I ask him to tell me his. Once I'm fairly confident about hiring someone, I spend a great deal of time talking about the job itself. If a manager

TWO OUTSIDERS LOOK AT GARY FELDMAR

Like most really successful managers, Gary Feldmar has created a unique management style, one that appears to work well for him at Excello Press.

The Feldmar style seems to be a healthy variation of Michael Maccoby's Gamesman. Maccoby, a sociologist who wrote a book on managerial types, defines the Gamesman as a manager who controls not through command but through persuasion. He believes that the best will rise to the top, as long as the rules of the game are fair. He distrusts emotion, however, for fear it might weaken his will to win.

Like the Gamesman, Feldmar wants very much to win. And he manages by reason and persuasion rather than by fiat. But, he isn't afraid to trust his feelings. He gives the Gamesman stereotype warmth and humanity.

Feldmar's "by the heart" management never gets out of control because he ties it to performance. The "family" he's created is based on a relationship of mutual obligation. Both he and his staff must honor the contract. If his trust in a worker is broken—if someone doesn't perform—then Feldmar is no longer bound by his emotional commitment.

Feldmar is obviously perceptive. He sounds like he takes people and their needs seriously, and thus has created a work environment that seems to foster initiative.

As a result, he's coping well with what's becoming a clear trend in the American workplace; workers at all levels who want a share of the action. It reflects changes in American society, especially within the family, where the word of one breadwinner is no longer law.

This trend and the issues facing any fast-growing company will combine to challenge Feldmar in the future, however. His head-and-heart management style, like any other, will have to evolve to remain successful. He seems to understand how limiting it can be to try to hold all power to himself; he gives his managers both responsibility and authority to act in his name. Yet they may eventually want more; perhaps equity and a voice in the plan for Excello's future. If they do, and Feldmar refuses, Excello could become a training ground for managers who move on to companies promising a share in the action.

As his company grows, Feldmar will also be challenged by the need for major infusions of capital. If he takes Excello public, Feldmar will find it more difficult to run his company as a family. Whether public or private, Excello is likely to reach a size and complexity that demands outside expertise. At the moment, Feldmar seems to rely solely on himself to make decisions. He listens to his managers, to his "head and heart," and then decides. Who provides a check on Gary Feldmar? He may need an outside director who can offer blunt, impartial, professional advice.

—*Jane Watkins and David Brunnel*

doesn't know exactly where he stands and what his job is, he can't succeed and he can't fail. Then everyone's dissatisfied.

If we decide to get together, money is the last thing that will stand in the way. I firmly believe that a good manager won't cost you a cent; he'll make you money. I don't want to overstate this, but I won't quibble over a few thousand dollars. The salaries I pay are not exorbitant, although I'd say they're above the industry average.

The time I spend hiring makes my job that much easier. I don't have time to look over the shoulders of my managers. I expect them to pick up several balls and juggle them while they're running. My managers carry tremendous responsibility. And I know they need tremendous authority to go along with that responsibility. Otherwise, I can't hold them accountable for their actions. Each manager operates as the chief resident expert in his area of operations. He hires and, in unambiguous situations, fires.

My role at Excello is a policy-making one. I operate in a combination management-by-objective and management-by-exception mode. I communicate my policies to managers who establish goals in their departments to achieve those objectives. Ideally, I become involved only when an exception arises. It works because I feel comfortable with my managers.

I need people who will challenge my thinking; what I don't need are a dozen Gary Feldmars. I've learned a great deal about this industry from managers who have come here with different backgrounds.

There is not a manager at Excello who hasn't walked into my office and told me—diplomatically—that he thought I was wrong about something. I know I make mistakes. And if I can make mistakes, my managers can, too. If people worry too much about making mistakes, they never take risks. When someone at Excello makes a mistake, I don't ignore it, but I don't dwell on it either. We sit down and try to understand why it happened.

If you can't accept mistakes, you end up with a bunch of yes-men who simply parrot your dictates. If you can, you encourage people to take risks, to show initiative, to think creatively.

Last year, Bob Johnson, our Creative and Customer Services manager, heard about a printing job for a company that wasn't a customer of ours. Without a whisper of what he was doing, Bob laid the groundwork for that job. When it was 80 percent complete, he came to me with the proposal and the preliminary prices he'd quoted. I was so stunned, all I could do was give him a hug and assure him he'd share in the deal financially. That job billed out at over $1 million.

Bob Johnson is an interesting case. Earlier this year he told me he had decided to leave Excello. This was a man who started here as an estimator, rose to head the department, hired his successor, and moved over to Production. He revamped Production and turned the department into Creative and Customer Services.

He came in and said he was leaving to take a job as the manager of a small printing company in New Mexico. His daughter has asthma and the climate would be healthy for her, and he has relatives in Albuquerque. I told him that we'd miss him but it looked like a terrific opportunity.

Well, a couple of months ago he called. The job wasn't what it was made out to be and he wondered whether his job here was still open. I told him it was. When Bob got back, no one said, "I told you so."

There are times when I think I should have a doctor's shingle hanging outside my office. I talk to managers and employees about all sorts of problems—problems with money, kids, marriage, and drugs. I really believe that if you can get whatever is bothering people out on the table and try to do something about it, you can avoid a lot of unnecessary problems.

One of our salesmen was putting in very long hours traveling to out-of-town customers and he was having some marital problems. One morning as he was dressing, he found his wife's wedding ring in his jacket. Nothing more—just that quiet message. He was so upset that he came in to talk to me about it. I asked him if he loved his wife. He said he did. I suggested he leave immediately, pick up his wife, and take a vacation. I told him to come back when it was time. He was gone for two weeks and Excello picked up the bill. So it cost the company two weeks. It was what they needed, a long trip together by themselves.

Except for my family, there is nothing more important to me than Excello Press. I agonize in its defeats and I gloat in its victories. I want people who work here to share my love for this company. I don't want them to think of their work as just another job, but as a career.

Everyone knows he has a chance to make his thumbprint visible at Excello. Some prints are hard to see unless you're willing to take the time to look, but I am. We have half a dozen customers come through our plant each week and I'll be damned if they don't mention how clean our plant is every time. I let our janitor know that.

We have bulletin boards in the plant and the office where we tack up letters that single out individuals for their contributions to a job. If I hear about someone's fine work, I go out of my way to tell him I think he's done a terrific job. We honor individuals as Employee of the Year and Salesman of the Year, and a team for Team of the Year, at our annual Christmas dinner-dance.

The opportunity for growth at Excello isn't limited to management. Three of our in-plant supervisors started as pressmen. One former press-man is now a salesman. One of our best salesmen started thirty years ago as an artist on the bench. The year before last our Salesman of the Year was a man who started in the ink room twenty-five years ago.

In the final analysis, Excello Press, for better or worse, is a reflection of me. That's not an egotistical statement; it's reality. A fish doesn't stink just from the tail, as someone once said, and a company doesn't succeed or fail from the bottom. So I try to set an example.

I set high goals for myself and for my company, but not so high that they can't be achieved. I like my wife's paraphrase of Browning: You must always reach beyond your grasp. I don't like complacency in myself or in other people, so I find it impossible to ignore mediocre performance. People who don't perform don't remain at Excello.

But I never forget that people are human beings. It's as simple as that. In the end, it is people who make up Excello Press. Without the people, there's just a shell of a building, some presses, and a sign over the door. If I can be sensitive to those people, I'm helping them achieve the goals I've set for my company.

—GARY FELDMAR

STOP WORKING
SO HARD:
LESS IS MORE

It's about time someone exploded the myth that you should fill every waking moment with "productive" activity. If your management time is a resource to be employed to gain maximum return on investment, let's look at a strategy more in keeping with that objective.

The concept of strategic reserve has been used in military operations for centuries. Translated into management terms, strategic reserve means keeping your time flexible enough so that you can apply management effort and skill when critically needed. Ideally practiced, this means committing only two-thirds of your time to planned and predictable activities, and keeping the remaining third open and in reserve.

"What," you ask, "I shouldn't do a full day's work?" Careful, you're talking like a production employee, not a manager. If your job takes more than two-thirds of the time available, you're probably committing yourself to more projects and objectives than are really required. Doing less *better* is the approach to take, not trying to play executive superman, a popular role today.

The strategic reserve approach to time management is tailored to your mission, a large part of which should be making yourself available to others when they need you. If a subordinate must make an appointment to get on your schedule, or stand for hours waiting for a break in the action, you are investing your time inappropriately. Even in small and mid-sized businesses, management's top priority must be to help others achieve results. This means resisting the temptation to carve out large chunks of work for yourself.

One manager I know was a charter member of the "eighteen-hour-a-day menace club." He arrived at 7:00 A.M. every day, after a one-hour commute. ("The better to think and look at the mail," etc.). Then, by careful scheduling, he filled the next twelve hours with meetings, presentations, telephone calls, dictation, and a hasty lunch at his desk.

His door was always open, so everyone could see his herculean efforts, but there was no way you could get in. If you arrived at 7:00 in the morning, he resented your intrusion on his quiet time. If you tried late in the day, at 8:00 P.M., you were taking away from the little time he had for his family (whose existence many doubted). Finally his boss sent the message that he should back off a bit, providing him with an assistant to lighten the load. The manager merely added to his duties the task of keeping his new subordinate jumping.

The counterproductivity of all this activity should be obvious, but the rule of 100 percent use of management time is hard to unlearn. One who did unlearn it was the chief executive officer of a small company who discovered he was doing more harm than good by constantly supervising his managers. He decided to take up flying the company plane in order to stay out of his managers' hair for a while. His managers are grateful and much more productive as a result. Another manager restructured his time so that he can visit outside organizations. The resources he brings back to his company from the field have had a great impact on his operations.

Several years ago, I worked with a senior operating officer of a small company who arrived each day at 9:00 A.M., went to lunch at noon, and left each evening at 5:00. He never worked on weekends, even though those who worked for him occasionally pressed him to come in then. Sales went from $750,000 to over $10 million in nine years because what he did, he did very well. Those who worked for him had to produce results.

GET TOP PERFORMANCE

Whoever thought of holding performance reviews semiannually should be put on bread and water and fed only twice a year.

Can you imagine shooting at a target every day and being allowed to check your hits or misses only twice a year? What could be more foolish or counterproductive?

The stock answer is that "twice a year is better than not at all." True, but not very encouraging when you consider that human progress requires constant evaluation and encouragement.

There is no need to make evaluation, support, positive remarks, statements of appreciation, and weekly performance reviews rare items in your organization. People thrive on them, just as machines thrive on regular maintenance.

"People machines" are the most productive devices on the face of the earth. How much effort do you invest as a manager in just doing ordinary preventive maintenance? Think about it. The technical aspects of your business may hold some challenge, but the return on investment from managing your people far exceeds anything you can do as a business technician.

In looking back on it, I can see that he really didn't do very much except make sure that everyone else was doing the things necessary to make the place hum. His employees were welcome to talk with him about their problems, but he never let them leave problems with him. He gave them the feeling that each one had personal responsibility for getting the job done, and that if he didn't exercise that responsibility, the place wouldn't run.

Protecting your strategic reserve takes discipline, but it can be done. Try it next week or next month. Open up two days during a week and hold them open. Keep two hours a day blank on your schedule. Protect these reserves so that you can do less and do it better. Why should nine to five be clerical hours only? Managers, real managers, deserve the same hours.

—JACK FALVEY

THE
TURNAROUND

You can find JoAnn's Expressway Lounge on the West Chestnut Expressway in Springfield, Missouri. It's located in a yellow cinder-block bunker, fringed along the roof with blue shingles. Inside, there are two pool tables and a pinball machine, a jukebox, a bar, and assorted tables. For most of any given day, it is exactly what it appears to be: another juke joint along another midwestern highway. But around 4:30 every afternoon, JoAnn's is transformed into a kind of true-grit tabernacle, when the regulars begin to arrive from Springfield Remanufacturing Center Corp. (SRC).

At the moment, about twenty-five of them are scattered around the bar, playing and talking as the jukebox pleads, "I want to bebop with you, baby, *all night long*." They range from assembly-line workers to senior managers, the latter indistinguishable except for an occasional loosened tie. Here, for example, are Pam Smith and Verna Mae Ross, who assemble fuel-injection nozzles, as well as general foremen Steve Choate and Joe Loeber. Over there, pounding on a pinball machine called Memory Lane, is Doug Rothert, the production manager, and the guy trying to bank the nine ball is executive vice-president Mike Carrigan.

It's an odd assortment of people, defying the normal stratification of corporate society—a fact of which they are all aware. "The barriers between management and employees just don't exist here," says Pam, the nozzle assembler, to which Verna Mae adds, "Here I am, pretty low in seniority, and I can sit here and bullshit with Jack over there."

"Jack" is John P. Stack, SRC's president and largest shareholder, who is presently lost in thought, calculating the more esoteric geometries of pool. He is thirty-seven years old, slightly under six feet tall, thin, and lanky, with thick brown hair and a boyish face. Of all JoAnn's regulars, he is the most regular. On any day, Stack can be found here from roughly 4:30 to 6:00 P.M., just in case someone should want to talk through a problem in less formal surroundings. Right now, however, he is more intent on making his next shot.

Standing there, leaning on his pool cue, blowing cigarette smoke over the green felt, he hardly seems like a man with a mission. And yet he is just that, for Stack has come about as close as anyone to solving one of the more perplexing business puzzles of our time.

The problem dates back to the early 1960s, when the idea took hold in boardrooms and business schools across the country that the secret of effective management lay in the numbers: first, in collecting the raw data on sales, profit margins, inventory levels, and countless other statistics; then, in arranging them into various pie charts and bar graphs; and finally, in conforming business strategies to their mathematical authority. Aided by the advance of computer technology, "quantitative" management soon became the shibboleth of the executive suite. Unfortunately, this preoccupation with numbers all too often reduced employees to the status of mere ciphers, thereby isolating the company from the creative energies of its work force.

It was a dangerous balance: too many statistics could prove toxic to humans, and too few could just as easily murder a business. To this day, the proper mixture of dismal science and effervescent humanity is the subject of heated debate, not to mention a number of best-selling books. What Stack and some 360 of his colleagues seem to have demonstrated is that a rigorous, even obsessive, quantitative regimen can still produce a strikingly people-oriented enterprise. Indeed, Stack is convinced that his number-crunching works so well *because* his people are so involved.

Ironically, all this has happened in a company that, up until three years ago, was a division of International Harvester Co.—the industrial giant that grew out of Cyrus McCormick's original reaper company. A rebuilder of engines and engine components, SRC was losing $2 million a year on sales of $26 million when Stack arrived in 1979 to turn things around. In 1983, he and twelve other employees bought the business from Harvester and struck out on their own. Carrying a crushing debt load, and facing potential ruin, they developed a meticulously detailed reporting system that at one point had them calculating a full-blown income statement every day.

The results have been impressive. Since the leveraged buyout, SRC's sales have grown 40 percent per year and are expected to reach $42 million in fiscal 1986; net operating income has risen to 11 percent; the debt-to-equity ratio has been cut from 89-to-1 to 5.1-to-1; and the appraised value of a share in the company's employee stock ownership plan has increased from 10¢ to $8.45. Meanwhile, absenteeism and employee turnover, once high, have all but disappeared, and the frequency of recordable accidents in the plant has fallen dramatically.

To hear Stack tell it, this turnaround owes much to SRC's exacting quantitative controls, but even more to its almost evangelical insistence on giving human potential its due. "Look, we're appealing to the highest level of thinking we can in every employee in our company," he says between pool shots at JoAnn's. "Why hire a guy and only use his brain to grind crankshafts?"

It is 11:15 on a weekday morning, and—in the company cafeteria—SRC is appealing to the highest level of thinking of the workers on the first shift. They are sitting at long Formica tables, talking, laughing, eating their lunch from brown bags and Tupperware containers. There is just one thing out of the ordinary: high on the wall above the microwave oven sits a red, electronic message board, quietly flashing the words, "FUEL INJEC-TION LABOR UTILIZATION 98%."

What the message means, as any of the lunching laborers can tell you, is that the fuel-injection pump assemblers spent 98 percent of their work time on direct labor (rather than overhead) during the first half of their shift. If they keep it up, they become eligible for a sizable bonus under an SRC plan known as STP-GUTR, an acronym for "Stop the Praise—Give Us the Raise." The electronic ticker tells them how they're doing.

"It's like the big red board at Caesars Palace," says Stack. "You know, the one with ten or fifteen games on it, for any sport you want to bet on. The odds are constantly changing, and the action is fantastic. Well, it's the same thing here. When you walk through this factory, you hear numbers everywhere you go. It's like you're in the middle of a bingo tournament."

SRC certainly does have more than its share of numbers. Those numbers guide its operational and financial reporting system, which is as elaborate, and as rigorous, as any in American business. What sets it apart is the level of employee involvement. Springfield's workers all play active roles in it; they are all directly responsible for helping to make it work.

The cafeteria ticker is part of that system, and—like most of the other parts—it is something Stack dreamed up as he went along. "I had no education," he says. "I had no master plan. My feelings were more basic. I just felt that, if you were going to spend a majority of your time doing a job, why couldn't you have fun at it? For me, fun was action, excitement, a good game. If there's one thing common to everybody, it's that we love to play a good game."

Gamesmanship lies at the heart of Stack's approach to management. Virtually everything that happens at SRC is based on the premise that business is essentially a game—one, moreover, that almost anyone can learn to play. As with most games, however, people won't bother to learn it unless they "get" it. That means, first, they must understand the rules; second, they must receive enough information to let them follow the action; and third, they must have the opportunity to win or lose.

It is hard to exaggerate the lengths to which Stack has gone to get everyone at SRC involved in the Great Game of Business. For openers, he has set up an extraordinary education program, designed to teach employees how the Game is played. At one point, he even went so far as to have every worker in the plant take a series of courses covering most elements of a business curriculum, from accounting to warehousing.

More recently, the company has organized an ongoing management training program, aimed at opening up opportunities for employee advancement. At SRC, those opportunities are real. General foremen Steve Choate and Joe Loeber started out as janitors; director of safety and training Lee Shaefer began as a "gofer"; Wendall Wade, the twenty-nine-year-old supervisor of engine disassembly, was a shipping clerk. Inspired by such examples, some 80 percent of SRC's employees have taken courses under the program.

But promotion is just one of the possible rewards for playing the Game well. More important, perhaps, are those offered by the STP-GUTR bonus program. Here, too, the approach is unusual. Instead of funneling a predetermined percentage of profits into a bonus pool, as is common, SRC ties its bonuses to the achievement of specific goals. In fiscal 1985, for example, there were two such goals: to control costs (specifically, to reduce the plant's overhead charge-out rate from $39 to $32 per hour), and to increase operating income from 6 percent to 15 percent of sales. Although the charge-out rate was eventually cut to $23 per hour, the company missed its operating-income objective. As a result, employees received bonuses amounting to 7.8 percent of gross salary, rather than the 10 percent they would have earned had the company met both goals.

Additional rewards are offered to employees whose ideas improve the company's operations—up to $500 per idea. Such programs are not uncommon in business, but SRC's works better than most. Thirty-two-year-old engine disassembler Freeman Tracy, for one, has turned in some fifty ideas, earning him $7,500 and saving the company almost $2 million in production costs—and that's just since the buyout. Before, says Tracy, he "wasn't in a thinking mood, but now you know you're helping yourself as well as the company."

Then, of course, there is the long-term reward of stock accumulation. Stack had originally planned to offer direct ownership to everyone as part of the leveraged buyout, but he ran afoul of a Missouri state law that limits the number of owners in a privately held corporation. Instead, he set up the ESOP. "To me," Stack says, "giving ownership to the people who do the work has always seemed like the simplest way to run a business. It frees you to concentrate on productivity."

If the education program teaches employees the rules of the Game, and the compensation program allows them to participate in the risks and rewards, everything else is geared toward playing the Game as well as it can be played. Like any successful team in any sport, SRC concentrates on the fundamentals, on doing the thousand and one little things that separate a champion from an also-ran: turning the double play, hitting the cutoff man, covering the bag, advancing the runner. In the sport of remanufacturing, the fundamentals include such things as using hand tools correctly, watching the labor utilization rate, figuring out better ways to make spare parts. To a certain extent, SRC works on its fundamentals through its education program and its system of rewards. Mainly, however, SRC keeps employees focused on the basics by giving them all the information they need to follow the flow of the Game.

To begin with, everyone—managers, supervisors, administrative personnel, production workers—has access to the company's monthly financial report, a weighty tome often running to ninety pages. In small group sessions, supervisors or department heads go over the figures, encouraging questions. In addition, there are the daily printouts from the cost-accounting department, detailing the progress of every job in each supervisor's area.

But perhaps the most extraordinary aspect of SRC's information flow involves its use of the income statement. Granted, every business concerns itself with the income statement at some point. Seldom, however, does a company do so as frequently, as intensely, or with as broad participation as SRC. "If you picture this organization," says Stack, "it's like a continuous Dow Jones ticker tape. For almost every single hour of every single day, there is a new number about the business crossing my desk. For us, the income statement is the same as the daily racing form is to a guy handicapping a race, or the same as the tape is to a guy betting on the market. I mean, it's addictive because it's fun, it's action."

The action begins every Tuesday morning, when some twenty-five managers and supervisors get together in a conference room near Stack's office. Everyone comes armed with a detailed, preprinted, projected income statement. The first column of figures lists the income and expense figures for the previous month. The next column gives the projections for the current month as they appeared in the budget at the start of the fiscal year. The following three columns are blank. Every week, one of the columns is filled in with adjusted projections, based on the reports given at the meeting.

Today, for example, quality supervisor Steve Shadwick notes a drop in the "average monthly deficiency rate" on General Motors diesel engines for the year to date—from 26 percent to 9 percent. What this means, chimes in executive vice-president Mike Carrigan, is that the company has saved between three and four "equivalent men" in extra labor costs because fewer parts have to be reworked. Production scheduler Ron Maus reports unexpected problems with a spare-parts supplier. Engine disassembly supervisor Wendall Wade confesses that his department has gone $268 over budget on protective gloves. And so it goes.

In about forty-five minutes, the morning's work is done. Stack, who has been recording the variances on a board in the front of the room, works the income statement down to a net operating income figure that is well above the 15 percent of net sales needed to trigger a bonus distribution for the quarter. Everyone appears pleased.

That same afternoon, the supervisors and managers carry the news to hourly workers all over the plant. In one lecture room, Wendall Wade stands before seventeen engine disassemblers sitting expectantly around two long conference tables. Most are dressed in grease-stained T-shirts and jeans, and several wear caps embellished with the logos of brand-name beers, whiskeys, or chewing tobacco.

First, production manager Doug Rothert presents a brief review of the income statement, with heavy emphasis on the bonus distribution. Wade follows with a solemn soliloquy on the virtues of conserving protective gloves. Then comes nineteen-year-old Bobby Voelker, the department's safety representative, who reports that there have been nine recordable accidents and fourteen days lost as a result. "We've got to do better than that," he says, adding self-consciously, "you've got to wear your safety glasses to and from lunch." Wade asks if there is anyone who does not understand the income statement. Two people raise their hands, and Wade offers to tutor them after work.

Meanwhile, in another room, general foreman Steve Choate is addressing the fuel-injection pump department. The pump has long been the most profitable item in SRC's product line, he is saying, but now it is threatened by aggressive domestic competition and cheap foreign imports. If the department could reduce the cost of remanufacturing the pump by 25 percent, SRC would still reign supreme for quality and price.

After the meeting, thirty-year-old supervisor Tim McVeigh explains that the department has already begun shooting for this reduction. For the past month, a four-worker task force has been studying the possibilities and will eventually enlist the other pump assemblers in the effort. "You've got to get people involved," McVeigh says.

That is, indeed, a theme heard constantly around the plant. There are no spectators in the Great Game of Business, at least as it is played at SRC. Everybody is encouraged to get involved, to take responsibility. As for the top executives of the company, they work diligently, and often ingeniously, to keep raising the level of participation.

Consider, for example, how executive vice-president Mike Carrigan went about getting managers and supervisors, and ultimately employees, more involved in planning the company's future results. He selected operating expenses as the place to start. After working up his own projections in some twenty areas—welding supplies, abrasive materials, hand tools, and so on—he asked every manager and supervisor to take personal responsibility for one account, and to report back in a month as to whether his projections were realistic.

Over the next few weeks, each of them went around asking employees about their needs, researching past expenditures, testing the production scheduler's assumptions, checking with the various buyers, forcing Carrigan to defend his calculations. When the group reconvened at the end of a month, the managers and supervisors were surprised to learn that henceforth their findings would be accepted as the budget figures for the coming fiscal year.

"You see, what happened here," says Carrigan, "is that now these people were in effect running their own small businesses. They had set their own budgets, and they had to live with them. If they wanted to complain, they had to complain to themselves. This is above all an awareness program. Every little bit counts, and only the people here can make the numbers work."

Getting people to make the numbers work is, of course, a major goal of the Great Game of Business. It is one, moreover, that the employees of SRC routinely achieve. Day in, day out, they run their drills so smartly, so effortlessly, so smoothly that an outsider is tempted to think of them as natural athletes, participating in a sport they were born to play. Watching them, it is difficult to imagine that a few years ago SRC was teetering on the brink of disaster.

But Stack remembers.

It was January 1979, and Stack, then thirty years old, had just arrived as the new plant manager. SRC was foundering badly. Opened by International Harvester in 1974 to remanufacture diesel engines and engine components for its truck and agricultural and construction equipment dealers, the plant had lost $2 million in the most recent fiscal year, and the big question was whether the employees, previously nonunion, would vote to join the Teamsters or the United Auto Workers in an election scheduled for March.

Stack had been given six months to determine whether the plant should be scrapped or saved. On his first day, he held a meeting in the cafeteria for all 140 plant employees. "I was giving them this Knute Rockne routine," he recalls, "and when I looked out over the crowd, I felt like I was looking into an aquarium. Totally immobile faces." At the end of his remarks, he asked for questions. There was a pause; then someone in the back hollered, "How old are you anyhow?"

"That was the only question I got," says Stack. "I knew then it wasn't going to be easy."

But Stack was not without experience in such matters. Four years earlier, at the age of twenty-six, he had been named superintendent of the machining division of Harvester's Melrose Park, Illinois, plant. There he had found himself in charge of five general foremen, all more than fifty years old; roughly 400 employees; and a division that ranked last in productivity out of seven divisions in the plant. Hoping to stimulate their competitive juices, Stack had hit on the idea of giving each foreman a copy of the division's daily productivity figures, broken down by foreman and then compared in total with the other six divisions. Productivity began to soar. The first time the foremen beat the previous high score, Stack bought them coffee; the second time, he bought them coffee and doughnuts; the third time, he invited them all to his house for poker, pizza, and beer. Within three months, Stack's division had risen from last to first place in the plant's productivity rankings. Thus was born the Great Game of Business.

By the time Stack got to Springfield, he had refined the concept somewhat, but he could not yet apply it to SRC. The place was in a shambles. Thanks to a critical shortage of parts, production had nearly stopped. "But the people wanted to work," says Stack. "Most of them had come off the farms. They were dedicated, hardworking people, and they were disgusted because they didn't have the tools to work with. The only reason they wanted the union was that they thought it might get them the tools they needed."

Stack convinced them otherwise. "It was very sophisticated," he says. "Me and the other managers got down on our hands and knees out on the shop floor and begged them to give us a shot."

"At least he was talking to us," says twenty-seven-year-old Randy Rossner, now a fuel-injection pump assembler. "Before, we didn't see much of anybody out here. It was as if nobody cared. Jack looked like somebody we could work with." Most of Rossner's colleagues evidently agreed. The union proposal was defeated by a 75 percent margin. Meanwhile, Stack managed to finagle a supply of spare parts from his erstwhile cronies in Melrose Park. So SRC's production line went back up to speed. "Now," says Stack, "we had to start winning."

Before they could start winning, however, they had to create the Game. Stack began by choosing three modest goals, which he called "account-abilities": product quality, safety, and housekeeping (meaning the organization and cleanliness of each work area). In addition, management cobbled together some production goals. Stack's purpose in all this was to focus attention on common objectives, and to suggest in some small way that performance could be measured. "Things were in such disarray," he says, "you had to start with something. We needed something to celebrate."

And celebrate they did. On the afternoon marking 100,000 hours without a recordable accident, the plant closed down for a beer bust. The theme song from *Rocky* played over the loudspeaker system, and members of the safety committee marched around, handing out fire extinguishers. Forklift trucks festooned with crepe paper were driven in a parade through the plant as onlookers cheered.

The celebrating continued as departments began exceeding their production goals. The department that won by the highest percentage was given an award—the "Traveling Trophy," a huge confection in marble and brass, topped off by a winged goddess holding a torch. Whenever the award changed hands, the winning department would strut en masse to the ex-winners' department and carry off the trophy amid much self-congratulatory brouhaha.

Stack's approach to quality control was no less dramatic. If, say, a transmission broke down in service, he would fly the hapless reassembler to the job site. One poor fellow spent a weekend repairing such a transmission in Kentucky, before the customer calmed down enough to let him go home. "I can tell you," says Stack, "when the guy gets back here, the word gets around fast that you don't ever want to experience that kind of pressure."

The effect of all this was soon apparent. Within four months, SRC had earned its reprieve. "Harvester was very happy," says Stack. "They left us alone and told us to keep going." At the end of nine months, the company recorded a profit of $250,000.

But encouraging as this start was, the Game was still quite primitive. There were no training programs, no financial controls, no systems for monitoring costs. As for the goals and rewards, they served to motivate people in a general way, but they were not targeted to SRC's specific business objectives, notably improved productivity.

Part of the problem, Stack realized, was that the plant operated under a system that measured labor, overhead, and materials by their actual costs, rather than their standard costs. As a result, he and his managers could not figure out what should be used (as opposed to what was used), nor could they accurately gauge their progress in using resources more efficiently.

So in February 1980, they organized a new cost department, which was given the task of taking SRC from an actual cost system to a standard cost system. This move—critical to the quantitative analysis SRC adopted after the leveraged buyout—sent a small army of engineers and accountants swarming over the shop floor. Measuring costs with the precision of diamond cutters, they were soon able to calculate, for example, the portion of the plant's heating and electrical expenses that should be allocated to a fuel-injection pump. When the cost commanders presented their findings to Stack, he nearly disappeared behind the mounds of data.

"Now I had all these numbers," Stack recalls, "and what was I going to do with them? Only the people could make them work. And how were they going to do that if they didn't know what the hell the numbers meant?" His solution was to educate the entire population, some 200 people.

Thus began SRC's Great Leap Forward. In the first three weeks of March 1980, groups of ten to fifteen employees rotated, during working hours, through a full range of business courses: production scheduling, purchasing, accounting, plant audit, standard cost, industrial engineering, inspection and warehousing, and so on. Most of the sessions, which lasted one or two hours, were taught by SRC supervisors, but occasionally outside instructors were brought in. All told, 96 hours of training were offered, involving more than 1,300 hours of student instruction and preparation.

The courses were immensely popular, and Stack was thrilled. He immediately set out to expand his list of "accountabilities," devising an intricate method of evaluating each manager's individual performance. The system seemed to be working well enough until two managers showed up in Stack's office one afternoon, each with a hand on the other's lapel. It turned out that one manager had reached his goal by cutting inventory—a move that prevented the other from meeting one of his. "The whole thing blew up in my face," says Stack. "These guys wanted to duke it out right there in the office." With customary flair, Stack ended the experiment by gathering up all the rating sheets and setting them on fire in a small picnic area in back of the plant.

"It served its purpose, though," says Gary Brown, manager of human resources, "because it showed us some of the dangers in statistics."

Despite this setback, the Great Leap Forward reached a splendid crescendo in October 1980, with an extravaganza billed as "Employee Awareness Day." The plant closed and reconvened in the ballroom of the local Hilton Inn. The employees lunched and suppered and listened to speakers. They also watched a documentary about Japanese business, which warned that—unless the United States improved its productivity—the next generation of Americans would be the first to experience a declining standard of living.

After the film, Stack stood up to speak. "Do you want this responsibility?" he asked. "Do you want to be the ones who started this decline? We've got to do something about it, don't we?" The audience rose as one, cheering and raising their arms, soldiers now in a great holy war. "I was standing there," says Wendall Wade, the engine disassembly supervisor, "and everyone was all around me, and I never knew working could be anything like this. It was great. It was simply great."

Little did any of them suspect how close they were to losing what they had just begun to build.

By February 1981, SRC could report that profits had climbed to $1.1 million, the highest in its history; return on sales had risen from .9 percent in 1979 to 8.0 percent in 1980; and productivity had increased 53 percent. The next month, Stack and six of his managers were called to a meeting at Harvester headquarters. Because of precarious economic conditions, they were told, SRC could not exceed 33 percent of its capacity for the next three years. "That was the handwriting on the wall," Stack says. "If you're not going to increase your sales, you're just going to die."

The United States had entered a recession. Farm income had fallen sharply, creating severe overcapacity in International Harvester's largest operations—the truck, agricultural equipment, and construction equipment divisions. The company was in trouble, meaning SRC was in trouble, too.

Stack returned to Springfield and held a meeting with his managers. They saw three possible scenarios: Harvester would reduce its capital commitment to SRC, causing the plant to deteriorate in an agonizing process of layoffs and cutbacks; the plant would be closed; or the plant would be sold. "Then the light came on," Stack says. "I thought, 'Why don't we ask Harvester to sell the plant to us?' "

Stack took the idea to the vice-president and the controller of Harvester's construction equipment division, to which SRC reported. Both men asked to participate as investors and operating officers. With Stack, they submitted a proposal to buy the plant for $6 million. While Harvester was considering the plan, Stack set about selling the idea to other potential investors. "I went to one of the biggest venture capital firms in Chicago," he recalls, "and the guy says, 'It's got no schmazzle. Redo the plan.' Hell, I was a grease monkey, and I produced a grease-monkey plan. But from all those rejections, I got better at it."

In the meantime, business conditions continued to deteriorate. By 1982, Harvester, burdened with close to $4 billion in debt, was desperately trying to stave off bankruptcy, and all signs pointed to the imminent liquidation of SRC. Seventy-six employees were laid off, and wages remained frozen at the November 1980 level. SRC's shining esprit de corps had descended to fretful paranoia. "There was a lot of uneasiness," says SRC manager Robert A. Bigos. "Employees here would ask me if they should get married, if they should have a kid, if they should buy a car. I mean, it's pretty strange when someone asks you if they should get married."

To no one's surprise, Harvester soon began encouraging bids for sizable chunks of its business, including its five remanufacturing centers, which it preferred to sell as a group. As a result, Stack found himself in the uncomfortable position of describing SRC's merits to potential purchasers. "I did everything I could to help them," Stack says, "but they always wanted to know if the existing management team would stay on. I'd say I didn't know. I mean I honestly didn't know. On the other hand, now they weren't sure about their bid either."

Such niggling uncertainties did not deter Dresser Industries Inc., which bid on SRC in late 1982. At the last moment, however, the deal fell through. On the day before Christmas, Harvester informed Stack that it wanted to proceed with his earlier proposal—but only if they could reach an agreement in one week. Stack nearly burst a major artery. How was he going to arrange financing and hire lawyers and incorporate and do everything else in one week? He absolutely had to have another month. Harvester agreed.

Stack described the opportunity before a meeting of his twelve managers, who reacted with tentative enthusiasm. "You know you want to do it," says executive vice-president Mike Carrigan, "but at times like that, you can't help thinking about what will happen if you lose your job." Nonetheless, they agreed to go for it.

Somehow, in the next month, all of the pieces fell into place. "No one remembers the Christmas of 1982," says Stack. The managers put up $100,000; the Bank of America lent them $6 million; and Harvester took back a note for $1 million. It was an all-out, mad rush to meet the deadline.

On the afternoon of Monday, January 31, human resources manager Brown sat anxiously by his phone, waiting for a call from Stack, who was negotiating with Harvester at his lawyer's office in downtown Springfield. Since SRC did not want to assume Harvester's liabilities to employees for sick pay and vacation time, everyone in the plant had to be terminated as soon as the buyout was completed. Finally, Brown decided he could wait no longer, and fired everybody, including himself and Stack.

The negotiations dragged on into the afternoon of February 1. At 2:30 P.M., Stack called Brown. "It's done. We own it." That evening, the managers and their wives celebrated in a second-floor room above a local restaurant. "It was probably one of the most fantastic moments you could ever have in your life," says Stack. "It was total euphoria. We knew that if we started thinking about tomorrow, we might get scared."

In the next few weeks, the business literally had to be founded all over again. New stationery had to be printed, a name adopted, a corporate logo designed. More important, all of SRC's outstanding contracts had to be renegotiated, including several with Dresser Industries, which had purchased Harvester's construction equipment business and now represented 60 percent of SRC's annual volume. Of the 171 terminated employees, 115 were immediately rehired as fast as the paperwork could be processed— about 30 per day.

Most important, the company had to choose a marketing strategy. According to industry observers, it chose wisely. Instead of selling through wholesalers to the thousands of job shops and assorted distributors—the common industry practice—SRC decided to sell only to original equipment manufacturers under private-label arrangements. With this stroke, the company spared itself a host of uncertain receivables and avoided the need to establish an extensive and costly distribution network. At the same time, SRC set out to diversify its market structure, eventually moving into four market segments: trucks, tractors and farm equipment, construction equipment, and automotive.

Meanwhile, the stakes had risen in the Game of Business, and Stack was not entirely sure the players understood the new rules. "I was frustrated because I couldn't get some people to see that it was a matter of survival," Stack says. "The question wasn't whether the johns were going to get cleaned or not. If things got down and dirty, we were going to have to come in and turn wrenches ourselves. This wasn't going to be any kind of administrative takeover."

To some extent, Stack realized, they all were victims of their environment, even the thirteen managers. "All of us came from huge corporations," Stack says. "There was still this mentality that we had an endless supply of cash. Probably half the people here didn't realize that this was it—that there was no turning back."

So now Stack had to revamp the Great Game of Business to conform with SRC's new reality as a freestanding corporation. "We had to set up a game," he says, "where we couldn't make a $10,000 mistake—or at least where we would know how to correct it right away. And we had to do this without establishing a dictatorship. Systems don't run companies, people do."

The solution, he decided, lay in the income statement. It could be a versatile tool, he thought; it could emphasize the urgency of SRC's position, transcend individual preoccupations, and measure performance. Once he set up the ESOP, moreover, the income statement could be used to encourage employee participation as well.

But the use of income statements would also require a much higher level of business sophistication. Again, Stack attacked the problem with mass education. SRC's managers and supervisors attended a series of in-house courses on income statement construction and analysis. Then supervisors returned to the shop floor and held abbreviated versions for the hourly employees in their departments. "And then they began to see," says Stack. "Their scope was no longer one of emotional protection of fiefdoms. It became one of logic and sequence. You can't live like a king. Most kings inherit their wealth. We had to scratch ours out. We had no time to lose. If we stumbled once, it was all over. So what we had to do is go by the numbers."

Thus did Jack Stack repair the rift between quantitative management and people-oriented enterprise, thereby solving the puzzle that had baffled so many for so long.

There is an ironic story about Stack, one that he tells with some amusement. It seems that, in the summer of 1968, when he was nineteen, Stack and a bunch of his pals from suburban Elmhurst, Illinois, piled into four or five cars and headed for Chicago to sample the commotion surrounding the Democratic National Convention. Grant Park was Stack's favorite haunt. There he would jostle his way to a spot up front, close enough to hear full blast the rants and raves of assorted political activists railing against the profiteers of corporate America.

Stack shared their resentment of corporate profit, but that was not why he had come. The engine of history, usually so distant and remote, had stopped near home that summer, and for once a kid from the suburbs could get close enough to feel its heat. Of course, he had his own opinions about Vietnam and politics, but they were often swamped in a churning sea of more conventional teenage concerns. He had no expectations then of making any meaningful contribution to the disposition of weighty national issues.

So today, leaning on his pool cue here in JoAnn's Expressway Lounge, Stack must find it endlessly curious how fate has worked its will on him, bringing him, in its own good time, to this point where his accomplishments illuminate a subject of persistent national interest—namely, the way people live and work in corporations.

He has time to ponder such questions these days, if only because SRC seems healthier than ever. Last year, it signed a new contract to re-manufacture diesel engines for General Motors, allowing it to diversify into yet another market. The deal also promises to add $75 million to SRC's top line over the life of the agreement. To accommodate the increasing volume, SRC has opened two new plants.

So much has happened so fast that even Stack sometimes worries about the dream turning a little sour. In a recent edition of the company's newsletter, he pledged himself to shoring up the retained-earnings account against the "off chance that the company runs into hard times." No, there is no specific reason. He is just the type to fret that, with so much going right, something is surely about to go wrong.

Perhaps his caution is reasonable. Paradoxically, SRC now must face the challenge of its own success. During the past few years, the company has been a close-knit family, whose daily life in the home could be easily influenced. Now, with new plants, more people, and more business, the company has to see if its management philosophy can accommodate a substantially larger, and probably less personal, enterprise. Some, like materials manager Dave LaHay, already feel the strain. "If I see one more person at the copier that I don't know," he says, "I'm going to freak out."

But here in JoAnn's, such vague and nameless threats could hardly seem more distant or more irrelevant. Pam Smith has just stunned the crowd with an account of a recent Frozen Carp Throwing Contest to benefit the visually impaired youth of southwestern Missouri. She explains how she herself came up a winner by pitching a ten-pound specimen of the frozen fish a full twenty-one feet. And Steve Choate has just sunk three balls with one shot—a feat that has set him to whooping and gyrating. And Jack Stack, leaning on his pool cue, must find it endlessly curious how fate has worked its will.

—LUCIEN RHODES, WITH PATRICIA AMEND

SUPER
MARKET

Considering how much he gives away or sells at a loss, it's a wonder that Dick Gromer makes any profit at all.

The coffee is free. Ice cream at the cone bar costs only a quarter, which barely covers the cost of the ice cream, never mind the labor. The whole meat department, with nearly $50,000 in weekly sales, loses money. The bakery earns a little, but not nearly enough to justify the space it occupies. The stamp-selling operation and the utility-bill collection service are dead losses.

Also, Gromer keeps his supermarket open and the lights on all night—even though few people in Elgin, Illinois, population 64,872, stay up, let alone go food shopping, much past 11:00.

Yet Dick Gromer, at sixty-four, is a wealthy man, and Gromer Supermarket Inc. regularly meets or tops most of the customary productivity and profitability averages in the industry (see box "By the Numbers," page 137). Just about any supermarket company—chain or independent—would happily trade Gromer's 2 percent-plus profit margin for its own. Gromer makes his money, moreover, in a perfectly ordinary, mostly middle-class city, with as much head-to-head competition among supermarkets as you will find everywhere but the smallest towns. For Gromer, there are no protected markets, no captive customers, no unique products or proprietary technologies.

There's only the daily challenge of making his store a little different—and a little better—than the competition's. Some of the differences are small, like floors that always shine. Some are striking, like the awesome variety of products displayed. None is accidental. Gromer beats the competition because he continually innovates, because he lets his managers manage, because he lets his customers tell him what they want, because he always knows how his business is doing, and because he brings his own art to the science of management.

Gromer's late father introduced Elgin grocery shoppers to self-service in 1936. Dick Gromer himself gave them checkout scanners in 1977, when only about 300 stores in North America had installed the price-reading computers. Dick's son, Gordon, just a few years ago brought twenty-four-hour shopping and an in-store salad bar to town. "If there's something new in the industry," says Tim Murphy, a food-retailing consultant, "people can expect to find it at Gromer's first."

"If you're a salesman and you've got something he doesn't have," says Jim Sanderson, at sixty-seven the oldest night-baker at Gromer, "you got a sale. He's the most progressive man I know."

Dick Gromer tries things. Not everything: Ideas have to feel right. And not everything he tries works. Someone suggested a catering service two years ago, and he agreed immediately. It's worked. On the other hand, persuading him to move the scales from the produce department to the checkout counters took nearly a year. Gromer worried that cashiers would confuse apricots with plums. They didn't, and the labor savings from the change were impressive. Bakery manager Pete DiBenedetto tried but failed to persuade Gromer to duct the aroma from the bakery ovens out to the front-door area. And he and the boss battled over hot-from-the-oven bread. Gromer thought it would sell; DiBenedetto didn't. It didn't. "He'd keep bringing it up," says DiBenedetto. " 'Pete,' he'd say, 'when are you going to start that hot bread operation?' So I took the hint, but it didn't work. One day he asked me how the hot bread was going. I said, 'Well, we're only selling six or eight.' He said, 'Why not stop it?' "

The message that Gromer's employees get from this behavior on his part is that they are supposed to try and it is OK to fail. "What I've learned," says grocery department manager Ron Lube (pronounced Luby), "is if you think it's good, go with it. The old man says be a leader, not a follower. . . . He's always having ideas, so to keep up with him, I gotta come up with ideas, too."

Because people like Lube keep coming up with ideas, Gromer Supermarket now has, in addition to the cone bar and free coffee shop: a salad bar, a fruit-salad bar, a gyros bar, a taco bar, a baked-potato bar, a soup bar, a hot and a cold deli, spit-roasted chickens you can smell all over the store, broasted chicken, catering, a twenty-four-hour bank teller, film processing, stamps, automobile license plates, utility-bill collection, and a machine that cores and peels pineapples. In the winter, they will jump-start your car. In the summer, they put out picnic tables and umbrellas.

Ten years ago, Gromer owned six supermarkets in the Elgin area. They ranged in size from 10,000 square feet to 18,000, about average for aging suburban stores. But he closed five of them and expanded one, then expanded that one again in 1983 to 50,000 square feet, creating what is known in the industry as a superstore. The average independent supermarket today stocks 10,555 separate inventory items—not *boxes* of cereal, for example, but brands and sizes of cereal. Gromer decided sometime back that product variety would be one of his competitive tools. He stocks 20,500 inventory items.

The average supermarket might carry 1,200 varieties of frozen food. Gromer carries 1,500, including 270 varieties of frozen dinners.

The average meat counter might contain 80 cuts of beef. Gromer has 110.

Gromer sells 18 varieties of seasoned croutons.

At the deli Gromer stocks: sliced bacon, shaved chopped ham, shaved roast beef, shaved corn beef, shaved turkey, shaved pastrami, shaved boiled ham, sliced roast beef, sliced turkey breast, sliced corned beef, olive loaf, old-fashioned loaf, ham 'n cheese, veal loaf, honey loaf, no-salt turkey breast, pepper loaf, barbecue loaf, smoked turkey, kosher bologna, sandwich pepperoni, pepperoni, German bologna, beer salami, meat loaf, beef summer sausage, jellied beef roll, chicken roll, roast pork loin, Canadian bacon, jellied tongue, pastrami loaf, blood tongue, capicolla, New England sausage, Lebanon bologna, head cheese, hard salami, summer sausage, Genoa salami, beef salami, cotto salami, all-meat bologna, all-beef bologna, smoked baked ham, Bavarian-style smoked ham, country-style smoked ham, baked ham, boiled ham, extra-lean boiled ham, spiced ham, minced ham, and honey ham. Not to mention the cheeses.

In produce, there are 152 barrels of bulk candies, nuts, dried fruits, coffees, grains, cereals, and pastas.

There is an entire freezer chest of frozen pizzas and a smaller, refrigerated case of chilled pizzas that assistant deli manager Dan Krueger makes himself.

But if some customers shop Gromer for its variety, a sizable number have something else in mind. According to the government, Americans spend a smaller part of their food budgets in supermarkets every year. The rest goes for food away from home—so Gromer has decided that he is really in the business of feeding people, not just selling the fixings.

"People will call in," says Peggy Casteel, busy slicing tomatoes, "and order a salad to be made up. Do you believe that? Do you believe people are that lazy?" Lazy or busy, they will pay for convenience.

They will pay $1.59 for four ounces of hydroponically grown spinach instead of 79¢ a pound for the dirt-grown variety. It doesn't require washing, and the stems don't have to be pulled out. "Customers like it because there's no work," Russ Baresel, produce manager, explains. Likewise the corn.

Fresh corn sits loose on the produce rack, but the cool air curtain over the rack dries the husks. So overnight Baresel's help husks the day-old corn, packages three to five of the naked ears in shrink wrap, and puts them beside the next day's fresh corn. "We sell twice as much of the packaged as of the loose," says Baresel. "I never thought we would, but customers don't want to husk it." And that's in Illinois.

The $500 device that cores and peels pineapples hiked pineapple sales by a factor of 10.

Everything on the salad bar, which Peggy Casteel helps clean and stock, costs $2.19 a pound except the soup. It is $1.59. In the summer, when produce prices are low, gross profit on the bars runs as high as 65 percent, according to Baresel. It may fall to 35 percent in the winter. Gross profit on bare groceries—soap, sugar, flour—by contrast, runs about 8 percent.

Gromer's hot deli features one daily special—Thursdays it is meat loaf and Fridays it is fish—and two or three other entrées daily. Chief deli cook Liz Libby will spit-roast 500 chickens a week and pressure-fry at least that many. The deli sells 400 sandwiches a week and untold 25¢ hot dogs. Customers who don't want one of the sandwiches Libby made and shrink-wrapped that morning can order the same sandwich over the counter. "They'll pay 50¢ more just to watch you make it," she says.

Between waiting on customers at the service meat and fish counter, Mike Baily takes small end cuts of steak that he used to toss into the meat grinder and alternates them with slices of pepper, onion, tomato, and mushrooms on skewers. "It's shish kebab," he says. "We get $4.98 a pound for them. Eighty percent of the weight is stick and vegetables. You could make 'em yourself, but people don't want to."

Beyond variety and convenience, Gromer's ultimate weapon in the fight to attract and keep customers may be the smile.

"I want some of the Sealtest ice cream that's on sale," the old woman says to the young man in the light blue blazer, "but all you have is chocolate."

"Yes ma'am," he replies, "That's all we sell here, just chocolate."

"It is?" She sounds disappointed.

"Well, no," says grocery manager Lube. He smiles. The customer smiles. "You tell me what you want, and I'll get it for you." She does, and Lube trots off, returning in less than a minute. The Sealtest, he says, is at the bottom of a pallet in the freezer room, and someone is going to be in trouble. But she should take whatever ice cream she likes, and she can have it at the $2.98 sale price. She thanks him and picks a vanilla, and they both smile again. The ice cream the woman walks out with cost Lube less than the Sealtest.

"I don't have too much trouble with employees," says Lube, later. "I just tell them to do as I do with customers."

"If we don't have customers," echoes Marjorie Lankton, a part-time clerk behind the service meat and fish counter, "I don't get paid."

The attitude permeates Gromer. Cashiers and baggers talk to customers, not to one another—not twice, anyway. Night stocking clerks straighten every set of shelves, every night, ensuring that every can, box, and bottle faces forward in perfect alignment with its colleagues on shelves above and below. "On income tax night," says night manager Nick Melikian, "I was at that stamp till all night . . . People in trouble come here, like parents with a son in jail for drunk driving, and they need cash for bail. We give it to them. People that need $10 for gas, even if they don't have a check-cashing card, we'll do it. It's goodwill for Gromer's." When a drunk wanders in, someone helps him call a cab.

Front-end managers—including Gordon Gromer, Dick's thirty-four-year-old son—carry a pocketful of little forms. "Hi. Can I take those bottles for you, ma'am?" Gordon says hundreds of times a day. He smiles, takes the returnable bottles from an entering customer, and gives her a chit she can exchange for cash at the checkout. "It's instant customer contact," Gordon says. He also carries a small spiral-bound notebook for jotting down customer requests. A notebook lasts him about a week.

An indignant middle-aged woman marches up to Doug Kern, another front-end manager. "Look here," she says, "these coupons were supposed to be doubled, and they weren't." The sales slip is two months old, and the coupons amount to 55¢. Kern smiles, takes the slip, apologizes, gives the woman her change, and apologizes again. She marches off.

BY THE NUMBERS

Gromer's Secret: Getting Customers in the Door

In a privately owned company, profit figures are usually kept private to be shared—reluctantly—only with the Internal Revenue Service. Dick Gromer will admit to profits of something more than 2 percent of his supermarket's gross sales. Based on some other numbers he discussed, the profit figure could be as high as 3.5 percent of sales. No matter, since even the lower number puts his store's bottom-line performance ahead of the profits of most of the country's largest chain-store operators. (The glaring exception, A&P has recently closed many of its less profitable stores.)

Net Income as a Percent of Sales

Gromer	2+
Safeway	0.94
Kroger	0.98
American Stores	1.53
Lucky	1.02
Winn-Dixie	1.59
A&P	3.67
Albertson's	1.68
Supermarkets General	1.21
Stop & Shop	1.69
Giant Food	2.11

To understand *how* Dick Gromer makes his profit, though, you need to look at Gromer Supermarket Inc.'s record in specific performance areas as compared to industry averages. In weekly sales per employee, for example, Gromer falls below the average, which isn't surprising when you consider the level of service provided throughout the store. But the comparison is misleading. When sales per employee-*hour* are compared, Gromer scores well above average. That is because the store uses a higher proportion of easily scheduled part-time employees than most operators. Gromer can bring in his workers when he needs them—and send them home when he doesn't.

Labor Productivity

	Industry average	Gromer
Weekly sales per employee	$3,237	$3,011
Sales per employee-hour	81.38	96

So Gromer's impressive sales volume is based on traffic, and the strategy Gromer uses to maintain the high traffic flow is the prodigious array of service it provides compared to other food stores. When someone drops into Gromer for a 25 cent ice cream cone, he or she can probably think of at least a couple of things to pick up at the store.

Services Offered

Service	% of supermarkets offering	Gromer
Magazine reading center	81	Yes
Carryout service	60	Yes
Service delicatessen	52	Yes
Film processing	49	Yes
Hot take-out food	39	Yes
On-premise bakeoff bakery	33	No
On-premise scratch bakery	16	Yes
Service meat	33	Yes
Scanning checkouts	33	Yes
Video games	31	No
Self-service delicatessen	27	Yes
Service center	24	Yes
Service fish	19	Yes
Catering	14	Yes
Movie cassette rental	12	Yes
Salad bar	9	Yes
ATM	9	Yes

But Dick Gromer does have a problem: sales growth. The market he serves is the part of Elgin on the west bank of the Fox River, and his growth in that market seems to have peaked. So Dick Gromer will open a second new store—with all the services of the first plus a sit-down restaurant—on the east bank of the Fox before Easter of next year. At 64 he is, he says, too young to retire.

Annual Sales Growth

	Industry	Gromer
1977	7.1%	11.8
1978	10.3	25.8
1979	11.3	20.3
1980	10.5	11.4
1981	9.1	5.4
1982	4.6	− 3.7
1983	4.7	4.6
1984	5.9	0.7

Similarly, comparing the size of the average register transaction at Gromer to the industry average might suggest that Gromer isn't getting any more out of its customers—indeed, maybe a little less—than the competition. But look at how many people pass through the Gromer checkout lanes during the average week. It is four times the industry average, and in a town as small as Elgin, Illinois, a lot of those 34,233 weekly trips to the supermarket have to be second or third trips by regular shoppers.

Trips Through the Checkout

	Industry average	Gromer
Customer purchase	$12.39	$12.31
Number of customers weekly	7,564	34,233

Another woman approaches Lube, shortly after his ice cream expedition. "Will you tell me where the mustard is?" she asks.

"No, ma'am, I won't," he replies.

"You won't?"

"No, ma'am, I'm going to take you there."

The country's ten largest supermarket chains account for about one-third of the industry's sales and operate more than a quarter of U.S. supermarkets. The largest chain, Safeway Stores Inc., operates more than 2,000 stores, and even the seventh largest, Albertson's Inc., outsells Dick Gromer's single store by more than 200 to 1. The chains' size gives them some advantages. They operate their own warehouses and can stock up on products when manufacturers offer price deals. They can advertise more efficiently, covering all their stores in an area with a single newspaper ad. They have access to large amounts of capital.

Competing with the chains, Dick Gromer has just two advantages to trade on. He is logistically more nimble, because he deals in dozens of cases of product where they deal in thousands. More important, he is organizationally more nimble. He has one layer of management to their ten standing between the chairman of the company and the product on the shelves. At Gromer's store, managers get to manage, and no one is afraid to set up a good deal or fix a bad one—like Ron Lube's orange juice fiasco.

A small Michigan manufacturer offered the grocery chief a terrific price on Fresh 'n Pure brand juice, thirty-seven twelve-bottle cases for $6 a case. Lube bought it and priced the bottles at $1.28, right next to the $2.29 Tropicana. By late afternoon, though, all the "juice" in the Fresh 'n Pure had settled to the bottom of the bottle. "Maybe it wasn't such a good buy," Lube allowed, and within the hour all thirty-seven cases of Fresh 'n Pure, worth $222 at wholesale, were in the compactor. "You don't want to jeopardize your image," said Lube, "for one stupid product." The manufacturer refunded his money.

"At Jewel," says Gromer, referring to a chain competitor, "they don't have a guy like Ron." Or if they do, it is a safe bet he is lost in a hierarchy, not managing on the floor.

At Gromer, Lube and the three other department managers are each responsible for their departments' bottom lines. They are responsible for generating their own sales, for doing their own buying, for pricing, merchandising, and controlling their own labor costs. "We treat each department like its own separate store," Gromer explains.

"And each department manager," says Pete DiBenedetto, who operates Gromer's scratch bakery, "acts like an individual owner"—including, he might have added, grabbing a profit at the expense of another department.

Lube, the thirty-year-old grocery manager, was A&P's youngest store manager when he was twenty-one. At Gromer he is responsible for, among other things, commercial bakery products. Last year he took on DiBenedetto's baked-in-the-store breakfast pastries by importing boxes of Entenmann's products. This spring he went after one of DiBenedetto's highest-profit items, angel food cake, with a commercial variety. "These cost me $1.02 and I shoot 'em out for $1.39. You give up some of the quality," he says, "but you get it back on price. That kills Pete. Say he sells his for $2 and makes $1. I only make 37¢ on mine, but I'll sell ten to his one."

"These little frozen doughnuts," he adds, replenishing the display he has erected just outside DiBenedetto's selling area, "they cost me 17¢ and I sell 'em for 33¢. That's what you call making money. I'm happy. The customers are happy. Only Pete's not happy."

When Lube attacks, DiBenedetto counters. He puts his own coffee cakes on a table where customers entering the store can't help noticing their special price before they ever get to the Entenmann's. "You do your best," he says, "to help your own sales." The net effect of this intramural competition is that Gromer sells more bakery products, in-house and commercial combined, than almost any other store its size.

The scanners at Gromer's ten checkout counters and an estimated quarter of a million dollars' worth of computer hardware and software are backup to the independence Gromer vests in his department managers— and to his own sense of what is a good idea and what isn't.

Scanners speed shoppers through the checkout lines, but only about 10 percent faster. Their real value lies in the tons of information they collect, which a clever merchant can monitor, manipulate, and analyze. In the process, according to John Lightfoot of *Supermarket Insights*, a monthly videotape "magazine" for the food-distribution industry, they have shifted the balance of power at the store level from manufacturers to retailers. The big food companies, Lightfoot says, used to tell retailers which brands, flavors, and package sizes to stock, and how much shelf space to allocate to each one. Thanks to the introduction of scanners, the retailers can fight back—and Gromer, according to Lightfoot, is "light-years ahead of most independent" operators in using scanner-generated data.

"Take cereal," says Gromer. "We were running out of space, so we did a movement study. Rice Krispies had five or six size categories, and we eliminated the slow movers. Not the ones we *thought* were slow, but the ones that actually were."

Two years ago, Gromer computerized its meat department. John Landeck, Gromer's son-in-law and the store's technology architect, helped Toledo Scale develop a system that can track a box of uncut meat coming in the back door all the way through the cutting and wrapping process. It tells meat manager Tom Smith who cut the meat, how long the cutter took, and how much gross margin the final product will produce. The system also includes a spreadsheet capability that lets Smith play "what-if" with, for example, a seventy-four-pound pork loin, which can yield different consumer cuts—for instance, ground pork, granny ribs, center-cut pork chops—in any number of combinations. With the computer, Smith can experiment with different combinations of cuts at different retail prices to maximize his gross profit on the whole loin.

Landeck also computerized Gromer's direct store delivery. Gromer orders most of its stock from J. M. Jones Co., a warehouse-distributor in Urbana, Illinois, which delivers a thousand or more cases of packaged goods at about 9:00 six nights a week. But some vendors—commercial bakeries, for example—deliver direct without orders. They have their own shelf space allocated, and it is the bakery salesperson's responsibility to keep that space neat and stocked with the right merchandise. With so many other things to keep track of, Landeck says, stores often just assume that these vendors are delivering what they are billing for, that the prices are right, and that they aren't using valuable shelf space to unload doggy products. Gromer checked these assumptions and found that it had products it didn't want and prices that were out of line. Now a receiving clerk takes a scanning wand to every vendor's goods at the back door. If it is not the right amount of the right stuff at the right price, it doesn't come in.

Gromer's scanner knows how many items go through the checkout lanes during every fifteen-minute period of the week, and Doug Kern, who schedules the utility clerks who bag customers' groceries, knows the rate at which a bagger can bag. So the computer helps Kern control his labor costs by scheduling just the number of utility clerks he actually needs. Lube also has a budget for labor, about 3.1 percent of sales. He checks his sales on the computer daily, and reschedules his help in the grocery department accordingly. Eighty percent of Gromer's 245 employees work part-time, a higher proportion than in most stores.

"With all this," says Gromer of his son-in-law's high-tech data systems, "all we're trying to do is know what's going on before it's too late."

The technology, for all its sophistication, is just a check. It can't tell anyone that an idea *will* work, only whether it did or didn't. And computers don't, in any case, create ideas. Tom Smith didn't need his meat computer to tell him he was going to lose a bundle last Thanksgiving when competition drove turkey prices down to 20¢ below cost. But he made some money by selling 179 hot, stuffed, just-cooked birds for $18 plus the price of the turkey. Similarly, no computer would tell assistant produce manager Bob Sponnholz to feed oranges to the juice squeezer every morning: A $10 case of oranges makes five and a half bottles of juice that he will retail for only $2.49 each, and he doesn't sell much of it. "But," he says, "it's something we have that no one else does. Some people come in just for this."

If science helps a grocer make a profit in a complicated business with few fixed rules, art is essential. The price on every one of the 20,500 different items in Gromer's store is the result of some manager's best guess. He considers the competition's ads, the product's cost, the volume he needs, how much he is making or losing on other products, the state of the weather, a manufacturer's deal, and a dozen other variables. Then he takes a shot. "Stack it high and kiss it goodbye," says Lube. "We'll football the peanut butter, but not pass on the full allowance on jelly. . . . We'll give away the paper towels but make money on the Windex. . . . You put your best-selling juice at the end of the case. . . . Put a sign on it, people think it's on sale."

AHEAD OF THE PACK

What the Best Supermarkets Have in Common

At its peak in 1930, The Great Atlantic & Pacific Tea Co., then the largest food chain in the world, operated 15,709 stores in thirty-four states. But times have changed, for A&P and for the rest of the food-retailing industry. The onetime leader is a shadow of its former self, having slimmed down to just 1,088 stores in only twenty-five states. The new top banana, Safeway Stores Inc., operates only 2,012 stores in twenty-eight states and the District of Columbia.

The Maine-to-California supermarket chains did well when food retailing was essentially a distribution business and customers picked a store primarily for its prices and convenient location. But the national chain operators, which pioneered in creating efficient operating and distribution systems for their stores, are at a disadvantage in today's more complicated and sophisticated retail food market. Their good management is no less important today than in earlier times, says food-retailing consultant Bill Bishop, but it is no longer sufficient. "What separates the extraordinary merchant from the average merchant today," Bishop adds, "is that the first has a very clear view of who his customer is and what he or she wants. The really outstanding retailers today are strongly market-driven."

The food business, in other words, has been experiencing the kind of segmentation found in such businesses as apparel retailing. It is a trend that favors the independents and smaller chains that can pick a niche and concentrate on it—like George W. Jenkins's Publix Super Markets Inc.

Ever since the seventy-eight-year-old founder opened the first Publix in 1930, Jenkins's customers have been middle- and upper-income Floridians. Today, Publix and competitor Winn-Dixie Stores Inc., by Jenkins's estimate, each have about 25 percent of the Florida market. But Jenkins stays well clear of the lower-income neighborhoods where Winn-Dixie stores flourish. "Somebody has got to service those people," he says, "and Winn-Dixie does a better job than we do."

Allen Bildner, chairman and chief executive officer of Kings Super Markets, which has fifteen stores in New Jersey, also goes after the high-income shopper—"people who are willing to trade some price for quality and service," as he puts it. To be sure he stays in touch with his market, he has put together seven consumer advisory boards, with fifteen to twenty-four members each, that convene quarterly. "We're astounded," he says, "by the fact that people are willing to meet after dinner and share their thoughts with us."

Pathmark supermarkets, a hugely successful division of Supermarkets General Corp., operates 137 stores in New Jersey and neighboring states and generates probably the highest weekly sales per square foot in the industry, $15.33, at least twice the industry average. What is unusual about Pathmark isn't its customer base—there is nothing upscale about its shoppers—but the lengths to which it goes to keep tabs on what its customers want.

"By prohibition," says Supermarkets General vice-president Robert Wunderle, "we do not have meetings in headquarters on Thursdays. By edict, vice-presidents are in stores on Thursdays—not just our own stores, but competitors', too. And that includes the fish stores, butcher shops, and bodegas that are competing with us." If there is a product in a local ethnic market that is selling, Pathmark wants it in its local store, too. But only if it is selling. "If you see a unique item on the competition's shelf but it is dusty, then that guy has made a mistake," Wunderle says.

"We spend lots of time," he adds, "visiting companies across the country, looking at new formats, new techniques. We're constantly asking ourselves what trends we see. But our forte is that we're not afraid to fail. To implement new ideas, we first get some store manager to buy in. We'll say, here's this idea. Anybody interested in trying it? Even if nine out of ten say no, we'll take the one and let him try. He becomes our test market. With the luxury of 137 stores times the number of departments in each store, that's how many test markets we have. At any given time there are probably three or four dozen experiments going on within the company."

"Strudel coffee cakes," points out DiBenedetto the baker, "are labor intensive, and I can only get $2.89. But appearance means a lot, so what I lose there I make up on butter cinnamon pullaparts. It's just dough, but it looks like a coffee cake, so people will pay $2.99. On fruit pies [about $3], I hardly make any money at all, but you've gotta have them for customers. I get it back on angel food for $2.63."

Artistry doesn't end with pricing. After customers have abused the tomatoes in the produce department, the tomatoes are washed, sliced, and put on the salad bar. Same for the cauliflower and broccoli. Day-old baked potatoes go into the soup. It not only helps the profit margin, "it also lets us be more picky about what produce we'll keep out on display," says Sponnholz.

The 25¢ ice cream cones sold in the foyer fall into Lube's domain, but they weren't his idea, and he has to absorb the labor cost. The quarter just barely covers the ice cream. So Lube created the 40¢ hot fudge sundae. With just a few cents worth of fudge, he earns a small gross profit, and the customer still gets a deal.

Lube also persuaded Gerber Products Co., the baby-food people, to finance a small display, above the normal shelving, of rattles, rubber pants, and other infant paraphernalia. "We added $300 to $500 of volume a month with a gross profit of 35 percent to 40 percent. . . . If we could pick up an extra $500 in each aisle, that would be $8,000." He is thinking of adding pegboard above the freezer chest and hanging microwave cookware. It is a 50 percent gross margin item.

What Lube and his colleagues do within their departments—constantly juggling a small loss here with a profit there, trading off margin for volume, looking for something new to generate a sale or attract a customer—that is what Gromer must do with the store.

If all that mattered was profitability, Gromer would shut down the meat department. After deducting product cost, labor cost, and supplies from its sales, the meat department contributes only 10 percent or less of its sales to company overhead. Overhead at Gromer runs close to 10.8 percent, which means meat is a net loser. The scratch bakery probably is, too. Its contribution to overhead is 22.4 percent, but its volume is tiny, just $16,384 a week on average. The salad bar alone will do half that in a good week without generating expensive gas bills for expensive ovens, and without occupying huge amounts of potential retail selling space. Bare groceries, which account for fully 25 percent of the store's sales volume, generate a gross profit of less than 10 percent. The gross margin on frozen foods is 30 percent, but they are only 9 percent of sales.

And no computer would ever suggest giving away free coffee or keeping an acre-plus store open twenty-four hours a day, 365 days a year, in Elgin.

"If we ever put a hard pencil to the scratch bakery," says Dick's son Gordon Gromer, "we probably wouldn't have one. Staying open twenty-four hours a day—that's a promotional thing. Business increased 25 percent a year for two years after we did it for two reasons, I think. In the last hour or two before you close, people get confused. Also in the morning. When do you open? Now, there's no confusion. And you get new regular customers from people that come in at night. We're going to restock at night anyway, so the only cost of staying open is the cost of the cashiers. And there are benefits. When you're open, all the employees have to maintain an attitude and appearance that they wouldn't have to maintain without customers. They probably work better. We probably have better managers for being open."

The bakery, the cone bar, the coffee, the postage stamps, and the jump starts. How much can Gromer give away?

"But all this is why we can do $400,000 a week," says the senior Gromer. "And if you still come up with 1 percent or more on the bottom line, you're doing all right."

He's doing all right.

—Tom Richman

ON
DISPLAY

The missing ingredient in most stores is the
enthusiastic encouragement from the boss to
attain and improve quality standards of merchandise and service. When the boss gets
excited, so does everyone else in a retail organization.
    —*Stanley Marcus*, Quest for the Best

Gordon Segal was getting excited. And when the boss of Crate & Barrel
gets excited, so does everyone else in his retail organization—particularly those within a twenty-foot radius of its main power source. On one
warm July morning, this included about forty employees from Crate's six
Boston-area stores, squeezed in among the candy-striped beach umbrellas
and picnic-to-go paraphernalia massed on the main floor of the Harvard
Square emporium. The troops had turned out for a bit of inspirational
oratory from the old field marshal himself, and he was not about to disap-
point the faithful.

"There are no promises in this business," Segal declaimed, halfway
through a rousing sermon on The State of Crate, 1985. "No guarantees that
we'll succeed. Me, I'm afraid all the time. I'm afraid we'll get too arrogant.
I'm afraid we'll get too snobbish. I'm afraid we'll take our competition for
granted. When you're in retail, you learn to run with a little fear."

With that he took off, running not with fear but with a $20 beverage
dispenser cradled in his hands. Clutching the container to his bosom, Segal
darted nimbly from saleswoman to store manager, stopping only to remind
his young charges that their main mission—indeed, their sole professional
purpose in life—was to sell fine housewares and accessories, and to sell
them with enthusiasm. Although no clear route lay open among the racks of
beach chairs and beer glasses, Segal flew on, apparently navigating by
some peculiar form of echolocation. The effect was utterly mesmerizing.
Crate employees who had handled the same piece of merchandise a hun-

dred times themselves were suddenly leaning forward to lay hands on it, as if it were the Ark of the Covenant and they, the lost tribe of Israel. One had the distinct feeling that had Segal elected to auction off his prop, $20 bills would have filled the air like confetti.

"We must never, ever lose sight of what we are," he continued, pausing to swap the beverage dispenser for a blue lawn candle. "We're not a distribution company, and we're not a computer company. We're a *sales* company." Segal held the candle aloft. "See this?" he said. "Ten or twelve years ago, two women were sitting on a beach in the south of France when they happened to notice a piece of rope with a glob of wax attached to it that had washed up in the surf. Because they had imagination—because they *saw the possibilities* in that glob of wax—today they own the biggest candle factory in France." He thrust it forward like a matador taking a stab at a hard-charging bull. "And that's what you people have to have. Imagination. This is a business built on personality. Personality and imaginative merchandising. You're selling a candlelit dinner by poolside, not a piece of wax on a stick. You're selling *romance*, not flatware."

He spread his arms dramatically. "This is theater, people," Segal thundered, "and you'd better be into it, because *you're* the stars!"

His soliloquy finished, the boss asked his supporting cast to "speak your minds." For a moment, they simply stood there, tongue-tied: how could they improvise dialogue that wouldn't sound woefully anticlimactic? Finally, though, after a few routine queries about Crate's imminent expansion into San Francisco and Houston, one woman decided to speak hers with enough imagination to suggest that she realized Crate & Barrel's future inventory wasn't just going to wash up on some beach in Nice.

How, she asked, did the $50-million-a-year company intend to underwrite this "major period of expansion" that Segal had so boldly outlined? Could it finance the growth itself? Would such established regions as Boston and Chicago suffer from Crate's great push westward? Segal thought for a moment before answering.

"Well," he said, "there are always rumors around that we're going public. And it's true that the risks tend to multiply geometrically as you grow. As it happens, private venture capital and going public are two alternatives we're constantly looking at. But retailing is a very fickle business. You can't guarantee earnings will be up 10 percent every year, and the investment community doesn't always understand that."

He stopped to tell a couple of stories. One involved a Young Presidents' Organization group outing on a U.S. Navy aircraft carrier in the Pacific Ocean. The other alluded to disappointing sales returns on a recent mail order catalog of his. In both instances, he said, bottom-line concerns over duplication of manpower or shortfall in revenues tended to cloud the more important goals of training personnel for actual combat, or, in Crate's case, of having the managerial flexibility to profit from error.

"That's the issue I have with going public," he offered. "That we're simply not that good, that we'll make mistakes. Hey, I *want* to make mistakes."

* * *

He has not made many. Since 1962, when the first housewares shop opened in a defunct elevator factory in Chicago's Old Town district, Segal's stores, now seventeen in number, have set standards of design and merchandising that have been the envy of—and often the prototype for—dozens of competitors and quasi-competitors, large and small. To anyone who has shopped for or sold housewares during the past twenty years, the "Crate look" is instantly familiar: glassware, dinnerware, flatware, and cookware piled floor to ceiling in drill formation; bolts of hanging fabric, acres of rough-sawed pine; potted plants, soft background music, hot spotlights, cool colors; theme displays in primary tones; signs in bold Helvetica lettering offering running commentary on a product's origin, function, and/or value. Every bit as palpable as the Crate look, however, is the Crate aura, an aura enveloping both the company and the man.

"Gordon doesn't deal much with the media," points out Ronald Fippinger, managing director of the National Housewares Manufacturers Association, "but his influence on this industry is enormous. He really helped create the whole gourmet-cookware craze in this country. And he *certainly* woke up the department stores to the fact that they weren't providing a high enough degree of service."

The toasts to Crate are as ubiquitous as the crystal on the store's shelves. John Gabbert, chief executive officer of Room & Board Inc., a Minneapolis-based furniture and accessories chain with two links in Chicago—Crate's home city—observes that while Crate does almost everything well, "they're the very best at product presentation. They're just *known* for that." One Dallas retailer told the *Chicago Tribune* that he holds his sales-training sessions outside Crate's front windows. His sole complaint: "My people manage to copy [Crate] for two days, and then it falls apart because they can't keep it up." And Stanley Marcus, retired chairman of Neiman-Marcus, the store that practically invented upscale retailing, flatly declares that Gordon Segal is "one of the great merchants of this century."

"I don't know what made him this way," says Marcus, who befriended Segal twenty years ago and later convinced him to open a pair of outlets in Dallas. "Maybe Gordon was born hungry, maybe he's always had the natural enthusiasm to do what he does. I do know that plenty of people have tried to copy Gordon, but nobody's really caught up with him.

"The big difference between them and most department stores," adds Marcus, "is that Crate is merchandise-oriented, whereas department stores are merchandising-oriented. Gordon makes a profit, but profit is not his first priority. He just plain loves to display his wares, and that kind of love is contagious."

The passion reflected in Crate's signature displays—"we put the stockroom in the showroom and lit everything with spotlights," is how one old-timer describes the method—is the same ardor that drove Gordon and his wife, Carole, to take a fling at importing back in the early 1960s. He had been in restaurants and real estate, she in teaching, but neither felt wed to a career. On a honeymoon trip to the Caribbean, they marveled at the variety of elegant, functional housewares available: items like French copper and German cutlery, which, if sold back home at all, were found only in "gourmet" shops, usually at several hundred percent above cost. Some months later, Gordon was doing the dishes (Arzberg dinnerware, a personal favorite) when he looked up from the suds and said to himself, "Hmmm, why not?"

"I was always interested in things like history and foreign affairs," Segal said one morning, sitting in his office at Crate's new $6-million Northbrook, Illinois, headquarters, "so [launching] this seemed more like an adventure than a business. Carole and I had absolutely no experience in retail. We were so green, we forgot to buy a cash register until three days after we opened our first store. At that point, we had one employee and $17,000 in capital. But we also had this burning desire to learn."

The learning process reached both sides of the Atlantic Ocean and both ends of the vendor-customer equation. At first, the Segals and their company, Euromarket Designs Inc., were content to import quality items they had seen and used themselves. Taking advantage of the newly opened Saint Lawrence Seaway, they had everything shipped directly to Chicago. The more they sold, however, the more curious they became about the anonymous craftspeople whose work they so admired. In 1964, what became known as the Marco Polo Effect took hold, and Gordon and Carole were off on a personal buying tour of the Continent. They quickly found that most small European manufacturers were loath to deal with a couple of footloose Americans following in the often muddied footsteps of department-store buyers.

"It wasn't exactly the Ugly American syndrome," offers Segal, "but we ran into a lot of horror stories about department stores placing large orders, manufacturers expanding production to meet those orders, and then, *zap*. No reorder. Or no more buyer, because he'd been transferred to another department. It was a tremendous liability for them. Europeans tend to deal more on trust than Americans do. Our first challenge was to win their confidence, even if that meant paying them several visits before we bought anything. We spent two entire days with Gerard Hofmann, a wonderful French potter living down on the Côte d'Azur, and got *nowhere*. On the third day, he finally agreed to sell [to us]—probably just so we'd leave him alone."

The Segals threw the Old Town store together in a scant two weeks; the name was a derivative of the open-shipping-container-and-dyed-burlap look they improvised out of necessity. Customers found them—one regular shopper was designer Miës van der Rohe's daughter, who often carried Crate stemware home to her papa. (If Gordon were into tattoos, van der Rohe's adage, "God is in the details," would be a strong contender for his chest.) But Gordon didn't always understand what they were up to. He could talk for an hour about a Bengt Bengtner goblet and not seem to care particularly if he sold one, six, or none. About half of the store's initial inventory went out the front door at cost: ignorance, not charity. Crate's revenue curve, moreover, was a picture of consistency; sales hit $8,000 the first month, half that the next, half *that* the next.

Ah, but at least it wasn't *boring*. In fact, the excitement was just starting. In 1965, with their customer base and pricing procedures more solidly established, Crate's proprietors were threatened with loss of their Old Town lease. Gordon again improvised an unusual deal—Crate would put up a new building, lease it back from the landlord, and finally would buy it fifteen years later—that foreshadowed a string of advantageous lease arrangements he would hammer out over the next two decades. In 1968, with the company grossing $500,000 a year, Crate opened a second store, Plaza Del Lago, in suburban Wilmette. The third store appeared in Oak Brook, in 1971. With each expansion, says Segal, they were "betting the company."

"Crate was highly leveraged all the way," he explains. "We'd never sought outside capital, in part because we wanted to keep the business small and exciting. We really did want to have fun with this thing." Contending that it wasn't until the opening of the Michigan Avenue, Chicago, store, in 1975, that "we finally got recognized," he mentions that his first bank wanted Crate to put up half the $300,000 cost of the Oak Brook expansion itself. Their response? "We found another lender."

Crate found other sources of inspiration as well. In 1966, Gordon and designer Lon Habkirk flew to Boston to look over Design Research. Founded by architect Benjamin Thompson, DR, as it was known familiarly, was the archetype of everything Segal aspired to: a clean, contemporary-looking, European-flavored design store specializing in imported housewares and furniture. As described in a Harvard Business School case study, DR "conveyed a glimpse at a life-style that was both gracious and yet conducive to the demands of modern society. . . . The results were a shopping experience unique for its time."

Habkirk, creative director of the Crate & Barrel Furniture store in Cambridge, Massachusetts, the only furniture outlet in the company chain, remembers the exposure to DR as being "enormously influential" on the Chicago operation.

"We went there because we were considering handling Marimekko," says Habkirk, referring to the fashionable line of clothing and fabrics that Thompson imported from Finland, "but both of us fell in love immediately. The genius of Ben Thompson was that he wasn't a retailer, so he didn't approach [retailing] in a conventional way at all. Beautiful women stood at the front door handing out fresh oranges. There were fresh flowers *everywhere*. It was retailing, yes, but it was retailing with *spirit*. Eventually we took the whole idea and translated it into a reproducible formula."

The formula they developed was not pure DR, however. DR featured top-ticket items and one-of-a-kind imports, but despite average sales of $236 a square foot, the store was unprofitable. Segal concentrated on building his business through volume buys and low margins, importing directly from manufacturers to keep prices 30 percent to 40 percent below comparable merchandise. Coupled with favorable suppliers' contracts, these measures committed Crate to a policy of setting one fair price on a piece of merchandise and holding it, not jacking it up or knocking it down as customer response might dictate. Volume was ensured through imaginative advertising and even more imaginative display techniques. Carole

BY THE NUMBERS

Segal's Secret: More Bang for the Square Foot

Housewares is a $42-billion-a-year retail business," says Jeff Adair, editor of *Housewares,* a trade publication in Cleveland, "where individual numbers are very, very hard to come by. Everybody knows what their competitors do, at least in general terms, but they don't like sharing their secrets with the competition."

On an industry-wide basis, it is no secret that the growth trend is in the direction of the discount houses. According to its recent listing of the top 100 housewares retailers nation-wide, *Totally Housewares* found seven of the ten biggest sales gainers in the discount category—and only three department stores in the top twenty-five. Supermarkets and drugstores have also become major players in the housewares game; Safeway Stores, for example, boasted 1984 houseware sales of $300 million, and Jack Eckerd did $185 million. Among leaders in other generic outlet categories are: Bamberger's department stores ($65 million); Best Products catalog showrooms ($450 million); Sears Roebuck variety stores ($1.8 billion); Cotter hardware stores ($300 million); and Price Club membership clubs ($125 million).

Although Crate doesn't show up on the charts, last year's revenues of $46 million would qualify it for *Totally Housewares'* list, well ahead of such department-store notables as Bloomingdale's ($38 million) and Marshall Field ($27 million). Plus, as *Totally Housewares'* survey notes, "There's no indication of such factors as profitability, [inventory] turn, or sales volume per square foot." Translation: Crate's controlled-growth strategy may well make up in quality of sales what it sacrifices in quantity. That growth has been about 20 percent compounded annually. Nine of the ten volume leaders averaged an aggregate 25.7-percent upturn in housewares sales last year, but none were specialty stores concentrating on imported merchandise. Adds Ronald Fippinger of the National Housewares Manufacturers Association, "There's been a great shakeout in so-called gourmet stores. So many of the little retailers can't make it. You walk into Gordon's stores and *know* he is."

Jeff Adair ventures that, as of a couple of years ago, anyway, sales figures in the $100-per-square-foot range were the benchmark for a successful housewares retailer. Despite his own penchant for secrecy, one number Gordon Segal *will* disclose is that last year, Crate's stores took in an average $450 per square foot of selling space—a figure that underscores a longtime contention of his that "if we're not doing three times what the department stores are doing, we're not doing our job."

Segal was a singular force in the latter regard. Until she left the company in 1965 to start a family, her touch was evident everywhere. In 1979, she opened Foodstuffs, a food store with a Crate-like merchandising approach; it may become the family's next great retail venture. And Habkirk himself influenced Crate's display concept after a sabbatical with the Peace Corps in Afghanistan from 1967 to 1970. Traveling throughout Asia, he was struck by the merchandising at open-air bazaars, where vendors hung racks of copper pots "like piles of jewels." Like Segal, he was convinced that shoppers would buy more readily if they didn't see one precious vase or pot sitting on a shelf "like some museum piece."

But the real key to reproducing the formula, and probably the missing element most responsible for DR's demise, was cultivating a sales force that could grow into a management team. Hiring bright young people was rarely a problem; keeping them motivated—and therefore employed—was. Segal, who worked the floor in one store or another for the first ten years himself, was fully capable of leading by example, but his personal élan meant only so much to a group of college grads with ambitions of their own. In a low-paying, labor-intensive field like retail, these people would either burn out, get hired away for better money, or rebel against managers brought in from outside the company. Whatever course the erosion took, it would doom even the most modest of Crate's growth plans.

So Segal developed an alternative strategy. Grow slowly, adding no more than a store or two a year until recently. Expand only in cities that appeal to employees. ("I love New York," he volunteers, "but I've never particularly wanted the hassle of doing business there.") Build up a respectable catalog business. (Crate's now accounts for about 10 percent of sales.) Finally, hire full-time people with the express aim of moving them into management positions. One such early hire was Barbara Turf, now Crate's executive vice-president in charge of merchandising and advertising. A former schoolteacher, Turf started eighteen years ago working part-time in sales. Soon, she was managing the Oak Brook store; about thirteen years ago, she began traveling overseas on regular merchandise missions. During 1970, a watershed year, Turf helped hire and train a core group of new staffers, 60 percent of whom are senior company executives today.

"The key people skills—love of customer, love of staff—are what keep this place going," says Turf. "Anyone who doesn't see them as important has either left the company or thinks we're all crazy."

The fact that Turf, like Carole Segal, began her career as an educator is more than a matter of coincidence. Crate's management structure is top-heavy with people—mostly women—who came out of classrooms, where the fine arts of patience and communication are prized skills. In significant ways, too, Crate's stores function as showroom and schoolroom: many have blackboards over the cash register listing the names of cargo ships, their destinations, points of origin, and merchandise on board. Salespeople are expected to be able to lecture knowledgeably on, among other things, the differences among stoneware, earthenware, and faience as compared with porcelain. As the four-part, 140-page *Crate Employees' Guide* puts it, "We knew that to be truly successful we would need to develop an educational philosophy towards our customer. Our stores had to be a place where customers could come and have discussions with intelligent personnel about our merchandise, creating a relationship which would certainly carry a longer impact than either our advertising or our displays."

Carol Sapoznik, Boston regional manager and Crate's first bona fide management trainee—she joined the company in 1971—traveled the typical corporate path of salesperson, stockperson, and store secretary and bookkeeper. One of her current duties is helping to implement a training program that embraces all full-time employees with at least one month's service. Although individual store managers do all their own hiring, says Sapoznik, responsibility for training is divided between in-store counseling and a companywide continuing-education program.

"At the corporate level," she explains, "it's a three-phase system. The first we call Fundamentals of Selling. In groups of ten or so, new employees meet at our warehouse facilities for a one-day workshop in issues like corporate structure and philosophy, salesmanship role-playing, add-on sales, how the buyers find new products, and so on. The atmosphere is meant to be loose and fun. Everyone is encouraged to ask basic questions like, 'Why do we sell this item?' or, 'How do I get promoted?' in a completely unrestricted forum.

"The second," she says, "focuses on product information. In Boston, we do this in four weekly sessions, and it involves part-time people as well as full-timers. One week we might do gourmet, the next dinnerware and glassware; one way or another, though, we cover every product category in the store. And the third [phase] is Design. Ray Aronson [Crate's corporate designer] put together a terrific slide-show lecture for us on merchandising philosophy, traffic flow, the effects of high and low crates, waterfall stacking, window displays, et cetera. The idea is to promote awareness of every single element involved in Crate's overall success."

AHEAD OF THE PACK

Secrets of Selling to the Home

Steve Eberman, cofounder and chief executive officer of Function Junction, a Kansas City, Missouri-based housewares chain with eight stores in the Midwest and two more on the way, pinpoints three crucial factors in the development of any exemplary retail organization.

"One is a store or merchant with a good concept, but they're a dime a dozen," Eberman avers. "The second is a good merchant who's also a good businessperson, and that's rather rare. The third is someone who's both of those, plus being an outstanding manager of people. As far as this business goes, I'd narrow [the last] list to Gordon [Segal] and myself."

Others give Eberman high marks as well. Donna Prince, editor of *Totally Housewares*, an industry trade journal, finds him "very unorthodox—but also very exciting. In some ways Function is distinctly Crate-like, but it's also more price-oriented, and more utilitarian. There's a lot less glitz."

Eberman opened in Kansas City in 1977, hoping that by avoiding such major markets as New York City and Chicago he could refine his merchandising concept without undue pressure to succeed immediately. His concept emphasizes color scheme ("the most flexible choice the consumer has to make") and product exclusivity. "Our stores don't carry appliances or have a lot of sophisticated fixtures like Crate," he says, "but we do have what I like to think is a more universal concept than they do. You won't find any Crate stores on the South Side of Chicago, for instance, but there could be a Function Junction there."

With 100 employees on his swelling payroll, Eberman notes that his greatest satisfaction comes from watching his employees develop into good managers. "To me, it's a thrill anytime someone in this company takes a job away from me," he says.

A major influence on Eberman during his wanderings around Europe in the mid-seventies was a chain of home furnishing stores known as Habitat. Designed around tile floors, splashes of color, and whimsical displays, the stores divide products into three generic categories: First Home/Life-style (functional, inexpensive home items); Country (furniture, rugs, and dinnerware); and City (high-design products in chrome, leather, and glass).

Founded in 1964 by entrepreneur and author Terence Conran, the Habitat chain moved into the United States in 1977 under Conran's own name and now has thirteen stores scattered throughout the Northeast. Conran's outlets, many in the 20,000- to 30,000-square-foot range, feature furniture, glassware, and kitchenware—"all the basic needs for the home," according to spokeswoman Pat Grabel. "About 90 percent of our products are exclusive to us, and a majority of those are designed by our own design group. All our stores reflect [Conran's] philosophy of good design at good prices."

"We're very different [from Crate], and will be increasingly so," says The Pottery Barn's Hoyt Chapin, veteran of many a European buying tour with his old pal Segal. "Like Crate, we developed relationships [with manufacturers] overseas that cannot be built overnight. Unlike them, we're more of an item store: We might have only two or three products in a category where they have ten. And though our stores are smaller—they average about 3,000 square feet—we're committed to a much more rapid expansion policy than they are. We really believe the moves we've made over the last year and a half ensure we have the systems and procedures to do that without sacrificing quality at all."

Founded in 1949 by Paul Secon, The Pottery Barn maintained a single housewares store in Lower Manhattan until Chapin bought the company in 1964. "[Secon] was a pioneer in this type of merchandising," says Chapin.

"Before World War II, it was something of a sacred approach to well-designed merchandise—almost like museum shopping—and he turned it into a supermarket." When he sold the operation to The Gap Stores Inc. in 1983, Chapin had thirteen company stores and another nine franchised outlets, all on the East and West coasts. That number has since grown to twenty-eight, with ten to fifteen more Barns on the drawing boards for next year.

"I was looking for a company that knew us, understood us, and would let us run the business the way we knew how," observes Chapin of his courtship with the publicly traded clothing retailer. "Now we have a much bigger resource pool to draw on, and we've been able to upgrade systems like electronics and computers without suffering any disasters. Since the acquisition, we've also lost only one old-time employee—a healthy sign. And it's no problem now promising our people plenty of opportunity to move within the company. Specialty stores are clearly the way to go in retailing. It's how you organize and manage them that makes the difference."

Gordon Segal himself is a student of management philosophy, and has often lavished praise on such retailing gurus as R. H. Macy's Edward Finkelstein. The Cellar, Macy's innovative housewares concept, is one of the more imaginative department store responses to the challenge of the specialty stores. Recently, Segal also singled out a company in an altogether different line of retail, Nordstrom Inc., a Seattle-based fashion specialty retailer. Founded by John W. Nordstrom in 1901, this chain, now six western states and forty-two outlets strong, grew into the largest independent U.S. shoe retailer before branching out into men's and women's apparel and accessories.

"Here they come into California," Segal tells his own people, "where there must be a new department store every three miles. And they succeed. They open in [Los Angeles] and do $300 to $400 a square foot in a 200,000-square-foot store. Phenomenal. How do they do it? They talk to you, they come up to you, they *care* for you. You can't believe you're in a major department store. Nordstrom does $900 million, $1 billion a year, *and they still care!*"

Thorough as it is, any training effort relies heavily on sound hiring judgment at the outset. According to Lon Habkirk: "Gordon always says he can't *make* happy people, he can only *hire* happy people. He doesn't want any 'victims' working here." In that vein, Crate looks for recruits with a high self-image and, perhaps, a family background in retail, or experience in teaching, or—talk about intense, service-oriented businesses—restaurants. What the company doesn't want, particularly, are refugees from department-store training programs, where the yardsticks of responsibility and achievement are apt to be very different from Crate's.

"The atmosphere in this company is competitive," Sapoznik avers, "but not *that* competitive. People understand they have the chance to advance, to assume a lot of responsibility, but they have to be motivated themselves. Unlike department stores, *all* of our people are in management training. We don't have clerks working the floor. We put our best people on the front line, and that's where we're different. In a department store, you can always spot the buyers and managers. They're the ones who won't come over and ring up your sale."

Sapoznik recalls being invited in by the Harvard group doing the postmortem on DR. "They asked me how long I'd been doing sales and pricing," she says, "and I said, 'Forever.' If a truck pulls in, I help unload it. If a store needs sweeping, I pick up a broom. Gordon's the same way."

Further testimony to Crate's work ethic and corporate culture comes from Pat Eckerstrom, the assistant corporate designer in Chicago. Ten years ago, just out of college, she started as a secretary in the Wilmette store—despite "never having typed a letter in my life." Having proved her mettle at Crate, she was hired away by a home-remodeling retailer at one and a half times her $9,000 annual salary; within a year she was back with Segal. The main lesson learned during her time away was how dreary retail could be when indifferent people sold inferior merchandise to an undiscriminating clientele.

> Bigger businesses entail bigger problems in finance, labor relations, building programs, employee training, executive development. The ultimate solution often leads in the direction of public ownership, either through the marketing of capital stock or merger. The moment an entrepreneur of fine quality takes in one outside partner or three thousand stockholders, the quality of his business can be affected, for the shareholders invest for three reasons only: security, dividends, and growth. They are notoriously unsentimental about their investments.
> —*Stanley Marcus*

Segal's conservative growth philosophy has not shielded Crate from change. He may be cautious about diluting the formula, but he is not a passive participant in the marketplace. By opening more warehouse outlets, the company has protected its flanks from the charge of discount stores. By emphasizing more seasonal inventory, it has attacked the department stores where they live. The whole scale is expanding. "Before it was, 'Here's this wonderful item, don't you want to buy it?'" notes one employee. "Now it's, 'Here are *all* these wonderful items, don't you want to buy them *all right now?*'" Among the swelling numbers: 600 employees, 250 overseas manufacturers, 100 domestic manufacturers, more than 8,000 individual items for sale, a 136,000-square-foot corporate office and central warehouse able to handle 3,000 mail order pieces a day, a $1.5-

million computerized point-of-sale information system that sweeps each store's register on a daily basis. With this expansion has come more pressure from below to hike salaries and commissions, along with more discussion about stock offerings—a good way to reward longtime workers, think some. It has also raised the question of growth by acquisition or merger, a strategy Segal claims to have considered and rejected.

Bette Gandelman, retailing specialist in the Chicago office of Harris Bank, concentrates on lending to companies in merchandising, with emphasis on closely held companies. Most of her clients, including Crate & Barrel, fall in an annual revenue range of $25 million to $200 million; most suffer a retail environment that seldom supports consistent growth in both sales and profitability. Crate became a Harris client in 1983, when Gandelman's division put together $7 million worth of industrial revenue bonds to finance the Northbrook complex. She was an avid customer long before that. "You couldn't live around here and not notice their growth," says Gandelman, "particularly if you're a working woman. Crate has distinctive designs and an incredibly high level of service, certainly much higher than most department stores. They were a name in Chicago with tremendous visibility, someone we'd been following a long time."

Among the institutional concerns at Harris is whether fast-growth companies can take what is essentially a local business and expand it: That is, can you take, say, a distinctive-looking store in Chicago and open one just like it in Houston and have it still look distinctive? Another worry is, distinctive or not, can the brain trust behind the store work as well with numbers as it does with merchandise—and vice versa? On neither score has Crate appeared to have been a cause of great concern. The company profit picture, says Gandelman, is impressive, but to the company's chief lender, depth of managerial talent is even more impressive.

"Most of our customers reach a hurdle point they have to get over, particularly when the founder's still around doing everything," she explains. "Many can't delegate authority. Others tend not to hire people who're better than they are. Not Crate. Gordon has done an excellent job bringing in new people. If you cloned Gordon you couldn't find a better merchandiser, but he can let go, too."

Letting go but keeping the faith—"the religion," Segal calls it—is, as Stanley Marcus suggests, the most difficult balancing act in retailing.

"One advantage is if you know [the dimensions of] the problem, you have a chance of beating it," says Marcus. "And Gordon may have more of a chance than most, because he's selling a restricted product line. Gordon's smart. If anybody can do it, he can."

And if anyone can do it with enthusiasm, Segal and his staff can. From the earliest days in Old Town, the play's been the thing. Lon Habkirk, who has been associated with Segal for twenty years now, sees that attitude as the boss's greatest legacy.

"Ultimately," says Habkirk, "this isn't serious for him. It's a grand game, and he plays it better than anyone, but it's still a game to Gordon. I remember when I was pushing him to take a chance [with] the Michigan Avenue store. It was way beyond anything we'd done, and as I was working on it one day, Gordon stood next to me and started talking about how he'd bet the company on the store's making it. Well, that scared the hell out of me. I mean, here I'd been *pushing* him to do it, and now the whole business was riding on the deal. He saw I was upset, so he stopped talking and pulled back. Then he got this big grin on his face and said, 'Hey, if we fail—so what? We'll do something else.' "

Habkirk smiles. "I've gone off to do other things myself," he says, "but I don't know anyone who's left Crate to open another store and been truly happy."

—JOSEPH P. KAHN

THE IMPORTANCE OF
BEING ARTHUR

Put yourself in my place for a minute. You're in a Holiday Inn in North Bergen, New Jersey, on a Saturday in January, and wondering why. It seemed like a good idea; you've never written about a trucking company. But now you've got your doubts. It's 7:00 A.M., the coffee shop's not even open yet and there's an ice storm going on outside. Still, you drive the three miles to the corporate headquarters of A-P-A Transport Corp. to interview its president, Arthur E. Imperatore.

A guard meets you just inside the front gate and says "Mr. Arthur" is expecting you. You're in the middle of a couple of acres of blacktop, surrounded by loading docks and long lines of trucks parked with military precision. Already you're trying to get your bearings. Where are the usual piles of discarded tires, the overturned oil drums, the burnt-out crankshafts? There's not even a gum wrapper lying around. The guard drives you over to the executive offices, dark and empty on the weekend. He takes you to the second floor and points you to an unusually wide black door edged in gold. "Mr. Arthur's office," he says, and leaves. You're about to become totally disoriented. That door's the first clue that you've arrived at an extraordinary place—something more than a trucking company.

You knock. No answer. You open the door slowly and step inside. Even if you had seen a picture of it before, you still wouldn't be prepared. Mr. Arthur's office is nothing less than the drawing room of a seventeenth-century Venetian prince.

At the furthest end of this long rectangular room is a black marble fireplace with floor-to-ceiling-length mirrors on either side. The mirrors throw back the gleam of the oak parquet floor and the early-morning light from the long windows to each side. In the middle of the room, on a Persian rug, stands an ornate conference table covered with green leather embossed with gold. The walls and ceiling are painted in light greens and beige and the woodwork is trimmed in gold. Off to one side is a plant-filled atrium with the statue of a contemplative Grecian nude perched on a pedestal in the middle of a fountain surrounded by statues of three nymphs playing flutes. You sit down and gawk, which turns out to be a good idea because this is only the beginning. Everything about this company is extraordinary.

Depending on what you read or whom you talk to, A-P-A is either the most profitable, the most productive, or the most astonishing trucking company ever to come down the pike. Or it's all of the above.

Ron Roth, director of research and statistical services at the American Trucking Associations Inc., after comparing A-P-A's superiority in net profitability, return on equity, and return on capital with an average of 409 intercity general freight common carriers in 1980, said, "As far as I know, there are very few companies that come even remotely close to A-P-A."

In *Commercial Car Journal*'s 1980 compilation of the 100 largest for-hire motor carriers in the United States, as determined by their gross operating revenues, A-P-A, at $62.9 million, ranked only eighty-fifth. But—and this "but" should be underlined—it had the best operating ratio of any company on the list.

To industry analysts, the operating ratio—operating expenses divided by revenues—is a basic and critical measure of a company's profitability and productivity. Said *Commercial Car Journal:* "Operating with Teamster labor in what is probably the highest cost area of the country, metropolitan New York-New Jersey, A-P-A president Arthur E. Imperatore continues to astound industry experts by getting the kind of productivity from the union that no one else in trucking is capable of doing." What's more, A-P-A has been number one for the past five years.

There are voices outside the black door. Arthur comes in. He's telling a man in charge of buildings and maintenance that the "Season's Greetings" sign outside has been up too long. He says this oversight could ruin the "symmetry and harmony of the workplace." What? Yes, he continues, workers' attitudes and habits reflect their environment. Given the right environment, workers move with a certain rhythmic harmony, even beauty.

Arthur's standing at a window demonstrating his point by analyzing the work of three men and a pickup truck with a plow attached, scratching away at the pack ice below. But one man has moved a stop sign out of the way of the plow and has left it turned so that it can't be seen by approaching traffic. Suddenly, Arthur is rapping at the window with a quarter and swinging his arms in wide circles and shouting: "No, no turn it around!" The sentences that follow are short and blunt, powered by four-letter words. The man understands. "We contracted the job out to them," Arthur says. "You can tell they're not A-P-A people. I won't tolerate a half-assed job."

He won't tolerate half-assed jobs, nor loafers or loungers either, because he can't. He appears to be answering some personal and irresistible genetic signal. "I've been working since I was ten years old," he says. "My first job was on a truck. I worked all day for 50¢ and a baloney sandwich and a soda. I've always wanted to do my job and do it right. I don't know where it comes from, but I've always been that way." He believes that any man who fails to commit himself totally to his work has failed to commit himself totally to his own life. Each time, it's a small tragedy not because he's let the company down, but rather that he's chosen to be something less than he could be. Arthur won't let it happen. "My whole philosophy here," he says, "is that we build men—incidentally, we move freight."

By 1946, Arthur's beliefs had already become his mission. He was a zealot and his own family was the first to hear the word. After serving in World War II, Arthur and four of his brothers came home to the five-room wood-frame house in West New York, New Jersey. "I was so anxious to get started on my life," Arthur says, "I couldn't contain myself." At first he decided he needed a college education and began attending night school. During the day, he was a Fuller Brush salesman. Meanwhile, two of his brothers, Eugene and Arnold, had bought a used army ordnance truck for $700 and were driving around town with "Imperatore Bros. Moving and Trucking" painted on the side of the truck. "But most of the time," Arthur says, "they were just hanging around the house. I couldn't stand it. One day, I told them to get out and sell, or take my name off the truck."

In March 1947, after several months of Arthur's badgering, the brothers, who now included George and Harold, convened a meeting. Arthur was elected president. "I'd always been the boss," he says, "but even then we made an agreement to run the company on merit. I told my brothers that if anyone could do a better job, at any time, then he could be boss."

With Arthur in charge, the brothers set out to build their company in earnest. They bought another used truck and, working out of their house on Fifty-first Street, scoured the west bank of the Hudson River for business. The loads were always heavy, the profits usually light. Arthur remembers hauling a 1,000-pound commercial refrigerator seventeen miles from West New York to Paterson, New Jersey, for $4. "We did anything to make a buck," he says.

Only one month after senior management had convened the meeting in the family kitchen, they bought A&P Trucking Corp. for $800 from Albert Amorino, a local trucker who had found himself in financial difficulties. In the deal, they got a small garage with four loading docks next door to Amorino's house on Fifty-ninth Street, only blocks away from their own house. They also got two very used trucks, and a new name. Even then, the Imperatores were practical businessmen. Since Amorino had already placed ads for A&P Trucking in an important trade journal, they decided not to let vanity stand in the way of potential customers. Adopting the name proved to be a mixed blessing, though. Eight years later, lawyers for the giant A&P food chain took exception to the obvious similarity. After four years of legal wrangling, the brothers simply added another "A" and became A-P-A Transport Corp.

During its first year in business, the fledgling company grossed $23,000. On the day before Christmas, the brothers brought their trucks back to the Fifty-ninth Street garage, sent out for pizza, and broke out a bottle of Four Roses to celebrate their success. A few days later, the roof fell in. Two big snowstorms in a row were too much for the old garage roof to bear. "Fortunately, it didn't do too much damage to our trucks," Arthur says, "but we worked most of that winter without a roof. It was so cold the toilets froze and we had to run next door to Amorino's house."

The next four years were filled with sixteen- and eighteen-hour days. Tiny A-P-A had been swept up in the great scheme of things. The pent-up demand of the post–World War II economy was exploding; the interstate highway system was expanding; and the trucking industry became a new frontier. "It was," Arthur once said in a speech, "a shoestring, bootstraps, seat-of-the-pants, call-it-what-you-will industry."

When the brothers had more trucks than a cramped terminal could handle, they parked them in the street and worked into the night by the light from Coleman lanterns. "It was brutal, physical work," Arthur says. "We worked like animals." At times the pace was so fierce, Arthur would comb the local bars looking for help. But very few men could work to Arthur's expectations and inevitably that would trigger his genetic code.

One day in the early fifties, Arthur spotted some of his men lounging around swapping jokes when they should've been loading one of his trucks. Arthur ran down the loading docks grabbing fistfuls of change from his pants pockets. When he reached the men, he threw the change at them and screamed, "Here, you sons-of-bitches. If you want my money for nothing, take it, take it all."

His fury reached its peak in the spring of 1952. A-P-A had just completed work on a new, 8,000-square-foot terminal that would serve as the nucleus of what is, to this day, the company's main terminal and corporate headquarters. Almost simultaneously, A-P-A was unionized by the International Brotherhood of Teamsters. "This single event," Arthur says, "started a new era for the company."

Previously, Arthur had told union officials that he simply couldn't afford to pay union pay scales and fringe benefits. He said that he would accept the labor agreement when he could, but that if the union forced the issue in the meantime, he would shut down. "Let's not kid ourselves," Arthur says, "it was inevitable. In those days, you couldn't operate in this part of the country without the union. No union, no company."

But for the first time in A-P-A's history, Arthur's irresistible will was being challenged by an immovable object, and Arthur couldn't accept it. He was specifically enraged over what he says was a drive by the workers to "run the jobs themselves and victimize the employer. I can empathize with the feelings of the men now, but not then. I wasn't giving enough then. I was wild. I had to do it. I had to build the company."

The atmosphere grew increasingly suspicious and potentially violent. "We'd walk around giving each other the eye," Arthur says. "I'd overreact, then they'd overreact. We set up shock waves."

The shock waves quavered dangerously for the next three years. "It was nose to nose and every day," Arthur says. "They were very combative times." Then on April 12, 1955, union members launched the first in a series of wildcat strikes. "Yes, I was shocked," Arthur says. "I was damn wild."

One of the issues that caused the first strike, Arthur says, was driver refusal to work on the docks in emergencies. "But," he says, "it could have been anything. Things were very tense." That first strike lasted only a day because Arthur confronted the strikers at the front gate of the terminal and told them that if they didn't return to work they were all fired. But on the day after Labor Day, the men walked out again. Clearly, Arthur's earlier ultimatum hadn't worked. And clearly, if Arthur was to control the destiny of A-P-A and live with the union at the same time, he'd have to find another way.

As Arthur recalls these events of nearly thirty years ago, he looks out the window from time to time. He stares pensively and quietly as if he can see and hear his memories being replayed in the deserted truck yard below. "When I think about it now," he says, "I can realize the men were both right and wrong. I mean they're human. Maybe we pushed them too hard. Maybe we didn't have enough respect for them."

In 1975, Arthur built a $750,000 recreation center next to the executive offices as a monument to the new covenant of respect. Replete with pool, sauna, gyms, weightrooms, and tennis and bocce-ball courts, it's free to every A-P-A employee. In addition, every year there are picnics and dinner dances. And every five years, Arthur throws a special party for the entire company. This year, for example, he's chartered the entire *Queen Elizabeth II* for a three-day float to nowhere and offered a trip to Las Vegas as an alternative. "I work at it," Arthur says. "I'm always asking myself if I'm treating my people right. I want them to know they're appreciated."

It's hard to imagine that this is the same wild man who used to throw his own hat on the ground and stomp it flat, who used to convene meetings with his men by jumping on the back of a truck, shaking his fist, and shouting, "Listen here, you bastards!"

"I'm a lot calmer now," Arthur says. "That kind of behavior just doesn't work. It drives the good men away with the bad. The lessons of the fifties were invaluable. We learned to talk with our employees." Arthur and his employees hadn't exactly fallen in love with one another, but he had taken a step in the right direction. "I saw it as kind of a *primus inter pares*," Arthur says, "where I would still be first." Over the next five years, Arthur engineered a system that would nourish and protect the fragile relationship.

During the winter of 1958, A-P-A opened a terminal in Reading, Pennsylvania, its first outside North Bergen. Arthur and one of the Reading employees were working together to clear the yard after a snowstorm. "No matter what we did," Arthur recalls, "shovel snow, move a truck, all this guy could do was complain. He certainly didn't want to work."

Too little thought, Arthur began to realize, was being given to the hiring process. It was too haphazard, too much was taken for granted. Given the job security built into the labor agreement with the unions, Arthur felt it was essential to screen prospective employees carefully. "Marriage," says Arthur, "is not nearly as close, especially these days, as the working relationship of an employee with an employer under today's labor agreement in the motor freight industry." So that year, Arthur sketched in the rough outline of the selection process that today produces an A-P-A "Ace."

Burt C. Trebour, A-P-A's director of labor and personnel, says that out of every 100 applicants, 4 become job candidates, and out of those 4, 2 are finally hired. The culling begins even before the application form is completed. The personnel department subscribes to thirty newspapers from cities and towns where A-P-A has a terminal. Anytime an arrest is listed, for whatever reason, that person's name and the information are transcribed on three-by-five file cards for future reference. Even the original newspaper clippings are preserved. Indexed and cross-referenced, the total file now contains 750,000 names and takes about twenty seconds to check. Before this check took hold, 1 out of every $4^{1}/_{2}$ applicants had a criminal record. Today, it's about 1 in 35. "The word gets around," Trebour says.

Provided his name doesn't pop up in the criminal file, and provided his application form isn't full of holes, and also provided that he gets through a twenty-minute interview with Trebour and a polygraph test in states where they're allowed, the future A-P-A truck driver has one week of orientation with no pay and two weeks of on-the-job training during which he rides one specific route with an experienced driver. "I would prefer the person who comes here," Trebour says, "to have never driven a truck before. That way he hasn't picked up any bad habits."

When the training ends, the driver begins his probationary period. This period is set by the prevailing labor agreement and at A-P-A varies between fifteen and thirty-three days. At the North Bergen terminal, for example, it's fifteen days. A prospective employee can be fired peremptorily during the probationary period. After that, his relationship with the company is governed by the union contract.

For those fifteen days, the prospective driver works his training route alone like any other A-P-A veteran. His productivity is measured on a daily basis and on the tenth day one of the company's industrial engineers rides with the man and does a thorough time-and-motion study. At the same time, the terminal manager and the dispatchers are also evaluating his performance. As the probationary period draws to a close, the man gets a series of back X-rays and a urinalysis for drug abuse. Then he's interviewed once more by the personnel department. "Everybody, all down the line, has to want him," Trebour says. And even then, he's not home free. There's one more interview to go and that's with a member of senior management.

For years Arthur himself conducted the ultimate hour-long interview, which also means that during that time he hired every A-P-A employee personally. "He's very serious about the interview," Trebour says. "I've seen him hold them from his sickbed, in the backseat of his car, and in front of the New York Athletic Club." Arthur asks questions about a man's habits, his relationship with his brothers and sisters, his marriage; he wants to know him heart and soul. "Every man chosen right," Arthur once said, "can have the most singularly dramatic and forceful effect on impacting productivity favorably." And further, "The successful candidate becomes quite proud that he's been selected in preference to many others. This helps to underpin a strong spirit within the company that we aim to be the very best."

A-P-A entered the sixties as a company greatly different from the one jolted by turmoil only five years earlier. Of course, it was bigger, having passed $1 million in gross revenues in 1958 for the first time. It had opened its first out-of-state terminal and, in the years ahead, would aggressively expand its service area in the Northeast and into the mid-Atlantic states. But more important than sheer physical size, A-P-A had changed qualitatively. Since every piece of freight required 225 individual actions involving up to 100 people, cooperation was mandatory. "Before, it was just tough, physical work done any way we could," Arthur says, "but in the sixties we learned to work through others, to coordinate the efforts of everyone."

Arthur identified and analyzed every one of the 225 individual steps—who could do what, when, and how. He constructed an operations flow chart that, when unfurled, was fifteen feet long. The system was a masterpiece of coordination but it would work only if everyone gave his best effort. Arthur was particularly concerned about the dockworkers and drivers. They were physically moving the freight and if they couldn't or wouldn't do the job, the entire system would bog down. The next question he had to answer was how he could ensure that these men worked at optimum efficiency. Further, the question was amplified by his own experience. He realized that left to their own devices, most employees create their own "comfort level," a work pace that, too often, is significantly slower than management expects it to be. So, Arthur began to think about a fail-safe system of daily productivity measurement.

He remembered when he was thirteen, pedaling a bike all over Union City, New Jersey, as a Western Union messenger boy. "One day," he recalls, "the company did time-and-motion studies on us riding our bikes to deliveries. That's where I got the idea. If it could work on bikes, why couldn't it work on trucks?"

Beginning about 1960, Arthur started the exhaustive process of building an archive of time-and-motion studies covering virtually every conceivable function a driver or dockworker was likely to perform. Every driver, for example, was carefully tracked time and time again, to see just how long it took him to complete his run. A series of standard times was developed; it reflected variables such as the number of pieces to be delivered, their weight, miles per stop, the area served, returns, pickups, and delays.

The first crude measurements were done manually from information supplied on the driver's manifest. Today, it's done by computer on a daily basis. Each day, the historic standard time for a given route is compared with the driver's actual time. The standard time represents 100 percent efficiency for a given run and is considered an "acceptable standard." "Ninety-six percent of our workers," says Arthur, "meet or exceed this standard every day." And if there's ever any questions about a given driver's results, they can be double-checked against the service recorder disks and the Argo Tachographs. The first device shows when a truck is moving and when it's stopped and for how long; the second device records miles per hour, rpms, miles driven, and when the truck was moving.

HOW A-P-A MEASURES PRODUCTIVITY

Experts say A-P-A is the most productive trucking company in the industry. And one of the major reasons why the New Jersey–based trucker consistently leads the pack is through a computer printout which measures the productivity of A-P-A drivers day by day.

August E. Pagnozzi, the company's chief industrial engineer, says the numbers actually re-create the events in each driver's workday. For example, when he translates the first line of one printout into English, it reads as follows: The driver of truck 908, assigned to the Wayne, New Jersey, run, delivered twenty-one bills at nineteen stops. The total weight of his load was 5,100 pounds and it consisted of 274 pieces.

He successfully completed all of his deliveries and had no returns. He also picked up seventeen bills at ten stops. The pickups weighed 4,059 pounds. He made one pickup stop where no freight was tendered.

During the day, the driver was unavoidably delayed for forty-two minutes. He traveled 173 miles at an average rate of 27.3 miles per hour. The driver's total work load should have been completed in an acceptable standard time of eleven hours. This driver's actual time of 10.2 hours was even faster. His efficiency rating was, therefore, 108 percent.

Productivity is measured every day, Pagnozzi says, and every day 96 percent of the drivers and dockworkers meet or exceed the acceptable standard time.

Over the course of two hours, you're listening to the development of the perfect productivity system with an increasing sense of awe and unease. You hear Arthur say, "We're realists. We know our business. We want a fair day's work for a fair day's pay. We expect work and we mean to get it." And you know it works because A-P-A's success tells you so. But gradually you find yourself not wanting to hear another word about the system. You wish it would go away. You think it's offensive. Arthur asks you why, in a way that says he knows what's coming. You tell him that it represents a depressingly harsh view of human nature.

Arthur says an employee once put it another way. "What do you need all these measurements for anyway?" the employee said. "All it means is that you don't trust me." Both you and that man, Arthur says patiently but emphatically, have missed the point entirely.

"It's not that I don't trust them," he explains, "but I know human nature. I know that good and evil are constantly in the balance. What I've done is to pit each man against himself so he can tip the scales one way or the other by himself. Every man craves direction, a sense of purpose, a sense of dignity. I've planned out the problems. I've planned out the frustration and waste. I've freed him to enrich his life, to achieve greater self-awareness. That's why I fought the men in the early days, because they wanted to be human hulks and I wouldn't let them."

And the system, because it's impartial, because the numbers don't lie, and because every man writes his own record, also did something almost unheard of. It neutralized the traditional antagonism between the union and management. "There's nothing left to argue about," Arthur says. "I've given the men more security, and a better kind of security, than the union ever could. After all, every man protects his own job every day by his own performance. He doesn't need someone else to protect it for him. That's why the union's never been an issue here."

Before you leave, you stop downstairs to look at an oil painting. Arthur asked you to. He said it sums up his story. It's called *The Honest Workman.* Arthur lined up twenty men so the artist could get the face of the honest workman just right. Even then, it was redrawn six times. The painting hangs on the wall just inside the front door to the executive offices. The man in the painting has one hand on his hip, and the other hand clutches a clipboard and papers. He is wearing a brown jacket and his shirt is open wide at the neck. The painting is done mainly in shades of sturdy, dependable brown. The man's face is the focal point of the composition. There is a bowl of fresh white carnations and yellow mums on a shelf underneath the portrait. There is also a plaque. The plaque assures the viewer that this man, who has just finished his day's work, is the real hero of A-P-A, "our typical workman who . . . has created this great organization."

"If you stare right at his face," Arthur says, "you can hear that man talk and you know what he's saying. He's saying: 'I know I've done my best for the company, for myself, and for my family, and if you don't know it, boss, then screw you.'"

—LUCIEN RHODES

THE UN-MANAGER

Early on the morning of July 26, 1976, twenty-three-year-old Jack Dougherty drove the five miles from his apartment to the Newark, Delaware, headquarters of W. L. Gore & Associates Inc. He noticed the horses grazing on either side of the road, and for a while he held the image in his mind. But he was preoccupied. It was his first day on the job, and the recent MBA from the College of William and Mary was bursting with resolve. "I was beginning my career," he says. "I told myself that all the fooling around had stopped. I was all business."

Dressed in a dark blue suit and smiling broadly, Dougherty presented himself to Bill Gore, the founder of the company. He shook hands firmly but warmly, looked Gore in the eye, and said he was ready for anything. "That's fine, Jack, fine;" Gore told him. "Why don't you look around and find something you'd like to do." "That," Dougherty says, "was probably the one thing I wasn't ready for. I was shocked, but he was so relaxed about everything that I decided to go along with it. He said maybe I should start at the Cherry Hill plant, where a lot of the new products were, and I figured they'd probably have something set up for me over there. But they didn't. I was confused for the next three weeks."

Jack spent his time earnestly interrogating various product managers who were more than happy to explain their activities in great detail. Finally, Dougherty careened into the office of Joe Tanner, who was busy marketing the latest wunderkind from the Gore laboratories. It was a white, gossamer-thin membrane with pores too small for a molecule of water to penetrate yet large enough to transmit certain vapors.

It was called Gore-tex, Tanner said, and when it was bonded to a fabric, lo and behold, the fabric became waterproof but "breathable," a combination of qualities that had long eluded researchers. He was only making tents with it now, Tanner continued, but it wouldn't be long until the great out-of-doors would see legions of campers wearing Gore-tex parkas, backpacks, and other gear. Dougherty heard them marching. "I liked what I heard," he says. The next morning, the new employee, dressed in jeans, was helping feed fabric into the maw of a huge laminator. Dougherty had found his "something to do." Today, Dougherty is responsible for all advertising and marketing in the fabrics group, the third largest segment of the company's business.

Bill Gore claims that Jack Dougherty's success, like the success of the company itself, is the happy consequence of a system of un-management Gore calls the "lattice organization." It is so named because every individual within it deals directly with every other, one-on-one, in relationships best described as a crosshatching of horizontal and vertical lines. Unlike traditional "pyramid" management structures with carefully defined chains of command, Gore's lattice contains no titles, no orders, and no bosses. Associates, as all Gore employees are called, are allowed to identify an area where they feel they will be able to make their best contribution. Then, they are encouraged to maximize their individual accomplishments. "We don't manage people here," Bill Gore says. "People manage themselves. We organize ourselves around voluntary commitments. There is a fundamental difference in philosophy between a commitment and a command."

Hearing about the lattice without seeing it in operation can leave a suspicion that Bill Gore may have created a kind of self-indulgent commune where the profits of commerce are largely irrelevant. But the suspicion doesn't last long; the numbers won't allow it. During the past five years, Gore's sales and earnings have been growing at a compound annual rate of nearly 40 percent. In the fiscal year ended March 31, 1982, the company's worldwide sales approached $125 million from five basic product groups: wire and cable, medical, Gore-tex fabrics, Gore-tex fibers, and industrial filter bags. The company has some 2,000 associates in twenty plants worldwide and seven more plants under construction.

"Money is essential," Bill Gore says. "Without it, you don't have an enterprise." When someone suggested recently that Gore's determined drive for profits seemed incompatible with his more rarefied ideas about human relationships, Gore said: "That's because there's something wrong with your education, sir. Actually, making money is a creative activity. It means people are applauding you for making a good contribution. In fact, it gives us the freedom to be what we are."

Wilbert L. Gore was born in Meridian, Idaho, near Boise. He is seventy but looks fifty. His face is tan and creased from a lifetime of outdoorsmanship, primarily backpacking. He is trim and compact, standing about five feet, seven inches tall. He is calm and totally devoid of pretense. When he was studying for his degree in chemical engineering at the University of Utah, he won the Rocky Mountain Conference diving title from the one-meter board. Bill recalls growing up "with a lot of love around me."

At age six, Bill began his mountain wanderings in the Wasatch Range in Utah. And it was in those mountains, at a church summer camp, that he later met his future wife, Genevieve. Vieve, as she is called, says that in those days, every time she came around, Bill would execute a series of back somersaults. Friends say they are inseparable. One company advertisement features a photograph of them in full backpacking gear against a cratered, mountainous landscape. The caption reads: "The force behind the dream."

* * *

The dream itself first started taking shape from 1945 to 1957, when Bill worked on a task force in the research labs of E. I. Du Pont de Nemours. As Bill remembers it, the task-force approach to problem-solving had just been introduced at Du Pont. It had become increasingly popular in scientific research after prototype groups had proven their effectiveness during World War II. Bill's group, which at times included twenty researchers from various scientific disciplines, was intent on fabricating useful products from a polymer Du Pont had patented in 1937 called polytetrafluoroethylene, or PTFE. Years later, consumers would know PTFE as "Teflon," of nonstick-frying fame.

At the time, though, PTFE was little more than a puzzle. It had all the markings of a super-substance: it was strong, impervious to chemical solvents, abrasion-resistant, stable over a wide range of temperatures, and a nearly perfect electrical insulator. But in polymer form, PTFE could be neither injection-molded nor extruded by melt-processing techniques, the two traditional methods of fashioning, say, a plastic bowl. It could be "ram" extruded, a process of taking a lump of PTFE, a battering ram of some sort, and then smashing the PTFE through an orifice. Tape and tubing could be made that way, but little else. "The task force," Bill says, "was exciting, challenging, and loads of fun. Besides, we worked like Trojans. I began to wonder why entire companies couldn't be run the same way."

But even as Bill's group burned the midnight oil, another task force succeeded in creating a thermoplastic copolymer of PTFE that could be conventionally fabricated. "Du Pont felt that was good enough," Bill says, "and our group was dissolved. Everybody went back to their departments." Gore did, too, but nights, holidays, and weekends, he went to his basement. "I had a pretty good shop set up," he says, "so I started fooling around with polymer PTFE down there."

Bill continued to pursue his career at Du Pont and tinker in the basement for a year or so. One night in the fall of 1957, Bob Gore, a junior studying chemical engineering at the University of Delaware, dropped in on his father in the basement lab. He was surprised when his father launched into a long lecture on PTFE. Not only did Bill recite the litany of qualities he considered superior to those of the thermoplastic copolymer, but he also related their importance to another technological revolution that was unfolding at an astonishing pace—computers.

Ever since he first entered a few numbers into a computer named Einiac, a forerunner of Univac, Bill had followed the evolution of computers and transistors with growing excitement. He felt that some of PTFE's characteristics made it an ideal insulator for electrical wires in computers. It would make them easier to build, he said, and would ultimately increase their efficiency. And that, he concluded, could mean a very profitable market.

Bill explained that he had tried various ways to make a PTFE coating but had failed. He held up an aborted section of ribbon cable and pointed out where his attempts had broken down. "Then I noticed some sealant tape made by the 3M company," Bob says. "Dad had said it was ram-extruded PTFE, so I asked him: 'Why don't you try this tape?' Dad said that would mean laminating the wires between two sections of tape and everybody knew you couldn't bond PTFE to itself. I went to bed."

As near as Bob can recall, it was around 4:00 A.M. when his father shook him awake. "I really didn't grasp what he was talking about," Bob says, "except I knew my father was very excited. I was sitting on the edge of my bed blinking at him, and he was waving this small piece of cable around saying: 'It works. It works.' "

"That's right," Bill says, "I stayed up all night to try out his suggestion. My son proved everybody wrong. But I really think it was 6:00 A.M. Bob used to sleep late." The next night, father and son returned to the lab and made ribbon cable "just as beautiful as can be."

During the next four months, Bill Gore tried to persuade Du Pont to take on the PTFE ribbon cable as a new product. "By that time in my career," he says, "I knew people who could make a decision. But it came through loud and clear that Du Pont regarded itself as a supplier of plastic raw materials and not as a fabricator." Soon after he learned of the company's decision, Bill and Vieve talked about starting their own wire and cable business. Bill said that if they mortgaged their house and took $4,000 from savings, they could make a go of it for two years. If they weren't successful by then, he said, he could probably get his job back at Du Pont or possibly teach at a university.

On January 1, 1958, their twenty-third wedding anniversary, Bill and Vieve started another partnership. "All of our friends told us not to do it," Vieve Gore says, "and that's a very difficult thing. But this man of mine had it in his head. He just had to do it. We had that basement festooned with lights. We put drill holes in the floor and drill holes in the walls. It's hard to describe what it's like to bring your husband home and turn him loose."

When Bill Gore left Du Pont, he was forty-five years old with five children to support. He left behind a career that spanned seventeen years, a good salary, and security. But he also took a lot with him. During the next twenty-four years, virtually every new product Gore & Associates introduced was based on the PTFE polymer, bought from Du Pont, that Bill first encountered on the task force. And, just as important, Gore set out to recreate in his own company the sense of excited commitment, personal fulfillment, and self-direction that he had experienced on the Du Pont task force. "From the very beginning," Bill says, "we were using the principles of the lattice. After all, there was just Vieve and me, and we had been using them for years."

The two years the Gores had given themselves quickly slipped away. They needed business badly. The few odd orders that trickled into the basement just weren't paying the bills. "We came very close to calling it quits," Vieve says. But help was on the way.

One afternoon, Vieve stopped sifting PTFE powder to answer a phone call from a man who said he was with the city of Denver's water department. He said he had a sample of ribbon cable and was very interested but needed answers to a few technical questions. "Obviously Bill was the technical expert," Vieve says, "but he was out on an errand. I didn't know what to say. First, he asked for the product manager and I said he was out at the moment, then he asked for the sales manager, and finally for the president. They were all out, I told him. Before I could ask if I could help, he was hollering: 'What kind of a company is this anyway?' "

It took a little diplomacy, but eventually the Gores got an order for about $100,000 worth of ribbon cable to be used as part of a system that monitored pressure in water mains. "That order put us over the hump," Bill says. "We took off from there."

By the time Bob Gore joined the company in 1963 with a Ph.D. in chemical engineering, it was clear the wire and cable business had taken hold. The company was properly ensconced in a new plant on Paper Mill Road in Newark, horses grazed lazily in pastures nearby, and the sun was shining on W. L. Gore & Associates. But all was not well. There were profits in the till, but there were also cracks in the lattice.

One warm Monday morning in the summer of 1965, Bill Gore was taking his usual stroll through the plant "to look around and say hello" when he suddenly realized that he no longer knew everyone's name. "I'm not talking about just one person," he says, "but several. I said to myself, 'Hey, the game has changed.' " Actually, the game was still the same, but there were many more players. The company had grown from simple connubial bliss to close to 200 employees. That growth was, in itself, a basement dream come true, something every entrepreneur hopes for. But, as often happens, it was still somewhat disconcerting.

"As the number of associates grew," Bill says, "we had to find a way to help people get started and then to follow their progress. This was particularly important when it came to compensation." At the same time, Bill wanted to avoid smothering the company in thick layers of formal "management," a common response to organizational problems that he felt stifled individual creativity. Instead, he promoted a kind of "buddy system," a casual Big Brother or Big Sister relationship in which a more experienced associate took a specific and personal interest in the contributions, problems, and goals of a new associate.

Gradually, the "buddy" system matured into the "sponsor" system, a largely semantic difference that, nonetheless, accurately suggests a more sophisticated sense of advocacy and involvement. Everyone at Gore has a sponsor and frequently more than one. The associate who starts out in, say, fabric inspection and quality control and then becomes interested in fabric lamination will have a sponsor in each department and perhaps still others as the associate's responsibilities grow.

Ultimately this associate will also become a sponsor, because at Gore leaders are not appointed but are allowed to "happen." "Leaders are so defined," Bill Gore says, "because they have followers. And why people follow one person and not another, I don't really know. Sometimes it's based on superior knowledge or skill, but there are many other nonobjective and perhaps even mystical factors."

The sponsorship system was a harmonious addition to Bill Gore's evolving method of un-management. It was flexible, expandable, and well suited to accommodate the future needs of a growing company—but it wasn't enough. During that tour when Bill discovered that he didn't know everyone's name, he also realized that neither did anyone else. Even more alarming, he found a subtle shift in perspective; the once tightly knit group had lost its sense of identity. Although he wasn't sure of the cause, his memories of the Du Pont task force strongly suggested that it had to do with the number of people in the group. Apparently, he reasoned, as that number approached 200, a group somehow became a crowd in which individuals grew increasingly anonymous and significantly less cooperative.

In part to test his theory and in part to reach midwestern markets, Bill Gore opened a second plant in 1967 in Flagstaff, Arizona. As people shifted to Flagstaff, the number of associates at the Newark plant dropped to 150. "That did the trick," Bill says. "People started smiling more. You could tell they felt better even by the way they said 'hello.' " In the years that followed, the accuracy of his intuition was proven time and again. Each time the magic number was breached, group cohesiveness and cooperation declined. Each time, Bill would open another plant. In fact, he has opened eighteen more plants since 1967, at an average cost of almost $4.5 million. The openings are all the more remarkable because the company never used a dime of debt until 1980.

The thought obviously pleases Bill Gore; he smiles faintly and says: "Opening plants costs money, but it makes money." Then he goes on to say that his goal in the next five years is to become one of the country's biggest companies. Almost impishly he waits for the message to sink in. Obviously growth of that magnitude means a cloudburst of new plant openings. "Yes, I know," he says contentedly. "We've already got seven under construction. Now do you see why profits are essential?"

The middle sixties marked a period of transition for W. L. Gore & Associates. By 1969, as the company approached $6 million in sales, Bill Gore had confronted the problem of growth and had found some innovative solutions consistent with his vision of a lattice organization. The sponsorship system, for example, preserved both order and individual freedom. And the realization that size had a measurable impact on group dynamics was another theoretical and then practical breakthrough. As a result, the lattice itself was evolving. These developments couldn't have been better timed. Bob Gore was about to have another brainstorm.

In the fall of 1969, Bob was troubled by a growing suspicion that the company's wire and cable business was slowing down because of market saturation and increasing competition. The anxiety made him restless and soon he found himself working nights in the lab toying with PTFE. If he could stretch PTFE, he reasoned, he could introduce air into its molecular structure, giving a greater volume per pound of raw material without affecting its performance. This, in turn, could sharply reduce the company's fabricating costs and ultimately increase profit margins on coated wire and cable products. That way, any sales slowdown could be offset by increasing profitability. The scientific community had already determined that PTFE couldn't be stretched very far. But since he had proven conventional wisdom wrong once before, Bob decided to go ahead.

For three days, he took slender rods of PTFE about a foot long and preheated them in the lab's ovens. Then, ever so gently, he pulled on both ends of the rod. Each time, the rod snapped in two. He tried again and again. He tried different temperatures. He tried to adjust the force of his easy pull. Nothing worked.

Finally, the days of futile, frustrating effort caught up with him. One evening in October, Bob Gore, dressed in a white lab coat and heavy asbestos gloves, took a rod from the oven, grabbed each end, and angrily yanked his clenched fists apart. The foot-long rod stretched the full length of his extended arms. "I couldn't believe it," he says. "I went right home. I didn't say anything to anybody because I thought it might be a fluke. I knew what I had done, but I just couldn't believe it. I always entered my results in a journal, but that night I didn't write anything. I must've been really worked up."

Early the next morning, Bob hurried to the lab so he could repeat his experiment before anyone else arrived. After several successful attempts, he called in his father and colleagues. With a quick flourish of his arms, he revealed the fruits of his labor. "We were all very quiet," Bill Gore says. "We were all trained scientists so we recognized the importance of what Bob had done. I was very proud."

Word spread rapidly throughout the company that Bob Gore had discovered a "miracle product." Even today, associates who were there recall the time with a certain breathless sense of wonder. "Everybody seemed to have an idea how to use it," says Burt Chase, business leader of the wire and cable division. "Bob kept a small gray file-card box in his office so people could drop off their ideas. I remember one that said we should string tennis racquets with expanded PTFE. We were all caught up in the excitement." The list of suggested ideas was so exhaustive that when the patent was filed on May 21, 1970, it correctly anticipated every product application that would be introduced during the next twelve years, with the sole exception of vascular grafting. In only six months, the miracle product, now called Gore-tex, had totally reshaped the company's future. A wire and cable company had been transformed into a multifaceted high-technology company reaching for a tantalizing variety of markets. At least that is how it appeared in the white heat of the moment. Translating imagination into viable commercial products was another matter.

Gore's first product using expanded PTFE was made by a process that didn't bathe the company in the glory of high-tech precision but was, nonetheless, a fitting example of the resourcefulness that would characterize the development of Gore-tex. This product was, and is, a joint sealant that is put on pipe flanges to ensure a tight fit.

Bob Gore affectionately describes the sealant's method of manufacture as the "sneaker process." Two men would come to work wearing sneakers; they would each grab an end of a preheated length of PTFE; they would nod to each other when ready, and then they would run like crazy to opposite ends of the warehouse. Voilà, they had made Gore-tex sealant tape. "Now that was something to see," Bob Gore says. "I guess it was about 100 feet, wall to wall, and those guys really flew. It wasn't fancy, but it worked."

While the boys were sprinting out in the warehouse, Bob and his colleagues were creating machines that could mass-produce the Gore-tex membrane in wide sheets and then bond it to fabrics. But it was slow work, and to keep the miracle product alive and growing, the associates foraged for new applications wherever and whenever they could.

In 1971, for example, Bill Gore chanced on the company's second-largest division on a snow-covered slope in Colorado where he was skiing with friends, including Dr. Ben Eiseman of the Denver General Hospital. "We were just about to start a run," Bill Gore says, "when I absentmindedly pulled a small tubular section of Gore-tex out of my pocket and looked at it. 'What is that stuff?' Ben asked. So I told him about its properties. 'Feels great,' he said. 'What do you use it for?' 'Got no idea,' I said. 'Well, give it to me,' he said, 'and I'll try it in a vascular graft on a pig.' Two weeks later, he called me up. Ben was pretty excited. 'Bill,' he said, 'I put it in a pig and it works. What do I do now?' I told him to get together with Pete Cooper in our Flagstaff plant, and I let them figure it out." Although a major problem would have to be solved four years later, 375,000 patients throughout the world now walk around with Gore-tex vascular grafts. "Cardiovascular disease is one of the major health problems of mankind," says medical products leader Jack Hoover. "The use of Gore-tex to treat it has only just begun."

By 1973, Bob's engineering team had devised machines that could stretch Gore-tex wide enough to cover the standard commercial dimensions of several different fabrics. All their tests indicated that at long last, the secret of a waterproof, breathable garment had been discovered. Bill Gore couldn't have been happier, but he wasn't going to wear it; he wanted to sleep in it. For years, Bill had yearned for a light, waterproof tent that would save him lower back pain on long mountain treks. Gore-tex looked like the answer to a veteran camper's prayer.

Since Vieve had routinely handcrafted their backpacks and tents, Bill commissioned her to stitch up a tent from sections of Gore-tex he had bonded to mosquito netting. Then they set off for the mountains of the Wind River Range in the wilds of Wyoming. "One night," Bill says, "it started to rain just after we had gone to bed. And it rained harder. Vieve and I felt around the tent and it was bone-dry. We were very pleased with ourselves. But then the rain turned partly to hail. The hail punched tiny holes through the Gore-tex, and later there must've been two inches of water in the tent. We didn't sleep well that night."

As it turned out, Bill and Vieve's soggy night at Wind River was more than a temporary inconvenience; it was the first sign that Gore-tex had entered a time of troubles. During the next five years, Gore-tex would suffer a variety of technical growing pains. Some were minor, but others were critical, even potentially fatal to the reputation of a miracle product, and all would test the resiliency of the lattice.

In June 1975, Dr. Charles Campbell, senior resident at the University of Pittsburgh, reported to Jack Hoover that a Gore-tex arterial graft he had placed in a patient had developed an aneurism, a bubblelike protrusion of the arterial wall that meant it wasn't strong enough to withstand the pressure of the blood within it. If the aneurism continued to expand, it would eventually burst, and the patient could die.

The problem had to be solved quickly and permanently if the company's plans for vascular grafts were ever to be realized. "I'm told from time to time," Bill Gore says, "that a lattice organization can't meet a crisis well because it takes too long to reach a consensus when there are no bosses. But this isn't true. Actually, a lattice, by its very nature, works particularly well in a crisis. A lot of useless effort is avoided because there is no rigid management hierarchy to conquer before you can attack a problem."

Only days after his call, Dr. Campbell flew to Newark to present his findings to Bill and Bob Gore and several other associates drawn from production and research. The meeting adjourned after two hours of discussion, and the associates went their separate ways to consider solutions. But one of the associates, Dan Hubis, already had an idea he thought might work. If he could wrap another layer of Gore-tex around a section of graft, he reasoned, he might be able to increase the rupture tolerance of the entire section. Hubis, a former Elkton, Maryland, policeman who had joined Gore in 1966 to work on new production methods, immediately started testing his idea in the lab.

He tried various wrapping techniques, and after each try he forced compressed air through the specimen section to see if it would hold. On his twelfth try, after three hours of work, he found the right method. Hubis had resolved a potentially serious setback in only one afternoon. "It was quick because it had to be," Hubis says. "I don't remember any clapping or cheering, but I know we were very happy." Bill Gore was pleased, too; not only was it a noteworthy technical accomplishment, but it also proved the worth of the lattice. "There were several people with different skills all working on a common problem," Bill says. "They came together quickly, and no one was slowed down because they had to get the approval of some higher-up before they could proceed. The creativity of such a group is much greater than the sum of its members."

As 1976 began, W. L. Gore & Associates still looked like the wire and cable company founded eighteen years earlier. It was more elaborate, of course, with more people, more markets, and a broader product line, but at least 90 percent of sales and profits were still being drawn from the basic wire and cable business. After several years of research and development, Gore-tex was only a modest success, contributing some $2 million in sales from uses in microfiltration, industrial filter bags, joint sealant, and medical products. But even though Gore & Associates may have looked like the same old company, it didn't look that way for long, because in 1976, Gore-tex took off and took the whole company with it. "From that time," says Shanti Mehta, Gore's financial leader, "the company's sales and earnings have grown at least 35 percent a year. Gore-tex products were soon contributing almost 50 percent of our business."

The initial surge was led by the medical products division as Hubis's strengthened graft won widespread acceptance in the medical community—eventually it would control 70 percent of the market. Then the Goretex fabric division kicked in with its first commercial product, a tent.

A mountaineer named Bill Nicolai had nearly frozen to death in the Picket Range of Washington State's North Cascades in the fall of 1971. Like the Gores, Nicolai had problems with his tent, only his was shredded to streamers in a storm. And also like the Gores, he wasn't going to let it happen again. That winter he created a two-man expedition tent especially designed to withstand nature's high-altitude perversities. He called it the Omnipotent, in praise of its virtues, and then he founded a company, Early Winters Ltd., to make it and sell it.

But the Omnipotent was a costly and complex affair meant for very serious climbers, and Nicolai soon learned that there just weren't that many people around who habitually spent their time on the roof of the world. For several years, Early Winters, like its customers, lived close to the edge of disaster. Even by January 1976, the company—one product, five employees, and rented space in a former neighborhood grocery store in Seattle—was still struggling to survive. Then Joe Tanner walked through the door. Since February 1974, when he joined Gore, Tanner had been traveling around the country literally trying to give Gore-tex away to anyone who would agree to make something with it. A few companies were willing to give it a try, but afterward they balked when they were asked to buy it. Then Tanner found Nicolai.

"I'd never met the man before," says Nicolai. "But there he was telling me about this stuff that was waterproof and breathed. He wanted me to make a tent with it. Of course, I'd heard all this before, but I had nothing to lose; my tent wasn't selling very well." Nicolai took some Gore-tex laminate, quickly fashioned a prototype tent, and headed for the hills. "The fantastic thing about it was that it worked," he says. "I took it camping at Icicle Creek in the Cascades. That night it was drizzling and twenty-nine degrees Fahrenheit—perfect for condensation. When I woke up in the morning, I felt the side of the tent and it was bone-dry. A shiver went down my spine." Nicolai's new tent, christened Light Dimension, was an instant success.

Although the Omnipotent is still favored by professional climbers, the Light Dimension reached a much bigger market because it set up quickly and was light, compact, and, at $195, some $60 less than its big brother. Sales at Early Winters jumped from $6,000 a month to $35,000, enabling Nicolai to introduce several new products. Today, the company's tents, parkas, and other equipment produce annual sales of roughly $10 million.

There was only one man who could have matched Nicolai smile for smile, and that was Joe Tanner. Two years of hope, disappointment, tests, and more hope had finally paid off. That summer he explained to a young business-school graduate recently hired at Gore that even though he was making only tents with Gore-tex laminate, it wouldn't be long until the great out-of-doors was draped with Gore-tex. During the next two years, as word of waterproof, breathable fabrics spread from Nicolai's store, Tanner signed up some half-dozen larger and better-known manufacturers.

Gore supplied the membrane and the lamination process, but it left design, cutting, and sewing to the manufacturers. Companies like Sierra West, Banana Equipment, and Recreational Equipment Inc. started making parkas, rainwear, sleeping bags, and a variety of outdoor accessories with Gore-tex. Once again, the sun was shining on W. L. Gore & Associates. But the summer of 1978, which began so full of promise for the Gore-tex fabrics division, gradually darkened into deepest gloom. "It was a nightmare," says Peter Gilson, the division's business leader. "Parkas were being returned because they leaked."

Gilson had just joined Gore. He was thirty-eight years old, but he already had fifteen years of conspicuous accomplishment in the fabrics business at Du Pont. But even with all his experience, Gilson was bewildered when leaky parkas started showing up in groups of threes and fours. "We had no idea why they leaked," he says. "At first we thought the customers hadn't sealed the seams properly or maybe they punctured it somehow. We sensed we had a problem, but because the parkas straggled in, we weren't sure how big it was." But there was one thing that Gilson did know: The entire company's reputation and credibility were on the line.

In September, Gore researchers discovered that certain oils in human sweat could clog the pores in the Gore-tex membrane, which, in turn, altered the surface tension of the membrane, allowing water molecules to pass through. In short, sweaty parkas leaked. But they also discovered that such "contaminated" parkas could be restored if they were washed in a detergent and double-rinse cycle or, in extreme cases, in a denatured alcohol bath. This became known as the "Ivory Snow Solution" and it was passed on to every Gore-tex manufacturer and dealer. For a while, there was hope that this solution would remedy the relatively few complaints being reported. Then, in November, Gilson received a disturbing letter from a part-time employee of Sierra West who also worked as a mountain guide. He told Gilson about a recent experience when he led a small group of campers into the Sierras and they were hit by a freak storm. "His name was Butch," Gilson says, "and I remember he wrote: 'My parka leaked, and my life was in danger.' That scared the hell out of us. Clearly our solution was no solution at all to someone on a mountaintop."

Gilson, at Gore only a few months, was faced with a decision that could cause serious damage to the entire company. Bill Gore calls decisions of this type "waterline decisions," using the image of a sinking ship. At any other time, Gore associates are allowed to solve their problems independently; free to seek advice or not, as they see fit. But if the problem could twist toward the company's waterline, associates must consult with other associates before proceeding. As evidence mounted, it became clear that the contamination problem was larger in scope and carried more serious consequences than had first been imagined.

Gilson sat down at a conference table with Bob Gore and four other associates. The circumstances were undeniably grave, but otherwise the meeting merely reflected the normal metabolism of a healthy lattice organization. Once again, associates with different skills had been brought together to solve a common problem. Bob Gore was there for his scientific expertise and the others brought talents in marketing, manufacturing, and quality control. The more they talked, the more they realized that there was only one thing they could do. "We took all of the noninsulated Gore-tex garments off the market," Gilson says. "We brought back, at our own expense, a fortune in pipeline material. Anything that was in the stores, at the manufacturers, or anywhere else in the pipeline, we stopped."

Meanwhile, Bob Gore set out to find a permanent answer to the contamination problem. One month after the garments were taken off the market, Bob Gore came out of the lab having restructured the molecular configuration of the membrane to exclude the oils that were causing the contamination. By late December, parkas made with improved, second-generation Gore-tex laminates were already on dealers' racks. In addition, Gilson told dealers that anytime a customer returned a leaky parka, they should replace it with a second-generation model and bill the company. "In the four years since 1978, we've taken back roughly $3.5 million of first-generation products. But hindsight tells us that we made the right decision. We didn't lose our credibility. We haven't lost even one customer."

As time passed, Gilson's perspective changed to give equal weight to what was gained as well as to what hadn't been lost. In four years, Gore's customer list grew from the original 6 to 125, including names like North Face, C.B. Sports, and Sierra Designs. Gore-tex fabrics blossomed into a profusion of products. There are Gore-tex jogging shoes, hiking boots, and high-fashion boots for women; Gore-tex hats and gloves; and trench coats, ski jackets, and golf jackets. There are even Gore-tex space suits on the space shuttle Columbia. The fabrics division has grown "substantially faster" than the company as a whole, and Gilson expects it to double its size in the current fiscal year alone. And, he says, there is more growth on the way. This year the army and the marine corps will begin outfitting troops in Gore-tex wet-weather parkas, pants, and headgear. "That," says Gilson, "is a sizable piece of business."

Still, the scare of '78 hasn't been entirely forgotten. Bill Gore, for example, likes to test a sample of every new garment personally to assure himself that it doesn't leak. Sometimes, he is spotted wandering around the grounds of the Newark plant during a rainstorm wearing a colorful, hooded parka, but at other times, when nature fails, he is perfectly content to wear a similar parka out to the garden behind his house and stand there with a hose over his head.

Ever since Bob Gore yanked a new future out of preheated goop, W. L. Gore & Associates has risen at a pace and in directions that no observer could have anticipated. But just as the company seems focused on a future of dramatic growth with fabrics as the largest and fastest-growing business in the company, yet another Gore prepares to yank something spectacular out of the goop.

"It will be the desalination of seawater; you know, making it drinkable," says Bill Gore. "We haven't talked much about it, because it's still in development. But my son, Dave, is going to give a paper on it next month."

Dave Gore is a thirty-seven-year-old physicist who has been working on the process for almost three years in Flagstaff. He says the idea first impressed him when he was a child watching his father scamper around the roof of the house setting up solar-distillation experiments. "It's always been a big dream of mine," he says. "It would have impact. You can make the desert bloom." But it was the invention of the Gore-tex membrane that made the dream come true.

Basically, Dave's process, which he calls "membrane distillation," involves passing water vapor from salt water through a Gore-tex membrane. Impurities are left behind and then the vapor condenses against a cold surface to recover potable water. He claims membrane distillation is considerably more efficient and less expensive than any other technique currently available. Even though he has only small units being tested, Dave says he is about ready to market them commercially. "We'll start with the $100 million-a-year market for pure laboratory water," he says, "and then we'll move to making drinking water from seawater. Worldwide, the market is probably worth billions. It's a little bit mind-boggling when you think of all the possibilities."

Could it be that virtually anything is possible in some kind of corporate paradise structured on the lattice? Is the lattice the answer to every problem? "No," says Bill Gore. "For example, established companies would find it very difficult to use the lattice. Too many hierarchies would be destroyed. When you remove titles and positions and allow people to follow who they want, it may very well be someone other than the person who has been in charge. The lattice works for us, but it's always evolving. You have to expect problems."

Sometimes, it appears, the lattice can even make life difficult for those it serves. Burt Chase, head of wire and cable, says the unhappiest moment of his twenty-year career was caused by a sponsor who wouldn't sponsor. "I still don't know what his problem was," Chase says. "At the time, I was selling on the West Coast, and I had three men working with me. Time after time I'd tell my sponsor that if he didn't come through for me on one thing or another, I'd have to let the men down. He'd nod and say: 'Uh, huh, I'll take care of it.' But he never did. Finally, I had to go directly to Bill Gore. I guess Bill told him that there were some very unhappy men out there and that woke him up. Anyway, it's still a potential problem that we work very hard at avoiding."

And sometimes customers don't quite know what to make of it. "I was taken aback that something that loose could really work," says Eric Reynolds, founder of Marmot Mountain Works Ltd. of Grand Junction, Colorado, and a major Gore customer. "I was also taken by the romance of it all, the idea of free spirits working together. But the more I've seen of it the more I think that the lattice works best in research and development projects. I think the lattice has its problems with the day-to-day nitty-gritty of getting things done on time and getting products out the door. I don't think Bill quite realizes how the lattice system affects customers. I mean, after you've established a relationship with someone about product quality, you can call up one day and suddenly find that someone new to you is handling your problems. It's frustrating to find a lack of continuity. But I have to admit that I've personally seen at Gore remarkable examples of people coming out of nowhere and excelling."

Associates asked to describe the lattice in operation act as if they have just been teased with an insoluble riddle. They do their best to capture a phenomenon that at times requires them to invent a new vocabulary. But in the end it becomes clear that the lattice to them is like breathing, something done every second and rarely thought about. "You don't come to work here and say, 'OK, now we've got to do the lattice system,' " says Carmela Avallone, head of fabric inspection. "The lattice is a feeling, a state of mind." And ultimately, they say, that feeling finds its way back to Bill and Vieve Gore.

Late one afternoon, Bill and Vieve were swapping stories about their adventures in the mountains of the world. Vieve suddenly changed the subject and began talking about a meeting the company had held for the associates on the previous Saturday. Some 600 associates filled an auditorium at the University of Delaware, she said, to listen to a detailed presentation about the company's results for the year and plans for the future. This was done regularly, she said, but this year was a little different. "My son, Bob, got up to speak," she said. "And then behind him were slides projected that he had put together showing Bill as a young man. There was even a picture of him going off a diving board. Bob looked at the pictures for a while and then he turned to the associates and said: 'My father was a young man once,' and that's how he introduced Bill."

As Vieve was telling the story she never stopped looking at her husband, and at the end of it she had tears in her eyes. And he never looked away from her, because they were talking really only for each other. He was looking at her and smiling faintly with utter tenderness. Vieve didn't say any more, but Carmela Avallone finished the story later. "When Bill got up," she said, "everyone started clapping, and then they stood up, and it went on and on, and there weren't many dry eyes that day."

"It's much better to use friendship and love," Bill Gore once said, "than slavery and whips. The results will always be much better."

—LUCIEN RHODES

"GOOD LEADERS
AREN'T PERFECT"

Businesses require a new kind of leadership if they're to thrive during the 1980s, claims Michael Maccoby, social psychologist and author of *The Gamesman*, the 1976 best-seller on management styles.

The Leader, Maccoby's latest book, describes a manager who is willing to share power, inspires cooperation rather than competition, and is more flexible and tolerant than his predecessors. It is based on case histories of six managers—three in industry, two in government, and one in a labor union.

His thesis in both books is that the most successful managers understand, and often embody, the positive elements of the existing "social character," Maccoby's term for the dominant attitudes and values of Americans during a given era.

In *The Gamesman*, Maccoby identified four management types: The Craftsman holds the traditional values of the early 1900s, with a concern for quality and thrift, and for his craft. In the past he may have been a furniture maker; today he may be the leader of a research and development team.

The Jungle Fighter sees both life and work as a struggle for power in which his peers are either accomplices or enemies, his subordinates resources to be manipulated. Past examples include such empire-builders as Andrew Carnegie. Now the Jungle Fighter may be the turnaround artist who is brought in to clean house and reorganize a troubled company.

The Company Man came to the fore during the tranquil fifties. His modesty, loyalty, sense of responsibility, and negotiating skills lent stability to corporate environments. He adapts to a company as if it were another family; his weakness may be greater concern for security than for success. Now he most often excels as a middle manager in a large company.

The Gamesman fit the management needs of the 1960s and early 1970s when fast-growing high-technology companies thrived on competition, innovation, flexibility, and aggressive leadership of project teams. Today he may manage a semiconductor firm. His career is a game, full of possibilities and options; his goal is winning.

In the current decade, one of limited resources and increasing international competition, the assets of the Gamesman are becoming liabilities, says Maccoby. He can no longer motivate his team by continually promising more. He may inspire counterproductive competition and distrust, and he can alienate subordinates by his lack of compassion in dealing with people.

The Gamesman is giving way to the Leader, a manager who understands the changing attitudes of the late 1970s and early 1980s. What are those attitudes, how do they shape this new style, and how can managers of smaller companies adopt traits that will make them more effective? Michael Maccoby answered these and other questions during a recent interview with *Inc.* senior writer Sharon Frederick.

INC: The leader you describe as the model manager for the 1980s sounds almost too good to be true. Is it a leadership style that's feasible for most managers, and, if so, how does one begin to develop such a style?

MACCOBY: Good leaders today are *not* people who are "perfect." They all have faults. The difference between them and old-style managers is that they acknowledge and struggle with those faults, rather than ignoring and becoming defensive about them.

There are no easy rules for becoming what I call a leader. You start by looking at yourself, at your strengths and weaknesses as a manager and a leader. One way to do that is to find somebody you're close to and trust, and say, "Look, I really mean this: you'd be doing me a great favor if you'd talk to me about my strengths and weaknesses as you see them." You'll be amazed at how much you can learn.

Another way is to look at other people and how they operate. That's the reason I use six models of good manager-leaders as the basis for my book. If you honestly think about yourself in comparison to Pehr Gyllenhammar, chief executive of Volvo, or Irving Bluestone, former United Auto Workers vice-president, you'll see differences between the way you manage and the way they manage.

INC: I find it hard to believe the head of Volvo, or a UAW official, has much in common with managers in small companies.

MACCOBY: They do have some things in common. What may be more revealing, however, is what they *don't* have in common. If you have an entrepreneurial temperament, you'll see you operate very differently from someone like Gyllenhammar. You may see that the same traits that got you where you are today can keep you from going any farther, particularly because you're going to have trouble motivating and managing today's employee.

Most limiting is the entrepreneur's tendency not to listen to anybody else. Successful entrepreneurs are often people who have done something when everybody else said it couldn't be done. If you've survived and brought a company to $1 million or $10 million in sales, you know you've succeeded where many others have failed. You've stayed on the edge of the cliff while they've fallen off. So you think: Why should I listen to anyone else?

You may also tend to think of yourself as father-knows-best. People are either with you—in the family and under your protection—or are enemies, outsiders. You want to control most situations and won't give up power to anybody unless you're sure the person is totally loyal. That paternalism limits an entrepreneur's effectiveness and creates dislike and resistance among employees.

There's also a certain ruthlessness to many entrepreneurs. They simply don't pay attention to what effects they have on other people. They don't try to be destructive; they just push ahead, regardless of the risks for themselves or others. That may have worked in the past, for the jungle fighters like Andrew Carnegie. I don't think it works well for managers today.

The best models for entrepreneurs today are the Hewletts and Packards. They've articulated values that go beyond getting rich or winning. They've learned to work cooperatively and to respect individuals who are different from themselves.

The weakness of the jungle fighter character is its lack of caring about people who aren't part of the company "family." If you're that kind of person, you're never going to be the kind of leader I'm talking about, unless you really wake up to your deep distrust of those you don't control and learn to take some risks with people.

But I think we all have the capacity to learn and to develop ourselves. So you can work at understanding how you operate and how you affect people. As Heraclitus said, everyone should know himself and act with moderation. You can't demand change, but you can demand moderation.

INC: You say some managers are people-sensitive, others are not. Don't most managers recognize that satisfied, motivated people are essential to the success of a company?

MACCOBY: Sure, all chief executives make speeches saying human beings are our most important resource. It's almost an incantation that they feel obligated to repeat. But that's the end of it.

You may say: We want to work like a real team here. But then take an honest look at how things *really* work. Start with your relationship to your managers. If your relationship to them is one of domination, maybe even controlled humiliation, that's the way they're apt to act with everyone else. Or, they'll act as a buffer between you and the organization, protecting people from you and filtering information so you don't hear some things.

Take a look at all your systems, both formal and informal. For example, are you evaluating people just in terms of their immediate payoff, their contribution to the bottom line, or on how they're helping to build the organization? If employees hear you say you want teamwork, but see that you don't reward people who care about building that team and developing younger people, they get cynical.

They become even more cynical when you try to solve problems of employee motivation by gimmicks. You may bring in a program like quality-control circles and say: We're going to be like the Japanese and get everybody to participate. If you don't then make the changes to move in that direction, you're messing up your organization.

Unless you're serious about change, don't use gimmicks that create cynicism and make people distrust you. People prefer a bastard who makes no pretense of being sensitive to people over someone who talks one way and acts another.

INC: How does the successful manager, someone who fits your model of the leader, motivate his employees?

MACCOBY: Most of us assume that what motivates us motivates everybody. We believe there's something called human nature that causes people to react in predictable ways, and that what we ourselves feel and want is a good example of human nature. You hear the idea all the time, in President Reagan's philosophy, for example. It's built on the entrepreneurial ethic which says: Give people opportunity and they'll work hard.

There's a certain truth there, but it's a partial truth. It doesn't take into account differences in individual character, which you see most clearly by living in another culture where people and their motivations are very different. To show those differences, in *The Leader* I used two models from outside this country: Gyllenhammar of Sweden and Jim Hughes, a plant manager in Scotland.

People who will be successful leaders and managers in the eighties recognize that what motivates them may not motivate others. They see that people very different from themselves can still contribute a great deal. And they see that only by respecting those differences and trying to understand them can they get people really working.

For example, you may be willing to make many sacrifices to build a business, but that may not be true of some of the people you hire. They can still be very valuable contributors, but they have simply made a decision not to sacrifice everything for their work.

Managers should also realize that they may have several different work ethics coexisting within a single organization. Some employees may identify closely with the new social character, others may not. Some old-style workers prefer old-style management and structured work; others want to work as a team supervising themselves. Your best bet is to be flexible, allowing employees different roles as much as possible.

INC: Frankly, this new style of managing begins to sound like more trouble than it may be worth, especially in an uncertain economy when many managers are worrying about simple survival.

MACCOBY: If you feel that way, I think the best approach is to be honest with employees. Say to them: Look, I'd like to think working here is enjoyable as well as productive and profitable. I know people are talking more and more about things like participation. But right now we're in a crunch; we've got to put all our efforts into improving our products and building our markets. If we get past this, I promise you we can start talking about how to improve the work situation here.

Before you do that, though, I'd look closely at the time and effort you're wasting by poor communication and lack of teamwork. Then, I'd look at the money lost on absenteeism, turnover, grievances, and the like. Finally, I'd look at whether you're attracting the caliber of people you'd like. You might well find that whatever resources you put into improving employee morale and motivation would pay off very quickly.

INC: Let's assume you do want to work on improving employee morale. Where do you begin?

MACCOBY: First you put aside time to talk with your employees. Be honest with yourself and recognize that many times when you *think* you're doing that, you're talking at, not with. I recently spoke with the manager of a small plant who was very concerned about his workers and about providing a well-run, clean, safe factory. Then I talked with his employees and they complained that the boss never listened to them, even though they thought they had good ideas for improving things.

Later the same manager asked me to describe what I'd seen in his company, and I answered that I'd seen a communication problem. He agreed with me, saying, "I keep trying to communicate with these people and they don't hear me." I replied, "No, you don't understand me. It's a two-way communication problem." His response was, "Yes, I've tried two ways—talking and writing memos, and neither works."

I never could get my point across, because he was so paternalistic, so convinced he knew everything, including what was wrong with his workers. Now that's a man who's not capable of running a bigger business; he'll never be able to handle more than a hundred employees.

The key is: Be willing not just to talk, but to listen to employees. Ask them what they want out of life and work.

INC: Will workers be honest with managers who ask that kind of question?

MACCOBY: That's up to the manager. You can't sit down and say: Now Joe, what do you want out of work? I know, of course, you want to make a lot of money and get promoted, but what else?

You've already destroyed the conversation at that point, and you'll never get honest answers. There are many subtle ways in which people pretend to have a conversation but show very clearly that they've already made certain assumptions, that they really aren't interested in listening.

A lot of entrepreneurs have gotten ahead precisely *because* they didn't listen to other people, as I said earlier. Often, in fact, an entrepreneur is the kind of person who is accustomed to selling himself all the time, so it can be awfully hard to get through to him. If he really wants to hear what people have to say, he's got to work at it. It's not enough to simply give employees the opportunity, because very few are going to have the quickness and aggressiveness to hold their own against him.

INC: Aren't you asking managers to play psychologist?

MACCOBY: If you're an engineer or scientist, you recognize that you've got to work with the nature of materials. You can't change or mold plastics or metals as you'd like; you've got to do it within the limits of the material.

What I'm saying is that the human material you have to work with now is different from what it was when our society was based on a craft ethic, or an entrepreneurial ethic. The better you understand that material, the better you can work with it and the more effective an organization you can develop.

The current change in your human material is not just a fad or fashion. When we moved from a society of small businesses and farms to a large organized society, where less than 10 percent of us are self-employed, that meant a shift in emphasis on what's important for success: away from independence and toward flexibility and cooperation.

At the same time, technology began to demand new skills. Brain work has been replacing physical work, and brain work requires more educated people. More education means more diversity in the way people think. That, in turn, is encouraging a value system that says: No authority has the right to tell me what to do without giving me a good reason.

These changes are deeply rooted. Unless you take account of them and understand them, you're not apt to inspire employees, especially younger ones.

These people are oriented much more to self than to a craft or money-making or winning. Why? Because the whole modern organization of society has made it a *problem* for people to develop a sense of identity, a feeling of belonging somewhere. For many people, it just doesn't happen naturally, the way it used to.

INC: Are you suggesting that we're moving away from the independence and individualism that lead to self-employment? Aren't others—for example, members of the Reagan administration—saying just the opposite?

MACCOBY: Yes, to both questions. There's been a great deal of romanticism, which isn't supported by the evidence, about a new entrepreneurial revolution. The question I think we must ask is: what percentage of our population is willing and able to succeed as entrepreneurs and small business owners? My own answer is that the percentage of self-employed will hold fairly level, at around 8 percent of the total work force, or decrease.

We no longer can look forward to the unlimited growth that spawned the great entrepreneurial era when we were building this country. Now we have a very complex, interdependent society. Nothing is simple, nothing is unlimited. I think entrepreneurs will continue to thrive in areas of business where there's no economy in scale and in new areas like software, genetic engineering, and other high-technology fields. The latter are open to only a small segment of the population, though—the highly technical, highly educated, and unusually energetic. We're kidding ourselves if we think self-employment is realistic for the vast majority of us.

Yet it's true that many people *want* their own businesses. They are not going to be able to succeed at them, however, and that will lead to a great deal of frustration. That frustration is one reason we're going to need such good managers; these people will have to be managed so they'll feel productive and challenged, not like losers.

At the same time, I think we're starting to see a waning in the desire to be self-employed as part of the new social character. People don't want to put as much of themselves into their work as it takes to run your own business. In *The Leader* I cite studies that show even currently self-employed people are less satisfied than they were ten years ago. They're unhappy with the insecurity, the risk, the long hours.

This has some serious implications for society, which we should deal with realistically, not by painting romantic pictures or lapsing into pessimism. Any social character has both positives and negatives, and this one is no different. The positives are that more people are concerned with developing and improving themselves. More people are experimental and tolerant, and want to participate in what they consider an equitable and meaningful enterprise. The negatives are a tendency toward selfish escapism, flexibility so extreme it becomes prostitution to whatever comes along, and a lack of respect for authority that can mean getting as much, and giving as little, as you can in order to beat the system.

Which set of attitudes do you get? I think it depends largely on what kind of leaders you have, whether in a company or a country. Never before has leadership been so crucial, in fact, because never before has the social character been so flexible and volatile.

I believe that leadership in the workplace is absolutely essential in terms of how people choose to lead their lives. You have so much opportunity: either to manage the same old way and create the cynicism that results in people saying, "All I want to do is draw my paycheck," or to really involve people and bring out the best in this new social character.

FACE-TO-FACE:
RONALD
HEIFETZ

Don't be fooled by Ronald Heifetz's youth. At thirty-seven, he has already had more careers than most people pack into a lifetime— surgeon, psychiatrist, cellist, and public policy professor. More to the point, this insightful man, who teaches at Harvard's Kennedy School of Government, is worth listening to, particularly for what he has to say about an insidious problem that entrepreneurs have been tripping over ever since the first start-up began to grow: defining the leader's role.

That is a subject about which a great deal has been written lately— much of it trite, little of it original. Rarely does someone come along with anything new or instructive to say about corporate leadership. At first glance, Heifetz seems an unlikely exception. He is the first to admit that he has limited knowledge of how businesses actually work. But don't let that stop you. Though his expertise is in political leadership, his insights are directly relevant to businesspeople, particularly those who run growing companies.

And Heifetz won't give you the usual blather about the personality traits of great leaders. He puts much more emphasis on the definition of leadership, in part because he understands the power of words. Label someone a leader—give him or her the leader's role—and a conscientious person tries to be or do what the label implies. That same label will likewise determine the expectations of the people in the group or organization being led. Problems most often arise, Heifetz suggests, when leaders and followers have the wrong notion of what leadership is. To correct the problems, therefore, you must begin by offering a better definition—which is precisely what he has done.

Inc. senior writer Tom Richman visited Heifetz's cubbyhole office in Cambridge, Massachusetts, to get the word.

INC: Can you give us a succinct definition of leadership?

HEIFETZ: I define leadership as an activity, *not* as a set of personality characteristics. So what I'm interested in is developing people's capacity to perform a particular activity, and I call this activity "leadership." And the activity of leadership I define as the mobilization of the resources of a people or of an organization to make progress on the difficult problems it faces.

Notice that I am not talking about routine problems; I don't think they require leadership. I'm talking about difficult problems. In those situations, someone exercising leadership is orchestrating the process of getting factions with competing definitions of the problem to start learning from one another.

INC: Let's try to simplify that. Are you saying that exercising leadership does not mean imposing a solution on the group?

HEIFETZ: Well, it might if the situation involves a simple problem. For example, if I take my car to my mechanic and he says, "This is what needs to be done to fix the car," the mechanic is imposing his solution on my car, and that's fine. With a routine problem, one can look to authority—to experts—to come up with the solution and to implement it.

INC: So you're drawing a distinction between exercising authority and exercising leadership.

HEIFETZ: Yes, but let me go on. I would not say that my car mechanic is exercising leadership. He's an expert, so I granted him authority. He's exercising his authority by telling me what's wrong with my car and what he's going to do to fix it. It's not a complex situation, and the mechanic is exercising authority, not leadership. But—and this is important—even in a very complicated situation demanding the exercise of leadership, an authority figure still has a role.

INC: Which is?

HEIFETZ: To maintain equilibrium in the organizational system. The function of an authority figure is to right the ship, maintain equilibrium, keep things on an even keel. People expect an authority figure to be comforting.

INC: And a leader, in contrast . . .

HEIFETZ: I wouldn't use the word "leader." I'd say someone who exercises leadership. Someone exercising leadership is probably generating *dis*equilibrium. Either he is raising issues or asking questions that disturb people and force people to come to terms with points of view or problems that they would rather not consider; or he's protecting other people in the organization who are creating disequilibrium.

INC: Let me see if I've got this straight. People exercising authority create equilibrium in an organization, and people exercising leadership create *dis*equilibrium. I guess I don't get it.

HEIFETZ: OK, say we're in a senior staff meeting, and the financial guy announces that we're losing market share. One possible reason, he suggests, is poor packaging.

The first thing that happens is the packaging guy becomes furious and rebuts the charge. The two of them start going at each other, and maybe others join in. Does this solve the problem? No. These are work-avoidance mechanisms. People will do all kinds of things that don't have anything to do with solving the problem. So someone has to exercise authority to reduce disequilibrium to a range within which people can pay attention to the information that the financial guy is presenting. Exercising authority can restore the equilibrium, but it can't solve the problem, which is that we're still losing market share. For that, someone—the CEO, the financial guy, someone—must exercise leadership, which is the mobilization of people to face, define, and solve problematic realities.

INC: I take it that by your definition, the person who exercises leadership is not the individual who provides answers but the individual who manages the group's efforts to define its own problems and reach its own answers.

HEIFETZ: Sort of. But it's a little more than that because it's not simply the neutral guy orchestrating a process. First, it would be fine to provide answers if you really had the answers. But if you have the answers, like my car mechanic, then it is probably not a situation demanding leadership. There are a lot of situations, however, in which no clear answers exist, but where the authority figure is expected to provide them anyway. The exercise of leadership then requires the orchestration of competing factions. That doesn't simply mean sitting back passively and saying, "You work it out," because organizations have ways of avoiding that work. Defining problems is creative work and very difficult. Orchestrating competing points of view is also hard work. Both generate stress in an organization, so organizations tend to find ways to avoid those tasks. Most often, they'll blame it on the authority figure himself, saying, "We shouldn't have to do this work. If only we had the right authority figure, the right *leader*, our problems would be solved."

INC: OK. Say I'm the CEO. I founded the company. I've hired half a dozen people to work for me. When I started out, I was the only one here. I defined the problems; I made all the decisions; I took all of the action. That's the way it was when those people came. Now, you're telling me, I have to change their expectations about my behavior.

HEIFETZ: Sure. Presumably, as you move forward, the environment in which you operate is going to become more complicated. That's why you need more people. If people continue to expect you to be the know-it-all in assessing a complicated environment, you're lost. You may be able to wing it long enough to stay aloft for a while, but there's no way, to my mind, you can exercise leadership alone. The exercise of leadership requires, in complex problem situations, more information than one person can have.

INC: So you've got to bring others into the process. What's so hard about that?

HEIFETZ: What's hard is getting people to do what's necessary to solve the problem. Understand that the solution to a complex problem is going to require adjustments in the habits of people involved with the problem. In your company of six people, all of whom may hold conflicting views, all six people will have to change some of their attitudes, their ways of seeing things, and their habits of action.

Those changes involve a learning process. Your people have to examine some of their previous conceptions, and they have to import into their frames of reference the frames of reference of other people—information that other people have. The CEO who is used to providing all the answers may be able to tell people what to do. But issuing a command is not going to change people's understanding. The solution is going to require that these people develop a capacity to continue to adapt to a changing and complicated environment.

INC: Which takes time.

HEIFETZ: Right. In the short run, the people in the company may be delighted to get clear commands from the CEO, because it protects them from having to think things through themselves. In the longer term, though, it's going to increase their dependency on the CEO as the authority figure, and it will weaken their own capacities to come to terms with a complex environment.

INC: So, contrary to expectations, the strong authority figure doesn't necessarily make the best CEO?

HEIFETZ: He may in certain situations. There is one situation in which it makes a lot of sense to exercise very firm authority. That is when the disequilibrium generated by the complexity of the environment is so severe that people cannot think straight, cannot organize themselves to work. In this case, the CEO's authority is a tool for leadership. He has to exercise authority to bring the level of disequilibrium into a tolerable range that allows people to go to work defining and solving problems.

INC: You mean what Lee Iacocca did at Chrysler?

HEIFETZ: Exactly. Iacocca had to make people feel sufficiently secure and safe. He had to play to their need to have a big daddy. . . .

INC: To a point?

HEIFETZ: To a point.

INC: What's that point?

HEIFETZ: It's the point at which people fall into comfortable habits. After that, you know you've gone too far. People still have to be sufficiently ruffled and disturbed that they're thinking and anxious and working, but not so discomforted and stressed out that they're dysfunctional.

Franklin Roosevelt is another good example, by the way.

INC: In what sense?

HEIFETZ: Well, in 1933, the country was in enormous crisis. A lot of the banks were going under. In his first 100 days in office, Roosevelt exercised a very firm and powerful authority that soothed and comforted the people and gave them a sense of hope and security. It was necessary because the level of crisis in the United States was so severe that the country was on the brink of falling into catastrophic work-avoidance patterns similar to those occurring in Nazi Germany that same year. There, the social disequilibrium was so severe that people looked to anyone who could provide them with some firm belief—regardless of what the belief was.

The difference is that Roosevelt, in providing people with a sense of security, knew that he couldn't do the solving. He knew the only way for the nation to make progress on this set of very messy, complicated problems was to engage the creative energies of the various constituencies. He had bankers arguing with industrialists arguing with labor arguing with Treasury. His own role was managing levels of disequilibrium and orchestrating the process by which these opposing factions sorted out the next steps.

INC: That sounds straightforward, if not easy.

HEIFETZ: Yes, but there's a trap for a Roosevelt or an Iacocca. Because his exercise of firm command made so much sense in a crisis, a CEO may begin to think that he should operate in that same mode all the time.

INC: Well, he was a hero once—he'd like to keep on being a hero.

HEIFETZ: Exactly. And that's natural. But please understand, it's not simply the person who resists letting go. The organization resists, too. The organization, once addicted to a hero, remains addicted, and it's quite difficult to disabuse an organization of its dependency on its hero. That's one reason why entrepreneurial CEOs of very successful companies often have to leave at a certain point—Steve Jobs, for example. They have to leave because there is a dependency they cannot counteract.

INC: You mean it was inevitable from the start that Jobs would have to leave Apple Computer?

HEIFETZ: I don't mean to be so categorical. I'm describing a tendency and a trend. It could have been managed differently in Jobs's case, if he had wanted to and if he had known how.

INC: Is there a point of no return, a point beyond which the only choice for someone like Jobs is to leave the organization?

HEIFETZ: People who end up in that position usually don't know how to disentangle themselves, because they don't understand the dynamics that got them so entangled in the first place. My assumption is that if they did understand the dynamics, and if they knew the kinds of strategies that would disentangle them, they could reverse the situation even at a late date.

I might add that Roosevelt, too, fell into the trap. When he got re-elected by a landslide in 1936, I think he began to believe he had a mandate to institute *his* answers. He tried to pack the Supreme Court to get *his* policy agenda realized.

INC: Isn't that exactly what we ask presidential candidates to do today—to have their own agenda with all the answers?

HEIFETZ: Sure. We're looking to Dukakis or Bush and expecting one of them to fulfill enormously unrealistic dreams, things neither can possibly know how to do. And, given their personal predilection to see themselves heroically, they will likely fall into the trap of protecting the American people from facing and taking responsibility for the problems in their midst. They'll provide people with convenient shelters, illusions, false senses of security, and hope that if only you elect me and my staff of policy experts, we'll get the country back on the road.

INC: Well, what would we do with Michael Dukakis now if he were to say, "I can't solve the trade deficit problem. You folks have to solve the trade deficit problem."

HEIFETZ: We wouldn't elect him. That's the paradox—you don't get elected if you don't protect people from the work they need to do. You risk your authority as soon as you attempt to exercise leadership.

INC: Shouldn't we expect leadership from a president?

HEIFETZ: That would be a big mistake. The President of the United States is rarely going to exercise leadership. Primarily he's going to exercise authority. He's going to maintain equilibrium. He's rarely going to challenge people to come to terms with harsh problems. If he does, he risks losing office. The exercise of leadership by high authority requires pacing the rate at which you challenge people to do work.

INC: So, we're looking for someone who will say, "Here, just take this pill. . . ."

HEIFETZ: Someone who will say, "I know what needs to be done, just follow me." And the tragedy is that eight years later, reality kicks you from behind. And that's what has happened in our current situation—with our drug problem, with our poverty problem, with our debt problem. We have had eight years with someone who has protected the American people from facing the challenges of the next century, or even of the next decade, and thereby diminished the country's adaptive capacity. He's told us we can blame external forces instead of helping us take responsibility for our own problems. And now, of course, we're upset because we have this huge debt. Reality has caught up with us and shaken some of our illusions.

Unfortunately, we're likely to repeat the same errors because our conception of leadership is fundamentally misguided. We'll elect the next guy who claims to have answers rather than the guy who is willing to challenge us by orchestrating our problem-solving processes.

INC: We're doomed?

HEIFETZ: Not necessarily. What gives me hope is something inherent in a democracy—I mean, the idea that we all share the responsibilities and obligations for making the society work. That is the nature of a democracy.

INC: Yes, but you've also written that in order to have a democracy, there must be a shared set of attitudes among citizens of a country.

HEIFETZ: True. We all have to share the attitude that responsibility is ours.

INC: Well, that's certainly not what I hear these days.

HEIFETZ: I realize that. As we face more and more frustrating problems, we tend to look for saviors, and—as a result—we have been losing democracy. We think democracy simply means having a political structure in which we vote. Or, we think democracy means the protection of individual rights and liberties. But that was never really the basic idea of democracy.

The basic idea of democracy was a shared notion that we all have a responsibility for the common welfare, for the common good, for the society as a whole, for the community—not just in times of war, but in all times. Instead, we have become more and more reliant on the president or on government, our authority figures, to do it for us.

One of the great Supreme Court justices, Louis Brandeis, stated that the highest office in the land is that of citizen. I think that's an important statement. If we lose that, and to some extent we already have, we do so at our peril as a nation. Democracy works successfully as an ongoing, adaptive mechanism because it develops our muscles. It keeps us thinking for ourselves. It doesn't allow us to fall into lazy dependency.

INC: So you see us as a nation getting lazy?

HEIFETZ: I see a growing dependency on administrative structures. We now have a wholly unrealistic faith that those administrative structures can address and even solve many community problems. For example, to expect the federal government to be able to solve the drug problem is absurd when the drug problem exists on every block in nearly every community in the country. It's absurd, that is, unless you're asking the federal government to get involved in how blocks of families within a particular community work together. Now that's pretty unrealistic.

INC: But there are some situations—you see them in military dictatorships and in lots of family businesses—where no one is exercising leadership. All you have is a strong authority figure. And yet these groups seem to do all right, in some cases for years.

HEIFETZ: That works if you're in an environment where nothing much is changing and the problems are routine. Take, for example, my car mechanic. He exists in an environment where most of the problems that are going to be pitched to him and his organization are known. Routines have already been established for solving them. In that situation, he can do a terrific job simply by exercising his authority. But if he wants to train new people, expand the enterprise, or plan for his own withdrawal and succession, there have to be activities of leadership.

INC: With regard to this distinction between authority and leadership, do you see many similarities between the public and private sectors?

HEIFETZ: The private sector could learn a lot from the democratic processes of problem-solving. The processes appear slower, but they're not. In fact, they're faster. That's because democracy is inherently more adaptive than other forms of social organization. If entrepreneurs would learn more about what makes this country great, they could apply that knowledge to making their own companies work better.

INC: I know you don't like the word "leader," but it does conjure a powerful image of the person who's up front and in charge.

HEIFETZ: We have an ideal of individualism—rugged individualism—embedded in our culture, and it is truly a wonderful thing. The notion of rugged individualism has given rise to a great deal of American ingenuity, creativity, enthusiasm, and values of integrity. The person who is able to make it against all odds is a hero in American culture. But rugged individualism has its downside, in that this same person tends to take the work of defining and solving problems on his own shoulders. He is inclined to see himself as the Atlas who can hold up the world by himself. He has a capacity to take a lot of responsibility, to gird his loins and go forth with courage, and that's great. But he gets trapped as soon as he begins to believe that this capacity is going to work in complicated situations requiring the efforts, wisdom, and points of view of a lot of different people.

INC: It sounds like you're talking about entrepreneurs.

HEIFETZ: Among others. In a way, the entrepreneur is idealized in our culture, and that sets him or her up for failure. He assumes the responsibility of satisfying employee aspirations that are impossible to satisfy. He buys into employees' expectations that he's going to guide them through the market, or through the next product innovation, or through whatever challenge.

Because the entrepreneur is inclined to accept responsibility and to see himself or herself as hero or heroine, he's also inclined to say, "OK, I'll do it for you again. I'll pull the rabbit out of the hat like last time. In fact, I pulled it out the last two times. And watch, I'm going to do it this time, too." The entrepreneur is energized by those expectations. And if he does save the day, he's reinforced the expectation that he'll be able to do it again and again. But it's a losing game.

INC: Because?

HEIFETZ: Because he's a human being. Because he's a jerk like everybody else—with his own failings and his own blind spots. And because the landscape eventually gets too complicated, even for him.

INC: When that happens, why can't he just pull other people in?

HEIFETZ: Because by now, there's no one around who has any capabilities. Every time he pulls the rabbit out of the hat, he generates more dependency and weakens his constituency, his own company. That's the trap in becoming the hero. If people keep expecting you to restore equilibrium, what they're actually doing is looking to you to help them avoid work. That's certainly where we're heading as a country.

INC: Is that where you come in? Do you see yourself helping us to avoid that trap?

HEIFETZ: I would say that I'm refining the notion of what leadership is.

INC: Refining what it is or what it ought to be?

HEIFETZ: Well, what it is, is a matter of people's opinions. Different people can say that they define leadership differently. You can't argue with someone else's definition. So, inevitably, the argument boils down to what it *should* be because the way we define leadership is going to shape the way people operate. People want to be leaders, after all. So our concept and understanding of leadership will affect the way people behave, and the ideals they hold out for themselves.

INC: Which means?

HEIFETZ: Which means my work here is to refine our understanding of leadership in a way that improves people's capacity to fulfill their aspirations for getting a group of people—an organization or a society—to get its work done, to make progress on the problems it faces.

PART

III

DELEGATING
AUTHORITY

PREFACE

One of the hardest parts of being a boss is knowing when not to be one. Even the most energetic manager cannot be everywhere at once, and if his company is growing, sooner or later the entrepreneur will have to entrust someone else with some of his responsibilities. *Delegating Authority*, the final collection in our book on managing people, consists of stories that examine why deputizing trusted subordinates is so important, and how it can be done safely and with a measure of grace.

A compelling reason for learning how to divide up responsibilities is executive stress. Constant stress can wear down even the hardiest of managers, often damaging professional and personal relationships in the process. And it is the classic hands-on entrepreneur who is the last one to admit that he could use an extra hand.

Our first three stories investigate what can happen when the boss works too hard. For one thing, physical and emotional breakdowns are a natural for the workaholic boss. "The Superman Complex" examines one chief executive who buried the grief and fear of his Vietnam War days in a total commitment to his company. But both experiences caught up with Max Carey and forced him to admit that he was not a superman and that he needed to hand off much of his work to others.

"Burnout: Working Too Hard for Too Long" looks at how burnout stress can creep up on any unsuspecting manager, and how it can be controlled. Left unchecked, the workaholic manager can, single-handedly, bring a healthy company to its knees. "The Boss Who Wouldn't Let Go" looks in on a CEO from St. Louis who reluctantly gave up total control, but only when he was backed into a corner and the company was in a state of emergency. By then it was almost too late, but Jack Kramer was saved by a last-minute bank loan and a major change in attitude. When Kramer finally learned to let go, he wound up getting professional planning, steady growth, and a turned-on staff.

Jim Waters, the antithesis of the white-knuckled Jack Kramer, knew how to delegate from the start. "One Boss Who Knew How to Let Go" examines Waters's style of delegating authority and responsibility—he hires professionals and puts them in charge. In the process, Waters himself has been known to change hats—from designer, to president, to chairman—and with each move, someone else climbs higher in his organization.

Jim Poure is another founder who knew he had to develop a first-class management team if his company was to continue to prosper. But how to do it? Poure decided to grow his own managers, using an in-house teaching system. In "The Mentor System," we find out how Poure developed a new generation of managers by pairing senior and junior executives into learning teams.

No wonder delegation of authority is the cornerstone of many successful companies. It helps attract and motivate talented managers and enables companies to move quickly on decisions that would be bottlenecked in a company where all authority resided at the top. The next three stories provide case studies of how delegation can work.

"The 'Smart Team' At Compaq Computer" explores a trend among high-technology companies to hire a seasoned group of executives from the very start. These companies, best exemplified by Compaq, do not centralize authority in one superstar CEO; they give broad authority to executives in marketing, sales, finance, and operations. The role of the CEO, says one consultant, "is to tap the potential of their teams. That's become the key factor for success."

Perhaps nowhere is top-down management more prevalent than in the military, and here, too, it drains motivation and initiative. When General W. L. (Bill) Creech took over the Air Force's Tactical Air Command in 1978, it was in deep trouble. Creech didn't need more money and more planes to turn things around; in "Four-Star Management," we find out that Creech worked his magic by pushing responsibility down to the lowest levels of his organizational chart.

Sometimes lower-level managers don't want to accept that responsibility. Because there was no incentive to work harder, store managers at Au Bon Pain, an upscale fast-food chain, either ignored operating problems or passed them up the chain of command. The solution, as we find out in "May the Force Be with You," was devising a new compensation system that richly rewarded managers for solving their own problems and running a profitable store.

Even bosses with the best of intentions and the most well-planned system of operations sometimes find themselves wishing they had done things differently. In "I Unchained My Chain of Command" and "They All Said Bill Sauey Couldn't Let Go," *Inc.* looks at two CEOs who painstakingly set up a management structure they were certain would result in high productivity. In the first case, Thomas Barrea, chairman of a data processing service, set up a strict hierarchy with himself at the top and an army of VPs beneath him. Soon Barrea felt isolated and bored. As he poked around his company he found a system of rules and regulations which his VPs had used to establish policy and which, handily, made no manager responsible for unpleasant tasks. Now Barrea has a horizontal management structure in place in which managers have more autonomy and responsibility, and overall morale—including Barrea's—is up.

Bill Sauey's situation was similar to Barrea's, except that Sauey didn't have much use for the team of VPs. He made *every* decision of any weight in his company's five plants. That meant a lot of traveling and constant high pressure—it also meant that Sauey was not much fun to be around. "They All Said Bill Sauey Couldn't Let Go" looks at Sauey's reluctance to delegate authority and how he has changed. Among the major changes is a whole new management structure—six independent divisions run by six independent managers—and a 27-percent increase in sales.

Sometimes answers to knotty business problems just aren't in the head of even the sharpest CEO, often because he's so caught up in the day-to-day operations of his company. "Who Do You Turn to When You're the Boss" and "The Advice Squad" investigate how outside advisers and boards of directors, if chosen carefully, can bring just the right kind of expertise and objectivity to overwhelmed CEOs and how their advice can help solve production and management problems, and improve odds for growth.

Many managers and entrepreneurs have fond memories of hands-on nights spent filling orders, or managing crises, like the time the payroll was barely met. But with time and planning that includes delegating authority to competent people, those memories should stay where they belong—distant. This collection of *Inc.* articles was compiled to show how important it is for the CEO or president to recognize the need to appoint and trust well-chosen assistants, and how even the most stubborn entrepreneur can learn to release an overprotective grip on his growing company.

THE
SUPERMAN
COMPLEX

The episode began on a bright Saturday morning in 1984. I went out on my deck with a cup of coffee and the morning newspaper, ready to ease into the weekend. When I opened the paper, there was a picture of the second Vietnam Veterans Memorial in Washington—not the famous wall, but the statue of those three combat soldiers. Immediately, something happened to me. I got a cold chill, a twisted knot in the pit of my stomach. My wife found me a few minutes later, sobbing uncontrollably. She was horrified. Since I could not explain to her what was happening, I grabbed a pen and paper. All I managed to scribble was a single word: "Vietnam." And then I really got scared.

Fear, you see, was as foreign to me as failure. The world had always known Max Carey as a winner, number one—able to do it all, anytime, any way. Fifteen years before, despite being the smallest football player in the league, I'd been an All-Ivy defensive halfback, setting five school records at Columbia University. As a U.S. Navy pilot, I'd graduated number one in my flight school and was the first in my class to qualify for high-risk missions. From 1971 to 1973, during the last years of the Vietnam conflict, I'd piloted an A-7 off the aircraft carrier USS *Midway*. I came home a decorated war hero: a golden boy. My business had almost failed in 1982, but I'd turned it around. There was no mission I couldn't fly, no challenge I couldn't overcome.

So my instinctive reaction to this episode was to push it aside. Vietnam? Well, it must have caught me at a weak moment. Within a few hours I was back to normal. Or was I? Driving to work some weeks later, I felt tears trickling down my cheeks. What on earth had happened to make me cry? Nothing I could put my finger on. Now, fear—real fear—overtook me. I thought: Oh my God, I'm having a nervous breakdown. Visions of Jack Nicholson in *One Flew over the Cuckoo's Nest* flashed before my eyes. "Max," I told myself, "you can't deal with this right now. You've got a wife and three young children counting on you for their sustenance. You've got eight people in the office who've put their future in your hands, and a world that's always expected the impossible from you. Oh Lord, not now. Please give me more time." But it was not to be. The episodes increased in frequency, and at times I was totally incapacitated.

In simple terms, I'd always been a "stuffer." Rather than deal with difficult emotional issues, I stuffed them deeply into my subconscious. This meant I'd stuffed all the grief and fear brought on by the horrors of combat and death. I had never told my family or employees there was anything I couldn't do. In combat, it was: "Keep up the bravado. Don't tell anyone you're scared or weak." In business, it was: "God forbid anyone should know you're not perfect."

In retrospect, I might have been able to go on indefinitely without dealing with the war and my grief. But the cumulative stress of my business is what broke me. It forced me to do something I'd never done before: ask for help.

In 1981, when I began Corporate Resource Development Inc. (after being top salesperson at Ryan Insurance Group, in the Midwest), I was an optimist whose ego exceeded his capabilities. My partner and I had borrowed $150,000 to start the company; yet, as it turned out, we had no idea how to target our sales and marketing services.

Coming home without a paycheck for the first time was far more destructive to me than trying to avoid my first surface-to-air missile in a combat mission into Hanoi. It hadn't been my fault that the guy on the ground was shooting at me, but it *was* my fault that I couldn't bring money home to my family. When you're the daddy and you're the husband and you walk in and you have no money and you have to look at your family eyeball to eyeball—I couldn't handle it. That's when my partner and I started drinking after work instead of going home.

The company hit bottom in January 1982. We'd been in business eight months and had forecast $50,000 in revenues that month. January was going to make us, was going to heal us—and we did no business. That's when it came apart. It broke my partner's back. He couldn't stay any longer. I couldn't believe that I'd parlayed a great career for this mire. If I were as strong as I said I was, and as smart, the company would work. Because the ideas were good.

One night in February I took my wife out to dinner on my overextended American Express card. Driving home, I apologized to her for what I'd done to the family. I told her I didn't believe I'd given the business my all yet, and that from that point forward, as long as we could keep the doors open, I was going to give it everything I had. I wanted to build this company; I wanted to build something that would be around after I was gone. And she gave me her unconditional support.

Since I knew it would take two or three years to get on top of things, I was even more determined, more single-minded, more compulsive than ever. I got more dogmatic, less willing to delegate, less understanding, more domineering. I was driving myself further and further away from everybody—at home and at work. I dealt in staccato communication:

"Did you do this? Why not? *I'll* do it.

"Why didn't you do it better? Why didn't you think of this?"

The fear of failure—of being broke again, of not bringing home a paycheck—was constant. When I was in combat, the terror I felt was instantaneous. I'm in an airplane over somebody else's country. They shoot a missile; I turn to beat it, and I avoid it. It explodes as it passes by. I'm OK. I proceed. That real gut-wrenching terror is over. But this fear is as if a tidal wave were after me. If I stopped and turned around to look at it, it would inundate me. Then on that morning in 1984 the built-up pressure of single-handedly trying to save my company intersected with the subconscious pressure from the Vietnam experience—and it was just too much to hold in.

To this day I am still in awe of the resources that were available once I was finally able to admit that I was not, and am not, omnipotent, omniscient, clairvoyant, perfect. Eventually, I went naked to those closest to me and, most important, to my God. My road to recovery started when I met a Vietnam vet at a party, and he touched on the subject of delayed-stress syndrome. We started to meet privately, and he'd say, "Max, let me tell you what happened to me, and maybe it fits for you." He'd been through it; he was very involved in vet activities; he'd been in therapy.

The biggest hurdle for me to overcome was the fear that I was going to be found out. I thought, maybe I'm not strong enough to be who I've become. Maybe this game I've been playing—accepting responsibility and attacking challenges—has taken a weak guy and made him look strong. And if I seek help, they're going to get inside my head and are going to show me that I'm just a weak charlatan who's gotten where I am through sheer discipline, willpower, and hope. But when I completely broke down at a church function—I had shaken hands with a woman who was wearing a POW bracelet—I knew I had to act.

Again, fate was with me. I went to a college alumni meeting and a classmate of mine—somebody I knew and trusted—was there. He was a professional psychologist, and I started seeing him. For the vet in me, confronting the horrors of war after the fact, the solution was relatively straightforward: open the subconscious and deal with the grief and the fear. My monthly trips to the Vietnam Memorial in Washington were part of that healing process. My lingering grief has to do with the fear I was forced to experience. Fear that deep changes a man.

For the entrepreneur in me, though, the learning curve was far steeper. One day my psychologist said, "Let me guess what it's like at your company. The people are detached, they're a little afraid of you, they do what you tell them to do, and that's about it. You feel they're not contributing." I said, "You're absolutely right. What's wrong with them?" "Max," he said, "the question is 'What's wrong with you?'"

Then this thing unfolded about my trying to be perfect, never admitting weakness. With his help, I eventually tried a very simple exercise. "Go back to your employees," he suggested, "and instead of using the word 'weak,' use 'real.' That is, don't say 'I need your help because I'm weak.' Say, 'I need your help because I'm real.' See, because you're not real to them, they can't understand you, they can't identify with you, and they can't help you."

That simple act of redefining weakness was a breakthrough. The next day, I called in my number-two guy. I told him I was in therapy and wanted to know what he felt about our communication, our relationship.

"Max," he said, "we don't have bad communication. We have no communication. You bark at me and I tell you what you want to hear. You second-guess every decision we make while you're away. Max, you and I don't have a bad relationship. We have no relationship."

So I let him know that I was real. I said, "I don't have the personal strength left inside me to run this company alone. I can't do it. The success of the company doesn't rest with me anymore. It rests on me and you and everybody else out there, and they're going to learn that today." And before the day was over, I had talked to each of my eleven employees. And I promised that I would no longer second-guess their decisions. I initiated an open-door policy in my office; I made sure that everyone in the company who wanted it could get some sort of psychological counseling—and that the cost would come from our operating budget.

And this amazing transition took place. All of a sudden projects were going on throughout the company, lifting one responsibility after another from my shoulders. When someone made a mistake, we started approaching it from a learning/therapeutic angle—not "You stupid bastard, any fool knows you should have done it this way." My philosophy now is that if we're doing our job taking care of each other, taking care of the client is easy.

In the past few years, Corporate Resource Development has become the success I'd always hoped it would be. By 1986, we were turning a profit, and we'll do $1 million in revenues this fiscal year. One of my goals, to make the INC. 500 list of fast-growing companies, was realized in 1987 (#395), when I also received the Atlanta Small Businessperson of the Year and Georgia's Vietnam Veterans Small Business awards. I've got excellent people around me, a thriving company, a wonderful family, all the material things I need.

But I have something else that's of crucial importance to me. And that is a mission. The large gray mass of vets who came back from Vietnam without my kind of credentials, who were branded "losers" and "drug-gies"—they're the ones I'm fighting for now. I teach a course for vets in entrepreneurship and sales and marketing; I do a lot of fund-raising. What these guys need is a chance—a chance, and the expertise of someone they trust. In that sense, it's important for them to know that Max Carey, the golden boy, also failed along the way. They're not so concerned about the guy who went right to the top, because they can't identify with him. But they can identify with someone like me, someone who went down and came back up.

To know you're not alone is a great relief.

—WILLIAM R. "MAX" CAREY JR.

BURNOUT!
Working Too Hard for Too Long

Ottis Stull, the top manager of a $2.4-million electrical contracting business, was normally a pleasant-natured man with an easy smile. He had a strong marriage and two healthy children. But after carrying out a subcontract on a large industrial rebuilding project, Ottis Stull changed. At the age of thirty-five, he had burned himself out.

"I didn't crash until the job was finished," he recalls. "I'd thought all along that when it was over, I'd sit down and relax. But I couldn't."

Stull's condition had developed slowly, and he had not realized that anything was wrong. But in the wake of his biggest job to date he experienced a letdown, and his psychological burnout began to manifest itself clearly. He became continually exhausted and frustrated. He couldn't relax. He was edgy and too quick to judge, frequently reacting to the slightest provocation with anger. Stull's wife Sally insisted that he get help.

Like most victims of burnout, Stull had worked too hard too long, had tried to endure too much stress over too short a time. Burnout does not strike suddenly, leaving its victims "sick" where they were "well" the day before. Instead it develops gradually. It knows no threshold, just as the line between social drinking and alcoholism is obscure. Even persons not suffering from burnout can on occasion exhibit one or more of its symptoms. But although the condition can make a shambles of a life, a victim can recover, just as Ottis Stull recovered thanks to a program of psychological counseling and changes in his work style.

Stull's case is not unusual, either in its cause or its solution. According to Dr. Edward Stambaugh, the clinical psychologist who worked with Stull, an estimated 10 percent of Americans succumb to burnout every year. And it isn't unusual for burnout to strike the CEOs and top managers of smaller companies.

Compared with their counterparts in larger corporations, smaller company managers have to do more of everything themselves, because they don't have large staffs to rely on. And even entrepreneurs who have support staffs, observes Stambaugh, don't always use them properly.

"All the entrepreneur possesses is locked up in his one little company," notes Stambaugh. "It is his dream, his vision, and there's precious little to fall back on if it goes bust. The very single-mindedness of purpose that makes the entrepreneur ideal for starting a company can easily become a threat as the company grows and there are more and more stimuli and demands on the owner's attention. All these can combine for a solid case of burnout."

Like his father and his father's father and their ancestors who had migrated from Germany, Ottis Stull believed in work. That was what a man did. He had been working since he was thirteen years old, when his father had made Ottis part of an electrical truck service crew. After graduating from the University of Kentucky at Lexington with a bachelor's degree in business administration, he joined Stull Electric Co. As could be expected, Stull pushed himself hard, prodding and molding his family's electrical contracting business. He could say, with a good measure of pride, that the company, which is based in Ashland, Kentucky, was profitable and growing.

But just as work was Ottis's pleasure, it was also his problem. During his waking hours he hardly ever stopped working; his job followed him to the dinner table and to bed.

Stull's workday started at 5:30 A.M. He would arrive at the company's main job site, thirteen miles away, by 6:30 so that he could catch the graveyard shift leaving and handle any problems that had developed overnight, as well as deal with the morning shift as it reported for duty. After things settled down at the site, he would travel four miles to his office to work on estimating and bidding for other jobs. He usually missed lunch.

"By one o'clock," Stull recalls, "I'd be back at the main job site going over more details, including the payroll. If any time was left in the afternoon, I would visit the smaller fringe jobs that we always had going around Ashland."

He would try to get home between 5:30 and 6:00 P.M. for a quick bite to eat. At 7:00, however, Stull would return to the main job site to check on the evening shift's progress. He considered himself lucky if he made it home by 9:00. When he did get home, he went straight to bed. And, as if his company schedule wasn't hectic enough, in whatever free time he had Stull was helping his father build a house.

Stull tried to play tennis once a week and he tried to get away once a year for some camping or mountain climbing. But at the time he burned out, he had stopped playing tennis and hadn't had a vacation for two and a half years.

Stull's condition didn't become acute until the major rebuilding project was completed. Though he might have admitted to being tired, he was planning to take time off to recuperate when this job was over.

But when the opportunity came, Stull discovered that he was literally incapable of relaxing. "I was so used to working," he remembers, "that I just couldn't sit down and watch TV or play games with my kids. I wanted to, but I just couldn't."

Instead, his mind refused to stop thinking about work. Obsessively, his thoughts continued to dwell on how to dig up more business, how to make his operations more efficient, how to solve the day-to-day management problems that always abounded. "I was almost like a computer," says Stull, "programmed for a certain routine. I couldn't find a way to change the program."

In another manifestation of burnout, Stull reacted to everything personally and defensively. If two of his employees were feuding, Stull felt that somehow he alone was responsible and had to solve the problem. He took even the most minor critical comment as a personal attack.

As his condition worsened, Stull became uncharacteristically irritable, depressed, and cynical. "It's hard to survive when you can't relax," he now concedes. "It's going to hurt you or your family or the people you work with."

Away from work Stull also became withdrawn and listless. "I didn't want to be outdoors. I didn't want to be sociable. I didn't want to do anything," he says.

All he really wanted to do on his off hours was sleep. "I had two speeds—full ahead or dead asleep stop. If it was Saturday afternoon, and I was home, I was either in bed asleep or on the couch asleep."

For all his symptoms, Stull did not seek out any cure, or even a diagnosis. The reason was simple: so insidiously does burnout develop, he did not realize the extent of his condition. He did not know he was acting the way he was. And, as is typical of burnout cases, his reaction to an occasional sense that something wasn't quite right was to put off thinking about it, to get some more sleep, or to press himself even harder.

Thanks to his wife, Sally, Stull began to see his behavior as others saw it. One day she sat him down and described his actions. For example, Stull had always considered himself a good father. But he had to admit that Sally was correct when she pointed out that he'd been yelling at his kids much more than was normal.

"To satisfy her" he finally heeded Sally's insistence that he see a physician. The family doctor concluded that there was nothing physically wrong with Stull, but did suggest tranquilizers. When Stull balked at that—"because I thought there had to be a better way"—the doctor recommended that he see a local psychologist. Stull considered the recommendation for a week; he and Sally went out for dinner one night and discussed the problem, and Stull decided to start therapy with Dr. Stambaugh.

Stambaugh's approach to resolving Ottis Stull's burnout was, fittingly, to approach it in a businesslike manner. Under Stambaugh's guidance, Stull identified his problem, determined the goals he wanted to reach, and developed specific methods for achieving his objectives. "Just like a management-by-objectives program," Stull says.

Among those objectives, Stull was to learn—or relearn—how to relax, and was to regain his ability to be satisfied in his relationships with others.

First, he would have to realize when he was tense and to learn what it was like to be relaxed. "I'd been barreling along so hard," Stull says, "that I'd forgotten what it felt like to be relaxed."

The trick was to begin with small changes so that Stull could experience some immediate rewards. Stambaugh suggested, for example, that Stull take twenty-minute baths whenever he felt tense. A warm bath, he counseled, could relax Stull's body and help his nerves. "I spent a great deal of time in the bathtub on weekends," Stull admits, "but it made me aware of the difference between being tense and being relaxed." Stull also started listening to quiet music. He began attending church again. "I was trying to teach myself how to relax," he explains, "so that it became part of me—not something I had to conjure up."

Second, he would have to work on his self-image. For starters, Stull was to quit smoking and get himself in better muscular shape by resuming his weekly tennis game. The purpose was to help him realize that he could regain some control over his life.

Though he'd smoked for fifteen years, sometimes up to three packs a day, Stull says that quitting smoking was one of the easiest things he did. And with that change came the realization that he could change in other ways. For instance, he had always thought that he had simply been "born nervous." But with Stambaugh's counseling, Stull learned that that self-diagnosis was a myth, and that he was capable of developing in himself greater peace of mind.

Stull also began to realize that he'd never put the right value on himself. At first he had trouble answering Stambaugh's question: "What are you worth?" Stull had usually thought of himself in terms of his business and the family, measuring himself with all kinds of external rulers. But as he reflected on Stambaugh's question more closely, Stull saw that he'd always responded to what others wanted and demanded. He had never looked at himself in terms of what *he* valued. Or as Stull puts it: "I'd always looked out and never in."

As the third step in his recovery program, Stull would have to spend more time with his family. He and Dr. Stambaugh decided he should plan and participate in weekly outings with his wife and children.

Then, once he had overcome the obstacles at home—once that base was secure—Stull would have to begin applying the same lessons to his work. His objectives were to learn to relax at work—to control the job, not let it control him; to delegate more responsibility; to remember that others are responsible for their own actions. He was to learn to place greater trust in others. And he was to concentrate on the reality of what he could control, to distinguish between what was and what was not his concern. "Sure," says Stull, "I still had a responsibility to the business. But I had to realize that if two employees were producing, it was their business whether they got along or not."

Stull knew that his recovery would require time and determination. "I had to make a conscious effort," he reports. "But I'm finding that it's easier and easier."

Today, Ottis Stull feels much more in control of his life. He is a man more at ease with himself and others, more confident, and happier. On the business front, Stull limits himself to an eight-to-five workday. He eats lunch, and when he has a few minutes free he relaxes at his desk or gets up and strolls out for a cup of coffee. Sometimes he even goes for a drive.

At home, too, Stull is enjoying the benefits of resolving his burnout. "My weekends the last six months have been a great pleasure," he says. "I'm spending time with my family and I can sit around on a Saturday afternoon and read a book."

And how can he avoid a recurrence of burnout? "Simple," says Ottis Stull. "I don't take my work too seriously. When I have time to have fun, I have fun."

—DONNA L. SAMMONS

WILL YOU BE BURNOUT'S NEXT VICTIM?

Most CEOs don't need a psychologist to tell them that down deep, they really thrive on working. But on occasion, they may need to be reminded that there is such a thing as working too hard, that overcommitment to one's job can be bad both for the individual and for his or her company. People, like machines, can burn out with overuse.

Professionals in the mental health field, such as Dr. Edward E. Stambaugh II, the clinical psychologist who treated Ottis Stull, describe burnout as a condition produced by working too hard too long in a high-pressure environment. Though the symptoms and intensity of the syndrome vary, there are certain physical and psychological warning signs to watch for in yourself and in your employees.

For example, explains Stambaugh, who now practices in Pleasant Hill, California, where he specializes in treating executives under stress, you may have a nagging sense of fatigue, feel physically run down, be unable to shake a cold, or suffer from frequent headaches or gastrointestinal disturbances. "You may also experience sleeplessness, a loss of weight, depression, or shortness of breath," adds Stambaugh. "You might come to feel bored, disenchanted, and resentful."

You or one of your employees may also exhibit behavioral changes. You may, for instance, find yourself talking less during meetings. You might notice that a normally gregarious employee suddenly seems withdrawn. Symptoms of rigidity or an exceptionally short temper are common in burnout victims. "And because burnout people often think that they do all the work," says Stambaugh, "the slightest incident can send them reeling."

"As a rule," he says, "burnout victims display all the signs of having their defenses ripped away. They aren't able to control their feelings anymore."

Stambaugh readily concedes that the pressures of life being what they are, these symptoms can manifest themselves in people who aren't suffering from burnout. "We all can occasionally act like we're burnt out. The problem with the burnout victim is that these symptoms are pervasive—they usually affect every aspect of his or her life."

Though no hard-and-fast rules exist, Stambaugh notes that some businessmen are especially prone to burnout. The overcommitted manager or employee can, at first, appear immune. He seems to accept jobs readily and approaches problems enthusiastically. Colleagues are likely to see him as competent, creative, and caring. Unfortunately, all of these positive attributes can't mask the fatal flaw that produces the overcommitted person's burnout. He can't say no. He keeps taking on more than he can handle. The quality of his work deteriorates and he senses the disappointment people feel about him. He becomes frustrated and tires of the overwork. He is in an ever-tightening vicious circle.

The person who is a candidate for burnout refuses to delegate authority and rarely, if ever, admits he needs help in his job. He therefore inhibits employees from receiving adequate training, from developing their own skills, and from progressing within the company. He makes everyone around him feel inadequate. His ability to alienate people only further reinforces his "I'm the only one who can do the job right" attitude. So he then tries to take on still more work. "And that sets him up for burnout," says Stambaugh.

Finally, a person with a rigid personal agenda, as is true of many entrepreneurs, risks burning himself out. Such a person has a dream—of greatness, of a life-style, of a company. Even when he's successful, he may drive himself to exhaustion. In other, more unfortunate cases, he realizes that his dream will never materialize, that all those eighty-hour workweeks were for naught. Yet, even though the dream is dead, he is apt to continue beating his head against the wall.

A major obstacle to curing the burnout victim, according to Stambaugh, is that denial and resistance often accompany the other symptoms. Before treatment can progress, the victim has to recognize his own psychological condition. Stambaugh advises that that can be accomplished with questions that will help the person see, in graphic detail, his actual plight. Explains Stambaugh: "When someone mentions to me that he's the only one who can do something right, I simply ask him if that's true. 'Are you really the only one who can do the job? What about all those people you have working for you? Didn't you hire them? If they can't do it, why do you have them on the payroll?' And so on. Eventually, the person begins to see that maybe someone else could help out."

Stambaugh also asks a burnout victim what's good about his life. "This can bring him up short when he realizes that there isn't much," the psychologist reports.

Often, too, Stambaugh adds, the victim tends to blame his feelings on his physical health. "The first step in treating burnout is to be aware that the problems are not physical," he says. "Have a check-up so that you can't use your health as a handy, but false, excuse."

In addition to having a physical, Stambaugh urges people who sense an impending burnout to take some time off. If you suspect that you're going to blow a fuse, he suggests trying to lighten your work load, especially by delegating more responsibility to others. "There's no admission of failure necessary," says Stambaugh. "In fact, the whole point is to get yourself back to a position where you can make an even greater contribution.

"There are people in this world who continually drive themselves to burnout," observes Stambaugh. "But there are others who can learn to avoid it." He suggests some preventive measures that can help reduce the possibility of succumbing to the condition. Among them:

1. Avoid being the person who always handles the tough jobs—even if you think you are the most capable. (And make sure that one employee, because of his or her record, doesn't receive all of the crucial assignments or get asked repeatedly to solve the toughest problems.)

2. Limit the number of hours you work.

3. Take vacations, and make sure your staff does, too.

4. Promote a team approach. When employees feel personally close to one another, they usually provide support to the boss. "That's a good way of assuring that the CEO isn't burdened with too much of the work," says Stambaugh. "Make the decision to trust colleagues and subordinates. That doesn't mean giving up all responsibility, but it does mean backing off—letting go."

THE BOSS WHO
WOULDN'T LET GO

Several years ago, Jack Kramer hit bottom. On a spring day in 1975, Kramer pulled over to the roadside on his way to work and looked out across the freshly plowed Missouri fields. For the first time ever, he dreaded walking in the door of his St. Louis plant. His stomach churned and he felt physically sick as he imagined telling his ten remaining employees that the bank had refused him the money he needed to write their paychecks.

The next two months were the worst in Kramer's life, and they marked the end of three years that hadn't been much better. But they were also a critical turning point: finally, thirty-seven-year-old Jack Kramer had to face what he had been doing wrong. He was slowly choking his own company, Cambridge Engineering, to death.

The problem was that Jack Kramer always thought he could do everything, and do it better than almost anybody else. It's an illusion most entrepreneurs share, and it destroys more growing companies than lack of money ever will. It was time for Kramer to let go.

Letting go sounds simple, but it's the hardest task faced by many company founders. For an entrepreneur, loosening ties with his company is like watching a child grow up and leave home. How does he forget the early sleepless nights, the years of sacrifice, and the center-stage role that comes with single-handedly nurturing a company through its infancy? How does he learn to live with an adolescent company—one that demands a life of its own?

Many entrepreneurs don't. They can't and won't admit that their entrepreneurial skills are no longer sufficient to run a young company and make it grow. In short, they stay entrepreneurs and never become managers.

That was Jack Kramer's problem.

Kramer had started out selling insurance after earning his degree in business administration at Washington University in St. Louis. After four years, he decided to scramble for himself rather than for somebody else. In 1963, he teamed up with his engineer-inventor brother, Fred, and they developed a heating and ventilating unit designed to act as an air curtain over shipping doors in factories and warehouses.

The two brothers worked in a drafty old building, with an aluminum siding company on one side of them and a piece welder on the other. If smoke floated Kramer's way, he fanned it back, and on stormy days he just went home because rain poured in all over his desk.

The first seven years weren't easy. Jack and Fred built their systems by night, sold them by day. Jack kept two sets of clothes handy: overalls for working on the "production line," and a coat and tie for meeting with bankers.

But Jack thrived on the pressure, playing the roles of president, sales and service manager, and accountant—making all the decisions, calling all the shots. From the beginning, he was the one with fire in his belly, the one who wanted to take on the world.

He took on a little more of it in 1970 when he bought out Fred. To Jack Kramer, the move meant only more freedom, the chance to be totally in charge. Much later he understood, painfully, that his brother had been angry and hurt at being pushed out by what he saw as Jack's greed. But Kramer knows greed was never the motive. Like the combat pilot who volunteers for missions precisely *because* he has only a 15 percent chance of survival, Kramer had an almost irrational need to prove he could do the impossible, and do it on his own.

For a few months, Kramer got this freedom; he wore all the hats, with only a production manager to help. And it looked as if his young company had nowhere to go but up. Kramer was seen as a dynamic leader by his twenty-employee staff. His product was recognized as a real innovation in industrial heating. His sales savvy led the company to $500,000 in sales that year, and his rudimentary projections showed a 20-percent-a-year growth rate.

At that point, however, Kramer was having trouble juggling everything. In fact, time was so precious he couldn't find a few hours to hire a new secretary when he needed one. His accounting firm urged him at least to get help on the financial side, and finally he hired a young accountant, Steve Glasmann.

At first, Kramer regarded Glasmann as simply another pair of hands to take over basic accounting work. But pressure was mounting—Kramer had to spend more time on sales, and he felt a greater and greater need for a sounding board to reduce his growing sense of loneliness and isolation.

He remembers the day he called Glasmann into his office for what he considered a landmark event. Kramer pulled eight files from his desk and handed them to Glasmann, saying simply, "These are yours from now on." The files didn't seem all that significant: they held order and purchasing information and some production schedules. Still, Kramer found it wrenching to let them go. To him, they were a vital part of his business, a part he knew inside out. "That moment hurt," Kramer recalls. "It was like turning over my children's birth certificates to a stranger."

Kramer felt he had taken a real step toward delegating authority. But he still retained control of key parts of his business—his optimistic sales projections, for example. He kept these files in his desk drawer, neatly drawn up the way he'd learned in school. Although he now admits his figures were based on "lots of aspirations and a little history," the more he looked at the projections, the more he believed them—until the following spring, 1972. At that time, he learned the results for 1971, and they left no room for fantasy: sales had remained at almost exactly the previous year's level.

That was the start of the three-year period Kramer now recalls hazily, through a blur of pain. He first decided to attack the problem of mediocre sales directly, bringing in a new salesman, later replacing him with another. But neither salesman met his expectations, and he was still generating most sales himself.

The difficulty was that Kramer wasn't sure what he actually wanted from those salesmen. He had neither the time nor the inclination to design a well-defined marketing plan. This influenced his recruitment of people; so did his conviction that he knew how to sell his products better than anyone in the company. Or outside it, for that matter. Because Kramer didn't trust sales reps, over 85 percent of Cambridge Engineering's sales came from within a 500-mile radius of St. Louis—the distance Kramer himself could reasonably travel.

Meanwhile, money got tighter and tighter. One of Kramer's early solo decisions continued to haunt him: he'd bought out his brother with company funds, so little profit was left over during the five-year payback period. The debt aggravated the company's already difficult cash-flow position caused by product lead times averaging six months. Cambridge Engineering limped along on its line of credit, as its bank grew increasingly impatient.

Kramer then decided to try another strategy. He would introduce a new product, a further modification of his brother's original system, that would combine two heating/ventilating units in a single frame. But his brother, the engineer, was no longer there to help. So Kramer drew his own design on the back of a cocktail napkin and turned it over to his machine shop. The shop responded beautifully. Unfortunately, however, it turned out that the system had a limited market. Kramer had struck out again.

To make matters worse, the Occupational Safety and Health Administration (OSHA) and the U.S. Environmental Protection Agency (EPA) passed regulations that forced the company to modify products, which hampered new sales. Then the oil embargo hit the country, taking its toll on the gas heating industry; on its heels came the recession of 1973–74 and a severe downturn in the industrial construction market that was Cambridge Engineering's business base. By the end of fiscal 1973, sales had actually *dropped*.

Kramer was desperate. He could see, though, that despite the company's rocky performance, Steve Glasmann and Bruce Kisslinger, his production manager, had developed into competent professionals. He then took what should have been a step toward letting go: he named Glasmann controller and gave him additional administrative responsibilities. And, admitting that he needed help with new product design, he hired a professional engineer, the first to step through the door of Cambridge Engineering since Fred Kramer had left.

Kramer's steps toward relinquishing control were more form than substance, however. He had acted only when his back was against the wall, never in anticipation of the needs of his company. He still expected to make the big decisions himself. But, mired as he was in the company's day-to-day operations, he still had no time for planning those decisions.

As problems mounted, Kramer threw himself even more frantically into sales. He had always been sure that direct sales were the key to success in the industrial heating business. That was his trump, he thought, and now he played it. He brought in two new salesmen and tried to set up a direct sales effort. It didn't help. In fact, sales dropped again in fiscal 1974 and Cambridge Engineering went deep into the red.

Kramer now was frightened. He'd failed at his own game. For the first time in his life, his sales and marketing savvy and perseverance couldn't pull it out. All Kramer's personal assets, including his home, were tied up in the company. He stood to lose everything.

With total failure looming, Kramer's entrepreneurial ego was subdued. He went looking again, this time for someone to take over his last private stronghold, sales and marketing. He came back with Jerry Batalsky, a hard-driving marketing man and mechanical engineer who ran his own manufacturing representative agency in St. Louis.

Batalsky devised a turnaround plan for the company, and Kramer listened to it. It called for a major change: moving as quickly as possible into the commercial kitchen ventilating market, which offered more potential dollars and a sales cycle that would help balance the industrial end of the business.

Textbooks say a company should diversify out of strength. Kramer did it out of desperation. But to Jack Kramer, the choice was simple: he could spend the little he had and risk disaster; or he could watch the company die a slow, certain death. With the help of Batalsky and Steve Glasmann, he put together his first long-term marketing plan, one based on reality, not hope.

The cure, coming so late, almost killed the patient. Six months into the new marketing plan, Cambridge Engineering posted preliminary fiscal 1975 results: its biggest loss yet. The expense of the new man and his marketing budget had pushed Cambridge Engineering over the brink. The company was out of money.

Kramer needed cash just to cover his payroll. He went to his bank, presented his plans, and asked for another six months—plus additional cash—to turn the company around. His bankers were cool; they had watched the company decline for four years. They not only refused Kramer's request for more money but also cut back his credit line.

That was the spring day in 1975 when Jack Kramer pulled over to the side of the road, convinced he and his company had hit bottom. It was also the day that Kramer gave up, once and for all, the notion that he could handle anything and everything better than anyone else. "A crisis like that is humbling," he says. "I vowed never again to create a company that was essentially an ode to myself."

Kramer had finally made the personal transition that was the key factor in his company's recovery. "It's like a child growing up," he says. "When I gave up my pride, started believing other people could do their jobs better than I could—and brought in those kinds of people—then things started to change."

Fortunately for Kramer, one banker was perceptive enough to see the dramatic change. After his money ran out, Kramer went to ten banks before finding Hord Hardin II, a Manchester Bank of St. Louis officer who had known and watched Kramer since his company's early days. Hardin believed in Kramer, as did two of his directors who were in the construction business and knew Cambridge Engineering's work. What convinced them, however, was Kramer's openness about his past mistakes, his detailed turnaround plans, and, particularly, his recently beefed-up management. The bank lent him the six-figure sum he wanted.

In the four years since then, their trust in the new Jack Kramer has paid off. As orders from the kitchen ventilating market started coming in, company sales and profits rose. By the end of fiscal 1978, sales had more than quadrupled to $2.5 million. Hardin had seen what the other bankers hadn't: Jack Kramer was finally letting go, he was finally growing into a manager by sharing his authority with people he respected as superior to him in their specialties.

But Kramer admits that he still wants to be involved in everything. "It's hard to relinquish what was yours for so long, like when I gave Steve those folders for the first time," he says. "I just have to keep reminding myself—Hey, that's his problem." And Kramer still spends 10 percent to 15 percent of his time selling. "If I had to give that up," he says, "it would kill me."

It also bothers Kramer that he's losing touch with the company's fifty employees, whom he previously considered his family. He can't always remember everyone's name when he wanders through the plant, as he still does almost every day. But he knows he has to limit that kind of activity in order to concentrate on management. Almost half of his time now is devoted to long-term planning and "keeping the pieces together," while his vice-president of finance, marketing vice-president, chief engineer, and production head handle day-to-day operations.

What has Cambridge Engineering gotten out of Kramer's "letting go"? Professional planning, steady growth, and, perhaps most important, a staff that takes charge and becomes an integral part of an exciting business. "Each manager works as if he owned 51 percent of the company," says Kramer. "It's amazing how hungry we all are to use our skills. Now each of them is an entrepreneur, too."

What has Kramer himself gotten from it? First, the freedom he thought he could achieve only by running a one-man show. Freedom to tackle major considerations and problems—a new building, a new computer, a long-term marketing plan. Kramer has learned that "planning isn't sitting down with a cup of coffee and a scratch pad, as some people think. Without a plan, the whole thing's futile."

Most important, though, is his realization that his company can now grow the way he'd always hoped it would. Now each month's results are better than the last month's. This year, his prediction of 20-percent growth is not a hopeful fantasy, as in the past, but a conservative projection. Kramer no longer fools himself with a set of imaginary numbers hidden in his desk drawer. Now he watches as the real ones, positive growth figures, line up on Cambridge Engineering's balance sheet.

—SHARON FREDERICK

COULD THESE DANGER SIGNALS APPLY TO YOU?

Jack Kramer's experience is dramatic, but certainly not unusual, say small business gurus who've worked with hundreds of growing companies. "Every company founder hits that crisis point when he is his own worst enemy because he refuses to let go," says John L. Komives, founder and president of Lakeshore Group Ltd., a Milwaukee-based consulting firm specializing in small, growing companies. According to Komives, the "letting go" crisis typically appears as early as the $1 million to $2 million sales level within a service business, usually before $5 million in a manufacturing company, often not until $10 million in a distribution firm. If not resolved, the problem persists for much larger companies.

Like Kramer, most company founders don't see or understand what's happening as their companies grow out from under them. Entrepreneurs often are egotistical enough to believe that the way they're running their business is the best way, and often enjoy the sense of martyrdom that comes from long hours and constant pressure. Few are able to identify themselves as the problem; fewer still can anticipate the crisis and avoid it.

Yet it's possible to do so. The warnings are there, the flags that tell a chief executive officer (CEO) to let go. But don't trust yourself to spot these flags if you're that CEO: ask your accountant, your attorney, your banker, your spouse, or your colleagues if any of the following danger signals apply to you.

Time pressure. Easiest to spot is the increasing scarcity of that always-precious commodity, the top executive's time. Like Jack Kramer, the entrepreneur who holds on too long feels overwhelmed. No matter how much time he puts in, he can't keep up with the multiplying demands of a growing business. "That means that despite the pressure, he's still meddling," says D. Westervelt Davis, a small business consultant with the national accounting firm of Price Waterhouse & Co. "His time's devoured by administrative matters; decisions take longer and longer to make."

Loss of control. The hard-pressed CEO often senses that the company is getting away from him. "Until now, he's been doing seat-of-the-pants planning and budgeting," says Davis. "He's gotten his information firsthand from a variety of sources and kept it on the back of an envelope. It's worked fine before, but now things are slipping away from him, and he can't identify what's going wrong."

Frequently the problem is most acute for the manager who has prided himself on one specialty, as in Jack Kramer's case. Kramer's market savvy had developed from constant contact with customers, prospects, and competitors, but the press of other management responsibilities meant he had less and less time to be out in the field. As a result, he found himself losing the market sense that made his company successful in the early stages.

Financial pressure. Lack of financial controls and of careful planning add up to a dollar dilemma. "At this point in a company's growth, a money problem is often symptomatic of poor planning rather than being a key issue in itself, as it was in the company's start-up phase," says Patrick R. Liles, former Harvard Business School professor and now a venture capitalist.

Even the CEO who has developed a basic financial plan often finds he hasn't included enough anticipated financing to cover faster-than-expected growth. He's then faced with finding his first growth financing, a time-consuming ordeal that is added to all his other tasks.

Second-rate people. Even if the company founder *has* brought in some help, he may not yet be psychologically ready to give up real power. As a result, he surrounds himself with less-than-competent people who aren't likely to challenge him—and who rarely develop into the top-level managers he needs.

To be successful, the CEO must hire people who are recognizably more talented than he in their own areas of expertise. Says venture capitalist Liles, "When we evaluate a growing company, we look at the top man and ask, 'Can the guy bring on someone competent as hell? Is he actually seeking, vying, for that kind of person?' "

Personal isolation and stress. Ironically, his failure to hire competent staff people increases the overburdened CEO's sense of loneliness and isolation, a universal problem for managers of young companies. In the long run, he has no one to help share the new pressures and problems he's facing.

"Often the entrepreneur knows on a gut level he's not doing as well as he could be," says John Komives. "But he's trapped by his own actions. He can't go to his banker or accountant and admit he's inadequate for the job. He literally has no one to turn to for advice, which compounds his problems."

Many, if not most, entrepreneurs ignore all of the above danger signs. "Getting an entrepreneur to let go has to be like Chinese water torture: you do it drop by drop," says W. Hardie Shepard, a New York financial consultant and director of seven growing companies. Unfortunately, as with Jack Kramer, what it usually takes is some mistakes bad enough to put the company in peril.

ONE BOSS
WHO KNEW HOW
TO LET GO

The founder of a small company doesn't have to feel the growing pains Jack Kramer suffered—not if he can recognize and put aside his entrepreneurial ego early in the game. Jim Waters did just that.

Waters, a tall, gray-haired fifty-three-year-old, has come full circle: from designing and building his first analytical instrument in his mother's basement, in 1947, through the growth of Waters Associates, Inc., to $55 million in annual sales, and back again to entrepreneurship with one-year-old Waters Business Systems.

At each step along the way, Waters let go just a bit more, opting to remain the engineer-entrepreneur he says he'll always be. He calls the thirty-two-year process "the growing up of Jim Waters." His friend W. Hardie Shepard, a financial consultant who was Waters's first venture capital backer seventeen years ago, calls it "a classic case of an entrepreneur recognizing the stages of a growing company and bringing in the pros as they were needed."

The first step came in 1967, when Waters Associates sold $2 million worth of its sophisticated measuring equipment. Waters had already hired a marketing manager, but he found he could no longer handle all of the remaining management responsibilities. He was constantly torn between his two most demanding tasks: overseeing production and designing new products. The company was growing at 50 percent to 100 percent a year, and Waters knew he needed more help if that growth was to continue. He brought aboard specialists in the areas of research and development, finance, production, and marketing while he continued as president and general manager.

In 1969 Waters encountered new problems. Several of the specialists he had brought in weren't working out, and his responsibilities were once again too broad. For instance, while he'd used his time to gear up for growth he had failed to see the signs of the economic downturn that hit that year and affected his business.

Enter Frank Zenie, a former "big company" manager whom Waters hired as production vice-president. "I learned a lot about good management from watching Frank," says Waters. "I slowly recognized that he did many things easily that I found very difficult, like working with people." With Zenie's help, Waters cut his staff from 175 to 125, focused his marketing effort, and reorganized, this time filling key slots with people who had been developing within the organization.

As a result, Waters Associates went into 1971 leaner and stronger. "We were a $4-million company," says Waters, "organized and staffed like a $10-million one." Zenie became general manager in 1971. Waters remained president through that year, trying to build a professional management team. However, "I slowly realized that I didn't enjoy it much," he says. By then, Waters was ready to take one more step back. He made Zenie president while he remained chairman of the board and a special projects manager—starting a subsidiary in Japan, doing computer and systems programming, heading a special marketing task force.

"That worked fine until we hit about $20 million," recalls Waters. "Then I started being more trouble than help. I was everywhere: talking to the janitor about the floors one minute, sitting in on planning meetings the next. The organization got very confused about my role." As a result, Waters moved himself entirely out of the company's day-to-day operations in late 1977. He now acts as chairman of the board, where his main activity is to "ask good questions" about the company's long-term goals.

Always the entrepreneur, however, Waters also is back doing what he loves, development work, in his new computer programming business. "It's back out there where problems are snapping like alligators and you love every minute of it," he says.

Does he have any regrets? None. "Ambition overcame pride," he says. "I wanted that company to succeed more than I wanted to hold on to control of it. The company would have stopped growing if I'd kept my hands in every pie. The entrepreneur makes his biggest contribution simply by picking good people—and then staying out of their way."

THE MENTOR SYSTEM

Ask any seasoned entrepreneur what the secret of growth is, and he will tell you that it all comes down to people and management. The logic is hardly breathtaking. Good management solves problems; bad management creates them. It's about as simple as that.

What's less simple, and more breathtaking, is the challenge of finding good management—a challenge that becomes increasingly critical the more successful you are. Some companies get lucky and hire the right people. Many more hire the wrong people and stop growing as a result. Then there are those such as General Alum & Chemical Corp. that invent their own solutions and develop management talent in-house.

General Alum was little more than a shell of a company when Jim Poure bought it in 1978 and merged it with a chemical distributor he owned. With annual revenues of some $350,000 and annual losses of around $10,000, the combined entity was, for all intents and purposes, a start-up—which is to say, short of cash. But, money aside, there were other reasons for not bringing in experienced professionals to run the company. "I had a good idea of the type of company I wanted," says Poure, a twenty-year veteran of the chemical industry and a former vice-president of sales and marketing for Inland Chemical Corp. "I wanted an organization with a particular style and mold. The problem with hiring experienced people is that they have preconceived ideas of how things should be done. So I decided to look for people with talent, energy, and basic intelligence and interest, people who wanted to get in on the ground floor and roll up their sleeves, with the understanding that the rewards would come later."

In the early years, moreover, Poure did not really need much of a management team. Relying on his own experience and street smarts, as well as the hard work of his employees, he quickly turned the company into a producer of high-quality alum, a chemical used in the treatment of water. This he sold primarily to municipalities, which kept coming back for more. By the end of 1982, annual sales had risen to $2.2 million.

But all was not well with the company, which had yet to see a profit. Its internal organization was a chaotic mess, and Poure was beginning to wonder how long he could go on. "There simply weren't enough hours in the day for me to handle everything that needed to get done," he recalls. Nor did he have anyone on board who could ease his load. He had a group of bright young managers whose enthusiasm and energy he valued, but whose inexperience only aggravated the problems. Sure, they had great potential, but their average age was barely twenty-eight, and there were limits to what they could contribute. Poure realized, too, that it could take a long time for them to develop into seasoned professionals unless they received the proper training—something he did not have time to provide.

To make matters worse, the company was facing some new and serious challenges in the marketplace. Among other things, it was beginning to suffer from the fact that it had only one production facility. General Alum's competitors, most of which were large companies, had several plants, which gave them a distinct marketing advantage. Customers were understandably wary of depending on any supplier that might leave them in the lurch if its plant broke down.

The obvious solution was to build a second plant, but Poure knew little about plant construction or financing. He needed help, and he wasn't going to get it from his young managers. So where could he turn?

As it happened, Poure knew a number of big-company executives with whom he often got together. Over the years, several had shown an interest in General Alum. One was a former colleague named Hap Murphey, who had, in fact, recruited and hired Poure as a cub salesman at Inland Chemical some twenty years before. "He was my mentor," says Poure, "and he's remained in that role." So when Murphey mentioned that he was planning to retire and would be happy to work with General Alum on a part-time basis, Poure jumped at the chance.

Their first project was the new plant, which Poure had decided to locate in Toledo. Together they developed the plans and discussed the financing. "We had limitations on capital, and we looked at some alternatives," says Poure. "His suggestion was to bring in a limited partner."

But Murphey's expertise lay in marketing, not finance, so Poure cast about for someone else to help put together such a deal. Again, he played his social contacts, this time turning to a family friend named Carlton Niemeyer, a sixty-eight-year-old former investment manager for Central Soya Corp., who had also retired recently. Niemeyer, too, was interested in working part-time with General Alum, helping to develop its financial structure. "That gave us a real strong financial adviser," says Poure. "We used his business talents to prepare business plans and *pro formas* to present to the banks." Forty percent of the new plant was sold to a limited partner, which "gave us the capital to secure the balance of the financing through the Toledo Economic Development Council and the Small Business Administration."

Eventually, Poure added a third person to his team of part-time advisers—John R. Berger, a sixty-four-year-old scientist who had been Inland Chemical's vice-president of research and development and environmental management. Berger was feeling underutilized by the company that had acquired Inland and welcomed the opportunity to work on developing General Alum's manufacturing operations.

With all three, Poure worked out arrangements that gave them a great deal of flexibility. They were paid by the hour, plus expenses, but they could determine for themselves how much time to put in and how to allocate it. From the advisers' standpoint, the relationship allowed them to stay involved with the business and still have the freedom to enjoy their retirement. As for Poure, he got the benefit of their experience, as well as critical advice on how to keep the company growing.

That solved one problem, but it did not address General Alum's need for experienced management *inside* the company. After discussing the options with various people, Poure decided to bring in a high-priced *Fortune* 500 executive as director of sales and marketing. It was a disaster. "The problem was ego," Poure recalls. "We all thought he was just the man we needed, but he couldn't make the adjustment to a small company. His field was sales management, and he was used to having a staff of people doing things for him. He was a specialist, rather than a generalist. It was like taking an ear, nose, and throat guy and putting him in a family practice. He lasted six months, which was three months longer than he should have."

Burned by the experience, Poure searched for another solution to his management problem. He was reluctant to go outside the company again. Was there a way, he wondered, for General Alum to grow its own managers? He thought of his advisers. What if he were to match each of them up with one of the more promising young people he already had on board? The advisers would continue to counsel Poure, but at the same time they would serve as mentors to his management team. If the system worked, it would give him the best of both worlds, combining the energy and commitment of the young people with the wisdom and experience of the retirees.

The more Poure thought about the plan, the better he liked it, and—in late 1984—he put it into effect. He assigned his twenty-two-year-old son, Tim, to work directly with Hap Murphey in the marketing area. Niemeyer took on thirty-eight-year-old Roger Meyer, the company's controller. Berger was teamed up with twenty-three-year-old Mike Feehan, General Alum's production manager. And Poure himself focused on the career development of twenty-nine-year-old Barbara Lehman, his administrative assistant.

It has been three years since Poure first set up the mentor system, and General Alum has never been healthier. Sales have climbed from $3.8 million in 1983, when the company finally turned a modest profit, to about $7 million last year. Since 1985, moreover, it has been "substantially profitable," according to Poure. Meanwhile, all the mentors continue to play an active role, he says, and the young managers are "two or three years ahead of their time."

Each of the mentors has had a significant impact on the company. Early on, for example, Murphey persuaded Poure to refocus General Alum's marketing efforts away from the municipal water business toward private contracts, primarily in the paper industry. "Over half the alum in this country is used in the paper business," says Murphey. "If you get a good industrial account like a paper company, you can still negotiate a competitive price, but service is more important to maintain that account.

With the municipal business, it wouldn't matter how good [the service was]: if our price was a buck a ton too high, we'd lose the business."

While he was advising Jim Poure on the company's strategy, Murphey was helping Tim Poure to implement it. "The first time I went in the field with him," says Tim Poure, "we were making a contract proposal to a paper company in Milwaukee. I didn't know what to expect. I mean, when you've got a bunch of forty- and fifty-year-olds sitting around a table, and some twenty-two-year-old starts tooting his horn about what his company can do for them—well, there's often a credibility problem." But Tim had been to the company's paper mills. He knew what the company needed and how General Alum could provide it. Murphey, for his part, could speak with authority about broader trends in the paper industry. "I was able to get the people's attention, and he was able to come in and do some sharp marketing," Tim recalls. "It was a real nice combination." Real nice, indeed. General Alum beat out two large competitors for the contract.

This is not to suggest that the mentors do the managers' work for them. True, they provide contacts and handle specific tasks that demand a higher level of expertise. But more often they serve as teachers and advisers. "Our role," says Murphey, "is to be elder statesmen, to critique them if we think they are doing it wrong."

Sometimes the young people choose to ignore the advice. Murphey and Tim Poure once disagreed about a young woman who had applied for a job as a salesperson. She was enthusiastic enough, said Murphey, but she didn't have enough experience in the chemical industry. "In his day, there were no female salesmen," says Tim, who hired the woman anyway. Within six months, she was the top salesperson on the staff.

Usually, however, the young managers are happy to follow their mentors' advice. "If I didn't have [Niemeyer] to turn to, I'd have to go to an outside accounting firm to get direction," says controller Meyer. "He helped us to revamp our entire budget process, so that it was as sophisticated and as accurate as possible."

Oddly enough, Niemeyer has also played a mentoring role with his old friend Jim Poure, forcing him to accept a financial discipline that does not come naturally to him. "Two years ago," Poure recalls, "when we weren't getting the profits we expected from the new plant [in Toledo], he spent about an hour in the parking lot, chewing me out for a couple of things we'd done. I don't mean he shook his finger at me, but he gave me a firm and constructive analysis of the mistakes we'd made and how we could have avoided them. If you are going to bring someone in as an adviser, you'd better be able to listen and learn. I recognized that he was correct."

More recently, Niemeyer helped Poure restructure the company. Prior to the restructuring, General Alum's two plants and its distribution division were separate corporations, a device Poure had used to obtain financing. Niemeyer came up with a plan to consolidate the different entities under one corporate roof and to buy out the Toledo investor, leaving Poure as 100-percent owner of General Alum. At the same time, Niemeyer put together a financial package to provide the company with capital for expansion, then helped present it to the bank. "Banks like it when senior people make a presentation," notes Niemeyer. "It gives you greater credibility. We came up with a logical plan, showing there was more to the numbers than just wishful thinking." The bank approved the loan.

Poure himself could not be more pleased with the way things have turned out. His own life is much calmer these days. "I had so much going on at once that I couldn't separate everything," he says. "I'm probably putting in as many hours as before, or more, but I'm a hell of a lot more productive."

Not that the system is perfect. "You have to remember that these people are retired," he notes, "and they like to travel. Sometimes they aren't around when you want to bounce something off them. But now I feel comfortable bouncing things off my own management staff, whereas a year or two ago I didn't."

The development of the management team has allowed Poure to think about long-term issues, including succession. With the encouragement of his advisers, he has designated his son Tim as heir apparent, although he himself has no plans to retire for another ten or fifteen years. "It helps Tim to know the time frame," says Poure, "and we felt that [his designation as successor] would give our employees a good feeling, knowing that the company would continue."

Meanwhile, General Alum continues to grow. With the decision to build a third plant, Poure decided that it was time to add an experienced manager to his team and—in April—brought in James J. Young, a fifty-nine-year-old senior vice-president at Owens-Corning Fiberglas Corp., as the company's chief operating officer. Nevertheless, he has every intention of keeping the mentor system in place, training the people who will run the company in years to come.

—LISA R. SHEERAN AND DONNA FENN

THE "SMART TEAM"
AT COMPAQ COMPUTER

In the beginning, there was the team. Bill Murto, Jim Harris, and Rod Canion were all senior managers at Texas Instruments Inc., in Houston. Each had been bitten by the entrepreneurial bug. Together they decided to strike out on their own.

Aside from that, little else was clear. Not the financing. Not the timing. Not even the type of business they would go into. As they gathered in the sweltering Houston summer of 1981, they considered starting a Mexican restaurant, a company to produce hard disks for microcomputers, and a business built around a beeping device to help find a misplaced briefcase or car keys. In the end, they decided to develop a portable personal computer compatible with the IBM PC.

The Compaq computer turned out to be well designed and well executed, a market sensation that generated $111 million in sales in its first year of operation. It was the hottest performance by a start-up in the history of American business, and success has since been piled on success. Compaq Computer Corp. has gone on to become the world's second-largest manufacturer of personal computers for business, with anticipated 1985 sales of nearly half a billion dollars. And, even more remarkable, profit margins have kept pace with growth.

Compaq's is the sort of story of which high-technology myths are made. But unlike many start-ups that have made countless fortunes in Silicon Valley and elsewhere, this one was different. There were no flashes of genius, no technical breakthroughs. If anything, say Compaq's founders, their story is something of a paean to dullness, a lesson in how a strong core of experienced executives managed their way to the top of high tech.

"I'm not a superstar with all the vision, just a guy who moderates the consensus among a pretty bright bunch of people," explains president Rod Canion in his austere office amid the pine forests of suburban Houston. "Our way has been to work as a team to find out the market needs and execute our product. If people say, 'Ho hum' and that we need more pizzazz, I think they miss the point."

Canion's point is that entrepreneurial success is far less dependent these days on the brilliant insights and force of personality of hard-charging chief executive officers. A growing number of companies are organizing themselves around a "smart team" of experienced, savvy managers who substitute collegiality for hierarchy and keep their focus on a single goal: building a company that's going to last.

The term "smart team" may have originated with management consultants Steven M. Panzer and Robert P. Kelley Jr. With venture capital tight, competition fierce, and product life cycles shrinking to spans of months instead of years, Panzer and Kelley argue that high-tech entrepreneurs have to adapt their management styles to a more demanding environment—one in which there is precious little room for error. Entrepreneurs must learn to invest their managers with a collective responsibility for even the most crucial business decisions. And managers have to learn to look beyond the narrow confines of disciplines to the broad concerns of the company as a whole.

"It's a new ball game out there," says Panzer. "The roles of CEOs are changing. They can't just be order givers. Instead, they are becoming coordinators, whose main task is to tap the potential of their teams. That's become the key factor for success."

High-tech entrepreneurs seem to agree. In a study of ninety West coast companies conducted in 1984 by the Southern California Technology Executives' Network (SoCalTen), CEOs were asked for their number-one priority in running their businesses. Fully two-thirds cited the development of a strong management team.

Nothing prompts this concern for team management so much as the realization that in the recent shakeout in the microelectronics industry, the

---

A ROGUES' GALLERY OF CALIFORNIA SWASHBUCKLERS

They were the highfliers of high tech: aggressive, creative, and supremely egotistical. The companies they founded made them rich and famous. But today, those companies are in trouble, and many are being run by somebody else.

Charter Members

Sirjang Lai "Jugi" Tandon,
43, Tandon Corp.

Adam Osborne, 45,
Osborne Computer Corp.

Steven Jobs, 31,
Apple Computer Inc.

Alan Shugart, 55, Seagate Technology

A veteran of IBM Corp.'s San Jose, California, labs, the birthplace of the modern disk-drive industry, Shugart pioneered many of the first small microcomputer disk drives. In 1973, he founded Shugart Associates, later bought and dumped by Xerox Corp. He launched Seagate in 1979, building a large manufacturing facility in Scotts Valley, south of San Jose, only to move manufacturing operations to Singapore in 1984. Singapore did not provide the salvation that was expected, however, and now, like Tandon, Seagate has its share of troubles, due largely to IBM order cutbacks and a marketplace with too many competitors.

Nolan Bushnell, 43, Atari Inc. and Pizza Time Theatre Inc.

The engaging, pipe-smoking Bushnell was once perhaps the most popular figure in Silicon Valley. A classic American gadgeteer, his big score was developing the Pong video game at Atari in the early 1970s. After Atari sold out to Warner Communications Inc. in 1976 for $28 million, things began going sour. Pizza Time Theatre, a restaurant chain with robot entertainers, fell flat due to poor marketing and even poorer pizza. Some insiders say that Bushnell refused to listen to others on his board. The company went Chapter 11 in early 1984. Bushnell is still pushing other ventures.

Jim Toreson, 43, Xebec Corp.

Toreson founded the company in 1974 and grew it to $158 million by 1984. Brilliant and charismatic, he was widely admired for his leadership in "Made in USA" manufacturing strategy. But the company is now having problems, in part due to being a one-man show and in part due to its overreliance on IBM. Like other "go-go" companies of the micro boom, Xebec is plagued with too much production capacity, excessive inventories, and flat sales. Losses last year amounted to $21 million on less than $150 million in revenues. Insiders lay much of the blame on Toreson's failure to develop a management team. "Everything is done Jim's way," says one. "It's a lone-ranger operation."

Lore Harp, 41, Vector Graphic Inc.

An extrovert German immigrant, Harp founded Vector in a bedroom suite of her suburban house in 1976. She was later joined by her engineer husband, Bob, and together they were brilliant performers. But marital problems led to Bob's departure, and by the early 1980s, the company was falling behind technologically. Today, the company is held together only by the efforts of venture capitalist Jean Deleage and the protection of the U.S. bankruptcy court. Lore, now remarried to *Computerworld* publisher Patrick McGovern, is said to be launching a new venture involving feminine-hygiene products.

Gordon Campbell, 41, Seeq Technology Inc.

Under this onetime Intel Corp. golden boy, Seeq was among the most ballyhooed of Silicon Valley's early semiconductor start-ups. But gregarious, publicity-loving Campbell soon alienated much of his original team. He married fellow founder Maria Ligeti, whose promotion to vice-president led to internal dissension. Campbell's showy style—he built a lavish sloping roof over his N. San Jose, California, headquarters rumored to cost an estimated $500,000—may also have offended tough-minded venture capitalist Frank Caulfield. In October 1984, Caulfield engineered Campbell's dethronement. Both Campbell and Ligeti have recently founded separate high-tech ventures.

Gary Friedman, Fortune Systems Corp.

Known as a super salesman, Friedman launched his microsystem manufacturing concern in 1980 and took it public two and a half years later, netting the company some $100 million. Now most of that money is gone and so is Friedman, who was eased out by his onetime venture capital admirers in October 1983.

victims have included some of high tech's most celebrated and charismatic entrepreneurs (see box, "A Rogues' Gallery of California Swashbucklers"). "The era of the swashbuckler is over," proclaims management consultant William G. Ouchi. "No longer can you have an engineer in control of a body of technology and have no competitors to worry about. You can't sell something now if you don't sell it well or make it well. The era of the Steven Jobses—the guys who thought of themselves as anti-organization—is ending."

In some ways, the era of the swashbuckler was a reflection of the technology itself. The microprocessor—the "computer on a chip"—came along in the late 1970s, and fundamentally altered the nature of the computer industry. Where in the past, entry in the industry was limited largely to those companies, such as IBM, Digital Equipment, and Prime, capable of building big-ticket items like mainframes or minicomputers, microcomputers afforded entrepreneurs the opportunity to launch companies in their garages, with only a good idea and a few thousand dollars in savings. Each week brought fresh news of a successful start-up that lent credibility to the notion that technological leadership and a flair for marketing could make up for deficiencies down the line in such mundane areas as inventory management and quality control. Computer swashbuckler Adam Osborne was even heard to declare blithely that IBM Corp. would soon "cease to be a significant force" in the small business computer market.

"They thought they were writing new rules," recalls Ronald J. Brown, now president and chairman of Osborne Computer Corp. "It worked great in the short run, but ended up as a disaster." Brown ought to know. He took over at Osborne after the company filed for protection under federal bankruptcy laws. One of his previous employers: IBM.

"The Japanese and IBM created an environment in which there is no tolerance for sloppy management," says Benjamin Rosen, a venture capitalist who lost all of his original investment of $400,000 in Osborne. "In the old days, you could get away with it, because you were competing only with companies like your own. Now, the IBMs and the Japanese are in every field. You have to have a much deeper, more solid management. You don't have the luxury of making mistakes." Rosen now puts that advice into practice, as chairman of the board at Compaq.

"When we left Texas Instruments, we were determined to start a company with people who could work in a *Fortune* 500 company," explains

Rod Canion. "We wanted to combine the discipline of a big company with an environment where people felt they could participate in a success. We wanted the best of both worlds. And we wanted to do it right."

For Canion, doing it right meant attracting seasoned professionals to his management team with generous offers of salary and stock. Among the first executives recruited to Compaq's smart team was John Gribi, a fourteen-year veteran of Texas Instruments who, as the new company's chief financial officer, set up a state-of-the-art accounting system that would not be overwhelmed by the company's growth. John Walker, once a senior vice-president at Datapoint Corp., was recruited to establish the sort of quality manufacturing operation that often eluded computer start-ups. And to make sure the new Compaq computers reached the retail market, Canion brought in H. L. "Sparky" Sparks, a twenty-year IBM veteran who had managed sales and service of the IBM Personal Computer.

In the early months, Canion and his two cofounders invited their new managers to join them in the executive suite, which consists, appropriately, of modest private offices arranged in proximity to a large and comfortable conference area. There, all the key company decisions were hammered out. As the company grew, new managers were added, but the management process remained essentially unchanged. "We brought in people not to execute orders, but who could replace us," Canion explained. "We wanted people in place who could take us to a bigger size. Our feeling was that if you have a consensus team, it is not going to leave a stone unturned."

Early in 1983, this commitment to consensus management was put to the test. Canion had become enamored of the prospect of producing a "lap-top" computer small enough to fit inside a briefcase. Although there was general support for the idea, a researcher named Mary Dudley was assigned to survey the market. She concluded that the customers just weren't there. After Dudley presented, refined, and re-presented her negative assessment, Canion eventually felt compelled to retreat. It was a good thing, too: lap-top computers by Gavilan Computer Corp. and Data General Corp. proved to be embarrassing market flops.

"I was the champion of that idea, but I was wrong," Canion remembers. "And what saved us was the consensus process—asking enough people, getting enough input. It's not like I'm the one who starts out with all the right ideas. I'm just part of the team process."

The smart-team concept at Compaq is an interdisciplinary approach to management: it assumes that the company's treasurer and top engineer, for example, have something valuable to contribute to decisions about marketing and manufacturing. And what works in the executive suite also works throughout the company. Because of it, Compaq now has a remarkable knack for developing, producing, and marketing new products in very short order.

Consider the case of the Deskpro 286. In the waning months of 1984, Compaq was facing the formidable challenge presented by IBM's new "super" PC, which many observers were predicting would leave companies like Compaq in the dust. The task of developing a response fell to Kevin Ellington, a twenty-one-year veteran of Texas Instruments. Ellington created his own smart team, drawing from every department of the company, its members working in parallel. Even as engineers were still designing Compaq's new product, manufacturing managers were setting up a new factory to produce it, a marketing executive was busily positioning it, an assistant treasurer was arranging to pay for it. Within six months, Compaq had begun shipping its Deskpro 286s to grateful retailers, while IBM's new product was still plagued by production problems and lapses in quality control. IBM had created a hungry new market and then stumbled; Compaq moved swiftly into the breach, shipping 10,000 computers in the first ninety days. Today, the product stands as one of the company's most successful, commanding some 3 percent to 4 percent of the business-computer market.

DÉJÀ VU

The Auto Industry, Too, Shifted from Entrepreneurs to Smart Teams.

In the first decades of the century, cars were to the American economy what electronics is today. The giants of the industry were Henry Ford, whose assembly line had defined how best to build cars, and William C. Durant, whose segmented marketing defined how best to sell them. But as the industry expanded, these entrepreneurial geniuses failed to develop the management resources and methods to keep pace. It would be left to a second generation of team managers to take these industries to maturity.

Henry Ford ran his company as if it were a "twentieth-century absolute monarchy," according to his biographer, Keith Sward. He disdained the idea of developing strong executives, insisting on placing his mark on virtually every major initiative. When one manager dared to question his ideas, Ford cut him off with the taunt, "Get out and send me an optimist."

It was not surprising, then, that independent-minded executives tended to have short stays at Ford. They were often replaced by men whose loyalty to Ford had an almost thuggish quality: one group of employees discovered that they'd been fired when they returned to their offices one morning to find their desks had been axed into pieces. Among Ford's more celebrated lieutenants was Harry Herbert Bennett, a former prizefighter who learned a knack for getting along with the boss during many years of service to Detroit's underworld.

Ford could get away with such practices as long as his competitors were not any better managed—and for a while they were not. At General Motors Corp., Durant ran the shop by the seat of his pants, with power and responsibility spread widely—some thought haphazardly—throughout the company. The weakness of this extreme decentralization became apparent when the recession hit after World War I, and Durant found himself with too many cars to sell and too little cash on hand. A desperate GM board was forced to turn to more professional managers.

Among them was Alfred P. Sloan Jr., who went on to serve as the company's chief executive for twenty-three years. Although personally well disposed toward Durant, Sloan believed that General Motors needed a more scientific and rational management process. He took the various entities that had made up GM and reorganized them into autonomous operating units, each with its own product development and manufacturing, sales, and pricing strategy. Each division was encouraged to develop its own identity and strategy, and individual managers were given the chance to shine. At the same time, Sloan made sure his central office was staffed with the best and the brightest, to coordinate the various divisions, spot problems, and plot the long-term strategy of the corporation and the industry. It was to become the most celebrated, and perhaps the most successful, smart team in American business history.

From Dearborn, Michigan, Henry Ford watched the reorganization at General Motors with disdain, convinced of the power of his own personal genius. "To my mind," he wrote, "there is no bent of mind more dangerous than that which is sometimes described as the 'genius for organization.' "

Dangerous, perhaps, but also profitable. Fed with fresh market intelligence from his various divisions, for instance, Sloan realized the necessity of producing a wide range of cars in a variety of colors for the growing automobile market. Soon General Motors was cutting deep into Ford's once-dominant market share. Ford thought it all just too frivolous. The customer, he is said to have declared, could have any color he wanted, "as long as it's black."

To the end, Sloan remained respectful of his entrepreneurial forebears. "Both Mr. Durant and Mr. Ford had unusual vision, courage, daring, imagination, and foresight," he wrote years later. "Both gambled everything on the future of the automobile at a time when fewer were made in a year than are now made in a couple of days. . . . They were a generation of what I might call personal types of industrialists; that is, they injected their personalities, their 'genius,' so to speak, as a subjective factor into their operations without the discipline of management by method and objective facts."

Responding to some unkind characterizations of his management style, Sloan had this to say: "Though I have often been taxed, by people who do not know me, with being a committee man—and in a sense, I most certainly am—I have never believed that a group as such could manage anything. A group can make policy, but only individuals can administer policy."

By mid-century, Sloan's concept of a multidivisional structure, with its emphasis on smart teamwork and rational decision making, had become the rule for the U.S. auto industry. It was also working at such nonautomotive corporations as General Electric Co. and E. I. Du Pont de Nemours & Co. Sloan's thinking influenced a generation of business theorists and historians, from Alfred D. Chandler Jr. to A. A. Berle to John Kenneth Galbraith. At MIT, a prestigious school of business and management bears Sloan's name, and continues to teach his gospel.

Will entrepreneurs of the future heed the lessons of history about the inevitable rise and fall of autocratic entrepreneurs? It is doubtful. More likely their attitude will be similar to that of their spiritual forebear, Henry Ford, who once proclaimed that "history is more or less bunk."

—Joel Kotkin and Karen Angeline

"I don't believe any other company could have done this," boasts Ellington, still amazed by the feat. "The first, second, and third reason for that was teamwork. . . . That's what has kept Compaq free from the perils of this world."

The momentum away from swashbucklers and toward smart teams is now so far along in California's high-tech industry that even the venture capitalists have caught on. It was largely venture capital that bankrolled the swashbuckler. And it is venture capitalists who lately have forced many of the swashbucklers to turn control of their companies over to more experienced managers as things have begun to go sour. For most, the period of transition has been costly.

"It used to be thought that you could start a company and then replace entrepreneurial types with [managerial types] later on," notes L. J. Sevin, who has backed such poorly managed companies as Osborne and Synapse Computer Corp. "But now I believe in original sin: if you don't get the right team from the start, you're wasting valuable resources to turn it around. Now if a deal doesn't include deep management, we don't get into it."

So these days it is such companies as Linear Technology Corp. that attract the venture capital. Like Compaq, Linear was founded by a group of executives and engineers who had worked together for many years—this group came from the giant National Semiconductor Corp. And like Compaq, Linear's first move was to assemble a management team much larger and more experienced than a relatively small new company would initially require. "In a start-up, you don't have time to train people," explains Robert Swanson, Linear's president. Venture capitalists responded enthusiastically to Swanson's plea for front-end loading Linear's management team, with three rounds of financing that raised $22 million. Investors read like a veritable who's who of high-tech backers, from Hambrecht & Quist to Ing. C. Olivetti & Co. Calls from other interested investors, including the Japanese, still come in three times a week.

"Linear is the kind of company that's flourishing with investors now," notes venture capitalist Don Valentine, himself a Linear investor. "People are reviewing the past and figuring out the clues of what works and what doesn't. And what seems to be working are those firms that have a combination of technical people, people with manufacturing skills, experienced sales- and businesspeople—where all critical areas are well staffed."

If today that sounds rather obvious, understand that it is a realization that has only recently come to such entrepreneurial hotbeds as California, where team management often was scorned and careful planning was thought to be the enemy of growth. This was a business culture dominated by brash autocrats who had made millions doing things their way and didn't think it necessary to bring in a team of seasoned professionals to keep things on track.

Perhaps none of California's entrepreneurs was more headstrong than Sirjang Lal "Jugi" Tandon, whose Chatsworth, California-based disk-drive manufacturer was one of the fast-growth darlings of the early 1980s. Tandon worshiped at the altar of expansion, ramping up production at a frenetic rate to meet the soaring demands of such ravenous customers as IBM. To keep costs low, much of its production was shifted offshore to Tandon's native India and to Singapore, putting the company in the anomalous position of laying off its U.S. workers even as its sales were expanding. As growth turned into hypergrowth, however, Tandon's widespread production system began to strain the company's slender management resources. Board members called for an infusion of experienced managers, but Tandon stoutly refused. Before long, the company's glaring weaknesses produced unpleasant results: defective quality and late entries of products. Today Tandon is reeling—from a general downturn in the industry, dramatically reduced orders from IBM, and foreign competition. Sales, which reached $400 million in 1984, were down to $269 million for 1985, with a loss of $135 million. Belatedly, Tandon has brought in some strong management: as president and chief operating officer, longtime IBM veteran Dan H. Wilkie; and as new senior vice-president, "Sparky" Sparks, who played such a key role as a member of Compaq's smart team.

No such late refresher course on sound management has been necessary for another disk-drive company, Quantum Corp., located in Milpitas, California, about 400 miles from Tandon's San Fernando Valley headquarters. While the high-profile, charismatic Tandon was busy grabbing most of the headlines, Jim Patterson, a former IBM executive who founded Quantum, was quietly building a smart team of managers drawn from such companies as Hewlett-Packard, Digital Equipment, Shugart Associates, and Control Data. Early on, Patterson and his team opted for growth that was slow and steady, and not overly dependent on one customer or one product. They refused any large orders that they feared would stretch management and financial resources beyond capacity. "We'd like to have that IBM business, but not on terms that make no sense for a company at this stage of development," Patterson explained.

For five years, Quantum was content to play the tortoise to Tandon's hare. But now the company's obsession with team building has begun to pay off. Sales in the fiscal year that ended in March of last year soared 79 percent, to $120 million. Profits have nearly doubled, to $21 million. And industry analysts expect a steady upward climb.

Quantum's president is anxious to hold on to his success. And Patterson thinks the key is to make it impossible for single-minded egoists to enter his organization. Prospective managers are subject to as many as a dozen interviews to ensure that they have the sensibilities and temperament of team players. Explains program manager Jim Parson, "Here you not only have to be good, but you damn better fit this culture."

Part of that culture involves a rare commitment to employees. In an industry traditionally dominated by engineers with limited interest in manufacturing and even less in the people on the line, Quantum has stood out during the current industry shakeout by retaining its entire 160-member manufacturing staff. Even when the company shifted its mature product line to a new factory in Puerto Rico last year, company officials used the occasion not to lay off "excess" workers but to train them to produce the next generation of product. That loyalty, Patterson feels, is more than rewarded—in quality production and in low employee turnover, which, at 5 percent to 10 percent, compares favorably with the 30 percent to 50 percent turnover common in Silicon Valley.

Many of the smart teams of California high tech are started by refugees from corporate America. But not all. Meet Albert Wong, Safi Qureshey, and Tom Yuen, founders of AST Research Inc.

In many ways, theirs is a typical start-up tale. There was no business plan, very little management experience, and only a shoestring budget. What they really had back in July of 1980 was a notion: that the IBM PC would create a huge market for add-on products that could enhance its computing power and expand its functions. Working out of a garage in Santa Ana, California, the chores were quickly divided. Wong, the technical genius, handled basic engineering. Yuen, like Wong a native of Hong Kong, directed marketing and sales. Qureshey, a Pakistani, took on administration and planning. Members of Wong's family pitched in stuffing boards when they could. And by year's end, sales had nearly reached $400,000 and business was booming.

Today, AST Research is a $140-million company, earning $19 million. And despite the building of elegant new headquarters in Irvine, California, and the hiring of dozens of high-powered managers, the essence of this company has remained very much the same: a partnership built on friendship and equality among three young immigrants who run their business by talking things over, as if they were still back in the old garage.

"I have to admit at first I was reluctant to join such a young group of guys, but their openness has really amazed me," says Don Williams, a veteran of Beckman Instruments Inc., who was brought in to take over manufacturing operations. "These are not your typical know-it-all, smart-ass entrepreneurs. They are very into listening."

With help from Williams and other seasoned executives, AST has emerged as perhaps the dominant player in the world market for add-on enhancement products, not just for IBM but also for Apple Computer and AT&T. Yet even though the company is now public and its founding fathers are worth more than $40 million each, there seems no intention to alter their management style. For like their smart-team soul mates at Compaq, Quantum, and Linear Technology, they do not appear to be driven by the prospect of making the next million or engineering the next great technological breakthrough. The ego is tightly tethered, fame and fortune do not inspire. What distinguishes the soul of this new entrepreneur is simply an overriding interest in building a company that lasts, an economic institution that endures.

"Our goal is to build an organization for the long term, a company like Hewlett-Packard or IBM, something that's good for all the employees," explains AST's Qureshey.

Quantum's Patterson agrees. "The important thing is not how big you are in your fifth year or where you rank among the fastest-growing companies. The issue is where you are going to be in twenty-five years. That's the standard to use to judge the really great companies."

—JOEL KOTKIN

FOUR-STAR
MANAGEMENT

In the clear skies over southern Nevada, a major air battle is raging. Fifteen Russian MiGs are swarming like high-tech hornets as air-force fighters close in at twice the speed of sound. One of the MiGs lets fly an air-to-air missile, sending an F-15 Eagle banking into a nine-G evasion turn. Another F-15, locking its sights on a MiG, launches a Sidewinder missile and blows the enemy out of the air. Moments later, a handful of A-10 Thunderbolts, cruising in at low altitude, open fire on a column of Soviet tanks as four F-16 Falcons suddenly appear from behind a mountain to bomb a Soviet troop formation.

The Russian troops are only simulated, of course, as are the missiles, bombs, and bullets. The planes, however, are real. At nearby Nellis Air Force Base, several controllers in a darkened room are watching the battle unfold on huge screens, the world's biggest and most expensive video game. It is something straight out of James Bond—and, as we'll see, straight out of Tom Peters as well.

This is one of the Air Force's Red Flag training exercises, a mock war that rages year-round over several million acres of Nevada desert. On one side are the men and planes of the Tactical Air Command (TAC), which is charged with defending American interests in the skies anywhere in the world. On the other, squadrons of F-5 Tigers sporting Warsaw Pact paint jobs, flown by American pilots who have been specially trained in Soviet air tactics.

On this day, the good guys win. But it wasn't always that way. A decade ago, when Red Flag was just beginning, the Tactical Air Command was in a sorry state. At any one time, half of the planes in its $25-billion fleet were not battle ready and more than 220 airplanes were classified as "hangar queens"—grounded at least three weeks for lack of spare parts or maintenance. Because of equipment problems, TAC pilots—trained at a cost of $1 million each—lacked the flying time necessary to keep their skills sharp, and the best of them were deserting the air force in droves. So, too, were mechanics and technicians, frustrated in their jobs and disappointed by the deplorable living conditions at almost every TAC installation. Perhaps worst of all was the soaring accident rate that resulted in tragic deaths, unnecessary loss of expensive airplanes, and embarrassment for the service.

Into this mess in 1978 stepped General W. L. (Bill) Creech. As the new commander sized up his domain from TAC headquarters at Langley Air Force Base, in Virginia, it looked to him like a potential national security disaster. "The U.S. military was coming apart," is how he remembers it. "It was worse than you think."

This is the remarkable story of how, in six and a half years, Creech turned his command into one of the bright stars of the defense firmament. TAC fighters today are in superb condition, its pilots fully trained, its installations sparkling. The number of hangar queens has declined from 200 to just a handful. Reenlistment rates are way up. And a dramatic reduction in the crash rate has saved dozens of lives and billions of dollars' worth of airplanes.

Perhaps most remarkable, Creech was able to work his magic with no more money, no more planes, and no more personnel than were available when he started. Creech's strategy was to force a bottoms-up management style on an organization that had always been strictly top-down—pushing responsibility and authority down into the tiniest crevices of his command. And so stunning was his execution that the Pentagon has now begun to apply his techniques throughout the U.S. military. Says one Defense Department official, "It's probably our biggest success since MacArthur's Inchon landing."

Any chief executive officer would have been daunted by the challenge of simply running so sprawling an operation, let alone reviving it. At the time that Creech settled into his post, he was in charge of 115,000 full-time employees working at 150 installations around the world—plus another 65,000 men and women trained and on call. The assets under his control were valued at more than $40 billion, including some 3,800 aircraft—more than twice as many as all U.S. airlines combined. He had a discretionary budget of $1.4 billion, with billions more reserved for fuel and spare parts.

Creech was no stranger to TAC. By 1978, he had already spent nearly thirty years in the air force, a career that took in the first jet-age dogfights of the Korean War, a military position with the United Nations, and wing commands in Europe. But perhaps most crucial to his views on managing TAC was a stint he had put in at the Pentagon during the days of Defense Secretary Robert McNamara.

The watchword of the McNamara regime was centralization, for which there was a dual imperative. Politically, the Kennedy administration came into office as suspicious of the military as the military was of the new president and his advisers. McNamara's assignment was to curb interservice rivalry and bring all of the services under greater civilian control. In addition, as the former president of Ford Motor Co., McNamara was a disciple of the management gurus of the day who preached that centralization was synonymous with efficiency. While his whiz kids fashioned new military strategies for the various services, battalions of cost analysts and systems planners cranked out new rules and regulations that reached into every facet of military life. Commanders in the field sensed that they had been stripped of much of their autonomy. Decision-making was jealously guarded within the Pentagon.

"The thrust was on saving money and people," Creech says. "It overlooked the requirement to do a good job. A lot of these guys, when you started talking about spirit and teamwork and cooperation, their eyes glazed over. They just couldn't relate to that."

By the time Creech put on his fourth star and took command of TAC, Robert McNamara was long gone from Defense, but his dogma of centralized management and command had become inviolate within the Pentagon. Only it wasn't working—not at TAC, anyway. Granted, some duplication had been eliminated, along with some jobs. But the cost had been high: the American military command had been robbed of much of its vigor. Innovation and initiative were discouraged, and people were dehumanized, thought of as mere costs of production, like so many bullets or mess kits.

It was not that Creech was unwilling to use quantitative means by which to judge TAC's performance. On the contrary, taking stock of the crucial measurement of production—the number of training sorties flown—Creech found that TAC had been losing ground at the rate of 8 percent each year since 1969. And to deal with the problem, he proposed nothing less than a radical restructuring of his command, one that would send authority down the ranks along with responsibility for meeting clear and simple goals.

Pentagon planners were appalled at the thought. Creech, they argued, would wind up adding thousands of new jobs and spending millions of new dollars. They were uneasy with the notion that one command might be different from all the others. And although they didn't quite come out and say it, they were suspicious that authority could be intelligently exercised by the likes of career military men.

"They were legion, the people against me," recalls Creech. "You couldn't single anyone out. The villain wasn't any particular person, but the whole system. It was all the staffers down below—these faceless regulation writers and approvers. I was going against the grain of the Pentagon culture. The system bristled."

Creech had an early ally, however, in air-force chief of staff General David C. Jones. Jones's support would not assure success for the decentralization campaign, but it did give Creech the kind of bureaucratic altitude he needed to escape the flak from the doubters within the Pentagon.

A $27-million F-15 is a beautiful piece of design and engineering, but without spare parts and skilled mechanics, it soon becomes a relatively useless hunk of metal.

In 1978, when Creech took command, the procedures for getting a fighter fixed might just as well have been devised by a British labor union steward. Consider the case of a jet grounded for a minor electrical malfunction.

The first man on the scene would be a general aircraft mechanic, known as a crew chief. The chief, after making his initial inspection, would put a call into Job Control, the centralized maintenance unit for each base. Job Control, in turn, would call the electrical shop, which would dispatch a man out to the flight line to work on the problem. On arriving, however, the electrician might well discover that an entire panel would have to be removed before he could really get to the problem, requiring yet another technician. There would be another round of calls to Job Control and the electrical shop. Then—perhaps after a stop at the post office and the coffee shop—the panel-remover would finally arrive on the flight line, only to find that he needed a spare part. So somebody would put in a call to the base's central supply depot, which stocked everything from jet engines to toilet paper, to see if one was available. Three more hours might pass before the part was trucked out by somebody else from the warehouse to the flight line. Meanwhile, the jet and its pilot probably would have missed their scheduled sortie.

Time, however, was only half the problem. Quality was the other half. The electrical shop, like the other specialized units for hydraulics, ejection seats, radar, navigation systems, and the like, would invariably dispatch its lowest-ranking people for routine calls. That left the senior sergeants, with their fifteen to twenty-five years of experience, back at their comfortable offices, pushing paper or maybe just reading the paper. And without their direct supervision, much of the work done on the flight line was the quick-fix variety—or worse.

"We were all aware that a human being was strapping into that jet, but there was a lot of sloppy work done to get it into the air," says Technical Sergeant Ruben Saldana, an F-15 crew chief at Langley and a TAC man before, during, and after the Creech command. "And if it missed its sortie, it was no big deal."

The pilots, too, were less than enthralled. "Used to be you could take an airplane off, but your radar wasn't working or the inertial navigation system didn't work," says Lieutenant Colonel Burr Crittenden, an F-16 squadron commander at Nellis. "So even when we did fly, the sorties were often low quality."

It all added up to a lackluster fighter force, beset with apathy, sagging morale, and horrifying statistics. Only 20 percent of "broken" planes were getting repaired in a typical eight-hour shift. Pilots who needed a minimum of fifteen hours of flying time a month were getting ten or less. The average plane, which had flown twenty-three sorties a month in 1969, was flying only eleven by 1978. And for every 100,000 hours flown, seven planes were crashing. Investigators blamed many of the crashes on faulty maintenance.

"One reason we were doing so poorly is because we were so good at centralization," says Creech. "It was a highly matrixed system, where the functional specialists only loosely worked for the person in charge of getting the job done. The supervisor was just a voice on the radio. Nobody really cared."

Creech's first move was to structure his command around a smaller and more manageable unit of organization—the squadron, which consists of twenty-four planes, rather than the wing, which is three times the size. Starting on a trial basis at a few installations, he created squadron repair teams, drawing technicians from each of the maintenance disciplines. The team would work only on their own squadron's aircraft. And instead of operating out of rear-area dispatching locations, Creech ordered them to move right down to the flight lines.

Almost immediately, there was an undercurrent of opposition from some of the senior sergeants, the princes of the maintenance realm, who had to abandon their cushy offices and move with their men to the flight lines. Worse still, the sergeant who once had supervised sixty electricians was now supervising twenty. Many felt demoted or diminished.

"We didn't care for it," says one of these so-called super-sergeants, who asked not to be named. "Here was this crazy general coming in and splintering an operation we'd spent years putting together."

Creech had anticipated some hostility, but in this instance a military culture worked in his favor: in the air force, there are severe penalties for insubordination. "I'm not saying everyone thought this change was great," he says. "But slowly they were won over. In the centralized system, we were top-heavy in management. We were keeping beautiful track of what we were not doing. But in our system, sergeants were sergeants. They were in charge of people, not paper. And they had to make those people produce. If they didn't, they were out."

The idea was to give each operational squadron and its companion maintenance team a common identity, purpose, and spirit. The maintenance people, who had been faceless cogs in a 2,000-person wing operation, found themselves sporting the prestigious flight squadron patches on their fatigues. They now belonged to the Buccaneers or the Black Falcons. They began wearing squadron baseball caps.

With the crew chiefs, the general practitioners of the maintenance staffs, this sense of identity was further reinforced. Where before they had worked on any jet in the wing, now they were assigned airplanes of their very own. They painted their names on the sides, just as pilots did. And all of a sudden, a twenty-three-year-old buck sergeant making $15,000 a year was in charge—yes, in charge—of a $27-million jet.

"It was exactly what we needed," remembers Sergeant Tony M. Brunner, a young F-15 crew chief at Nellis. "It makes you feel important to be in charge of something. There's got to be more to what we do here than a paycheck."

The crew chiefs took to their new responsibilities with a passion, doing whatever was necessary to make their jets the best. They went everywhere with them—on deployments, through inspections, to the wash racks. And they kept a sharp eye on the technicians—in military parlance, "kicking ass and taking names." Excellence became an obsession. When Creech went to visit some crew chiefs to find out how they liked the new arrangement, a sergeant summed it up nicely. "General," he said, "when was the last time you washed a rental car?"

The pilots couldn't help but notice the change in attitude. "Crew chiefs now come in sometimes on days off to buff up the planes," says Lieutenant Colonel Paul V. Hester, a former F-15 squadron commander at Langley. "When we get back from a sortie, they are standing at attention, saluting, holding the forms. That's not anything they're directed to do. That's pride in their airplanes. They want us to feel that pride when we fly."

It was not long before a strong camaraderie grew up between pilots and their crew chiefs. They talked electronics, they talked football, and they went drinking together after work. At the same time, squadrons began to build strong identities. Squadron colors were painted once again on the tail wings of aircraft, a time-honored tradition that had been outlawed under centralization. And pretty soon one squadron was working overtime to beat the other two squadrons in a wing, on everything from pilot performance to quality of maintenance.

What Creech did best, perhaps, was to remind even the lowest-level employees that their jobs were directly tied into TAC's central mission: flying and fighting. Wing commanders were ordered to resume active flying, and to emphasize the point, they were encouraged to wear flight suits when visiting Langley. For their part, squadron maintenance officers were routinely summoned to headquarters for three days of classroom work and inspiration from the top brass.

"We didn't send captains in to brief them," recalls General Jerry Rogers, Creech's logistics chief. "We did it ourselves. And on the third day, General Creech himself came in and spent half a day with them. They had to figure that if he does that, then he thinks maintaining airplanes is pretty important."

TAC's new spirit was soon reflected in the statistics. In Creech's first year as TAC's commander, the sortie rate shot up 11 percent, and another 11 percent in the second year. By 1980, the average fighter was in the air twenty-four hours a month, up from seventeen in 1978. Some 60 percent of the planes were now rated mission capable, up from half.

Creech, however, was just beginning to decentralize his command and improve the sortie rate. Moving beyond maintenance, there was also the question of the sorties themselves—how they were planned and scheduled. In the past, a handful of officers at wing headquarters had plotted schedules out in detail, squadron by squadron, a year at a time—16,000 sorties. Each squadron was given not only its quota, but also detailed instructions on how and when the sorties should be run.

In Creech's decentralized TAC, squadron commanders were given a sortie goal and set free to design their own flying schedules. And they were given some added incentive to meet their targets: if a squadron met its monthly goal early, Creech decreed, then the entire squadron, from pilots to maintenance techs, could take an extra three-day weekend.

Mind you, meeting these goals wasn't easy. These were highly sophisticated jets with hundreds of components that often require repair or replacement. And the training hops were no snaps for fliers, either. An F-16 pilot, for instance, had to master precision bombing, air-to-air combat with complicated missiles systems, and the delicate maneuvers required for tactical nuclear strikes, should they ever be required. Still, the incentive plan worked splendidly. Virtually every squadron in TAC now averages ten extra three-day weekends a year.

By the early 1980s, the TAC turnaround was attracting plenty of attention at the Pentagon. "There were people who would say, 'You're fudging the numbers. It looks too good,'" General Rogers recalls. The pattern was repeated many times: they'd try something and gather enough evidence that it worked. Then, to make it official policy, they'd have to write a regulation and send it to the Pentagon for approval. "That was a vehicle for endless bickering about details," Creech recalls. "There was a good bit of hostility and foot-dragging." But with the help of the successive air-force chiefs of staff, Creech most often prevailed. And, slowly, the converts to decentralization grew in number.

Creech and Rogers weren't shy about inviting Pentagon officials to see their new program in action. At one important outing in 1980, for instance, they took members of the Pentagon's vaunted Program Analysis and Evaluation Office (PA&E)—prime proponents of centralization—along on the first training deployment of F-15s to Europe. Eighteen fighters screamed into Bremgarten, a Luftwaffe base in southwest Germany, and four hours later all of them were loaded for combat. The next day, those same jets flew seventy-five sorties, nearly four apiece.

"Under the old system, we couldn't have dreamed of that kind of launch rate," says Rogers. "The PA&E folks had been very suspicious of our statistics, but that made believers of them. They went back and became evangelists for us in budget battles and such. It was really a watershed."

By this time, of course, centralization was under attack everywhere, as newer management theories began to emphasize motivation, competition, delegation, and employee ownership—all concepts Creech had used. And as stories began to surface about $600 toilet seats and $200 wrenches—the stuff of centralized procurement—the Pentagon searched to demonstrate that it was changing with the times. Creech's decentralization efforts became part of the official program. And the general found there was plenty more decentralizing to do.

He started with spare parts. An F-15 crew chief who needed a new tire for his jet, as an example, at that time had to phone in his request to the base warehouse and wait hours for delivery. Moving a part through the system required 243 entries on thirteen forms, involving twenty-two people and sixteen manhours for administration and record keeping. It was cumbersome, frustrating, and worst of all, slow.

"We had lost focus on why we existed—to support aircraft and the maintenance guys," says Colonel Donald W. Hamilton, TAC's director of supply at Langley. "We'd grown too bureaucratic."

In 1981, Creech decided to break up the warehouse system and move aircraft parts from the storage areas at the rear of the base right up to flight line. Not that there was always a convenient place for parts stores big enough to stock 10,000 different items. But with scraps of wood and leftover cans of paint and underutilized shelving, folks made do.

What serious money Creech had, he spent for minicomputers that let crew chiefs and their technicians know exactly what parts were available, and let supply specialists know what parts needed to be reordered. Now, all a crew chief had to do was climb off a jet and walk a few yards to a terminal to find out if a part was available. A push of a button ordered the part to be set aside. Then it was only a short walk down to the parts store with a simplified order form to have the part in hand. More often than not, it was waiting on the counter by the time he arrived. Total time lapsed: about fifteen minutes. Today it's down to eight.

At the same time, Creech mounted a crusade he considered equally critical to the rebuilding of TAC. On the theory that quality begets quality, he ordered a top-to-bottom sprucing up of every TAC facility, ranging from airplane hangars to barracks to mess halls. Once the Reagan defense dollars began to flow, that crusade took on a momentum of its own. But long before, Creech had begun by ordering that nearly everything within his domain receive a fresh coat of paint, from airplanes to cars to buildings. Nothing was spared. TAC even went so far as to paint the backs of stop signs.

"I could paint all of TAC for the price of one F-15," he says. "My philosophy is that if equipment is shabby looking, it affects your pride in your organization and your performance. You can't preach to a young man that an airplane can be shabby on the outside but has to be spic-and-span on the inside. You either have a climate of professionalism, or one of deterioration and decay. You can't segment it. Only on TV do you have these Black Sheep squadrons. Good outfits look sharp and act sharp. The great pilots—the Chuck Yeagers—are not sloppy people."

Fresh paint gave way to murals and lounges and comfortable furniture in flight-line facilities, and then to new barracks complexes with carpeted rooms and semiprivate baths. And while pilots had formation flybys to show their stuff to the public and the brass, squadron vehicle fleets held annual "roll-bys" displaying their gleaming trucks and vans.

It was all part of General Creech's emphasis on respect and recognition for his people. "Pride is the fuel of human accomplishment," he preached to his command. And competition was the spark plug. To drive home the point, annual awards banquets, complete with citations and trophies, were held at every wing, to recognize the year's best maintenance and supply specialists.

By the time General Creech left TAC, 85 percent of his airplanes were rated as mission capable, and jets were averaging twenty-one sorties a month, with twenty-nine hours in the air. In wartime, TAC was capable of launching 6,000 sorties a day, double what it had been when he arrived at Langley. In peacetime, the crash rate had dropped from one for every 13,000 flying hours to one for every 50,000—and crashes traced to faulty maintenance nearly vanished.

TAC, under Creech, had gone from the air force's worst command to its best. For much of the time, it had been a battle, and heads had rolled. The lazy and the incompetent, who had found numerous hiding places in a centralized structure, were smoked out when maintenance operations moved to the flight line and squadrons were held accountable for their performance. Some had to leave. But many more decided to stay. In 1983, two-thirds of the first-term mechanics decided to reenlist, or nearly double the rate of 1977, the year before Creech took command. Second-termer retention rates went from 68 percent to 85 percent over the same period. And some of the older technicians found they liked Creech's program so much that they recalled retirement papers to see it through.

THE WORLD ACCORDING TO CREECH

Some practical business management advice from the general who tamed the Pentagon.

INC: What's the most important management lesson for business that you take away from your experience with the air force?

CREECH: What we proved at the Tactical Air Command is that some organizational approaches stifle initiative and motivation while others nurture it. In the final analysis, it boils down to productivity, and to improve it, you have to create more drive and enthusiasm—a turned-on team. In that context, American business has not been well served by the management theories of the 1960s and 1970s that taught of the tremendous virtues of consolidation and centralization. It wasn't only the Defense Department that was bitten by that bug. Most of our companies, large and small, have those theories insinuated into their warp and weave to one degree or another.

INC: How does that manifest itself most commonly?

CREECH: Well, the most common phenomenon is for a manager who has two operations doing similar things to conclude that if he consolidates them, he'll save manpower and some cost. It's a given that it is wise to consolidate wherever possible.

INC: There is a germ of truth to that, isn't there?

CREECH: There is a germ of truth, but what happens is that managers take it to a ridiculous extreme. I often ask people how they would like it if there were one airline in this country. By the theory of centralization, it would be very efficient. How efficient? Just ask anyone who flies on Aeroflot, the Soviet airline. The problem with consolidation is that, while it can yield some immediate and tangible savings, it has indirect and negative effects on people—on morale, motivation, enthusiasm, creativity. Additionally, if you consolidate too much, you lose your ability to make meaningful and objective comparisons between similar operations. How efficient is your airline? Well, you'll only know if there are two airlines. And with a little competition thrown in, hopefully the people who work at the airline that is less productive will face up to that fact and face up to the need to try harder.

INC: A chief executive of a smaller company, listening to you just there, might say, "Oh, that's interesting, General, but you're talking about TWA or General Motors or something on that scale. But I have only forty people here."

CREECH: In most cases, the urge to consolidate is driven by the urge to centralize, which has nothing to do, really, with bigness. It's an attitude toward management, and it exists in large companies and small ones. The theory of centralization says that there are certain kinds of decisions that have to be made up high, because that's the only place they can be made in an intelligent fashion. And to facilitate that, they like to have lots of rules and regulations and stipulations to govern people's behavior. Meanwhile, all decisions gravitate upward. What I was able to prove at TAC is that, within certain general guidelines and goals, you *can* give people real authority down below—give them some breathing room to make their own decisions. Rather than a tightfisted operation where one person is in charge—which is what you find in a lot of small companies—you can have a decentralized organization in which there are many leaders charged with achieving your goals.

INC: Then the manager says to you, "Look, General, if I decentralize and give authority and responsibility down below, some percentage of those people are going to wind up being inappropriate, and some are going to screw up. There will be customers who are mad and profits that are frittered away and expenses that are going to get out of control and sales that will be lost. It's just inevitable." What do you say? Isn't it true that those things will happen?

CREECH: Some of those things happen the way things are now—and fewer will happen if you do it the other way. Remember, you're talking about greater productivity, greater loyalty—conveniently, the centralizers like to forget about that. And even in a decentralized organization, the CEO has to keep track of how well people are doing, so that nobody can make such fantastic mistakes that it dooms the whole corporation. Oh, sure, once you start delegating authority and hold people accountable whom you didn't previously hold accountable, there will be more of an attrition rate. And what is the moral of that? It's that incompetence finds it easy to flourish in centralized organizations, because it's all so communized and homogenized that you cannot sort out the real performers from the nonperformers.

INC: Can you take decentralization too far?

CREECH: I suppose there will always be some people in any organization who are going to take it too far. And in those cases, you have to guard against the temptation to pull that authority back up and say, "Well, I can't trust any of these folks. I'll handle it all up here." That's a major part of what causes centralization in the first place.

INC: Are there any other pitfalls to watch out for?

CREECH: Probably the most common is that managers don't give themselves the tools with which to track and view objectively how people are performing below. You need a way to know if the barn's on fire *before* it's in ashes. And in business, I've found that too many managers are still watching P&Ls or growth curves, which don't necessarily give them good indications of where their systems are breaking down, where productivity is lagging. When the bottom-line numbers finally come in and they are disheartening, managers don't have answers as to why it all happened. And so, again, the instinct is to centralize across the board, to set down regulations, to try to micromanage everything from the top.

INC: One of the fashionable new ideas is to delegate to an ad hoc team of people from different departments the responsibility for solving a problem or creating a new product line—all this as a way of getting around some of the problems you've pointed out with a highly centralized organization.

CREECH: Well, the problem with much of that matrix management is that it gives people responsibility without giving them real authority. And without the authority, most people won't really accept that sense of responsibility—and you really can't blame them.

INC: Can you be more specific?

CREECH: Well, in most of these situations, you have a basic vertical management structure that is common to most centralized organizations. You'll have, as an example, a chief engineer, and all the engineers in the company will work under him. And a vice-president for marketing with all the marketing people under him. Suddenly, there is a specific job to be done, a project, and some number of engineers and marketing specialists are assigned to that project, along with people from manufacturing and accounting and whatever. That's matrix management. But who is in charge? You can try to hold everybody on the team accountable, but that's not the way human behavior works. You have to hold a few key people accountable.

INC: Presumably, you hold the project manager accountable.

CREECH: Well, I have some experience with that. Some years ago, I commanded the air force's electronics-systems division in Boston, where we bought about $5 billion worth of electronics each year, ranging from the Airborne Warning and Control System aircraft—the AWAC—all the way down to telephones and switchboards. We had lots of projects with lots of corporations. And occasionally, a program would get in deep trouble, and we would send in a team to find out what was wrong. Nine times out of ten, we found that it was a highly centralized and highly matrixed organization in which there was no real sense of accountability or authority. I remember one case in which a major corporation had about 900 employees working on a major program, and there were exactly nine people who reported to the project manager in a hire-and-fire context. All the rest were assigned to him in a matrix context, and they reported to their functional chieftains—the chief electrical engineer or the chief computer programmer and so forth. And the project manager ultimately wasn't in charge of any of them. And so what the project manager had to do was form a coalition. Coalitions sometimes work, but they're not long on accountability, because it's too easy in a coalition to point fingers at the other guy.

INC: So what's the alternative?

CREECH: The answer is to keep an engineering department, for example, to handle some of the housekeeping chores, to worry about whether all the engineers in the organization have the know-how and the background the company needs. But once you form a mission or a task force, you've given the authority to the project manager to evaluate the performance of those engineers, distribute bonuses, assign work load, and even fire somebody.

INC: There was a time, of course, when matrixing was a hot management idea, just as centralization was hot. Now, maybe decentralization is the buzzword. Isn't this just a case of the pendulum swinging back and forth? Wasn't centralization a good idea in its time?

CREECH: I don't think it was ever a terribly good idea, although in certain settings I'd agree that a certain amount of centralization is useful. It's just that it became almost a religion. It was overdone—and still is grossly overdone.

INC: And you find that is true in entrepreneurial settings as well as in large corporations?

CREECH: Oh, I find it very common among founders or small groups of founders. They grow their companies to a certain size by operating as one-man bands, controlling authority and making all key decisions, but beyond that they begin to feel very uncomfortable. Founders feel as if they are losing control. And then one of two things happens. Either they consciously or unconsciously make decisions that stifle growth, or they try to use their old management techniques long after they have become ineffective, so the companies reach a point where they can't survive under that kind of stifling centralized management. In my judgment, you can't micromanage a company as small as 100 or 200 people. Long before that, you have to start giving some real authority to the people below you.

INC: Would it be correct to say that if you don't start that early, you probably will never do it?

CREECH: I learned a long time ago that you have to not let the perfect be the enemy of the good. The fact is that it is never too late to change, because in any organization, there are lots of people just waiting for you to give them some responsibility, some sense of ownership, something they can take personal pride in. And it's amazing how, once you take those first steps, suddenly a thousand flowers bloom, and the organization takes off in ways that nobody could have predicted.

TAC commanding officers thrived under the new system. Of the 148 wing commanders who served under Creech, only about 3 percent were relieved for poor performance—fewer than under any of Creech's three predecessors. "It was not a ruthless system," Creech emphasizes. "You just don't get results by going around chopping people's heads off."

Even in retirement, Creech's philosophy sets the tone for air-force management. General Larry D. Welch, now the air-force chief of staff, served in staff positions under Creech. He later went on to head up the

Strategic Air Command, the nation's nuclear strike force, where decentralization also became a battle cry.

Even the Pentagon has got the religion. A recent Pentagon directive gives commanders new authority to abolish regulations, streamline procedures, and do whatever they think best to enhance mission accomplishment. "People doing the job day in and day out know better how to do it than some guy who is sitting behind a desk," asserts William H. Taft IV, deputy secretary of defense.

As for Creech, now fifty-nine, he continues to spread the gospel to leaders of industry and government as a lecturer, consultant, and corporate board member.

In his travels, Creech remarks how common it is for executives to think of decentralization and delegation as loss of control and abdication of command. If anything, he says, just the opposite is true: "When I left TAC, I had more control over it than my predecessors. I'd created leaders and helpers at all those various levels. Without that kind of network below you, you're a leader in name only.

"It's not really that hard to run a large organization," the general explains. "You just have to think small about how to achieve your goals. There's a very finite limit to how much leadership you can exercise at the very top. You can't micromanage—people resent that. Things are achieved by individuals, by collections of twos and fives and twenties, not collections of 115,000. And that's as true in industry as it is in the military."

—JAY FINEGAN

MAY THE
FORCE BE
WITH YOU

Nobody expected much from Gary Aronson, and he didn't surprise anyone. After dropping out of college before the second semester of his freshman year, he knocked around awhile, eventually winding up as manager of a Kentucky Fried Chicken franchise. In 1983, he switched jobs again, this time moving to Au Bon Pain Co., a Boston-based fast-food chain specializing in fancy coffees, croissants, and spotty customer service. That fact notwithstanding, Aronson viewed it as a different kind of company, or so he told himself, perhaps as a way of justifying his cut in pay from $410 to $280 a week. Different Au Bon Pain may have been, but three years later, Aronson was still making a meager $26,000 a year, with which he supported his wife and two children.

At thirty, Aronson was frustrated, bored, and wondering why he persisted in the food-service business. Fast-food companies don't want managers, he thought; they want trained dogs who will go through their routines and keep their mouths shut. Aronson himself had a hard time keeping his shut. He was known in the company for being "difficult" and "opinionated"—a whiner and a complainer. He didn't care. "My heart wasn't in it anymore," he recalls. "I had the feeling of being in a dead-end job. I thought if I was lucky, I might earn $3,000 more in five years." This was assuming, of course, that he didn't get fired, a distinct possibility. So he put in his forty-five hours a week and tried to figure out what he was going to do next.

Today, Gary Aronson is still in the food-service business, and still with Au Bon Pain, but he no longer works forty-five hours a week. Three mornings a week, you can find him in his store at 3:15, and on other days he's there from 6:00 A.M. until the store closes at 7:00 P.M. He works weekends, too, putting in a total of sixty-five to eighty hours each week, making sure that the food is fresh, the place is clean, and the customers are satisfied. His face looks weary these days, but he is not complaining. He's too busy thinking up ways to bring in more customers, sell more food, and make the whole operation run more smoothly. "This is the first time in my life I've been treated like a professional," he says.

It's also the first time he's been *paid* like a professional. If he continues at his present rate, he will make at least $80,000 this year. Suddenly he and his wife, Donna, also an employee, are the talk of the company. The betting is that they will be the first pair of Au Bon Pain shopkeepers to arrive at a managers' meeting in a chauffeur-driven limousine.

Companies have traditionally viewed compensation in a fairly narrow context—as just one of the many levers available to influence the direction of a business. Of all the factors that affect a company's performance, compensation is seldom listed among the most important. If the company fails (or succeeds), the owners will usually blame (or credit) the product or the strategy, the financing or the timing. Seldom will they say that the crucial difference between success and failure is the way they structure the system for paying their employees.

And, in some cases, that may be true. After all, many companies succeed with a compensation system that's little different from their competitors', while those that fail usually have a multitude of other problems. And yet it is a fact that a company with an extraordinary record of performance almost always has an extraordinary compensation plan as well. In most cases, it has been installed by the founder, who had a vision of the kind of company he or she wanted, and an acute understanding of the kind of reward system that would inspire employees to create it. Then there are the handful of companies such as Au Bon Pain, which grope their way through a maze of obstacles before finally hitting on a compensation structure that makes most of the other problems go away.

The truth is that Ron Shaich (pronounced *shake*) had not given much thought to the issue before he became president of Au Bon Pain in 1982. He was only twenty-eight years old at the time, with limited experience in business. As a student at Clark University, in Worcester, Massachusetts, he had founded and managed a nonprofit campus convenience store in competition with a local Store 24. He had been so successful, and had had so much fun, that he decided to get his MBA, graduating from Harvard Business School in 1978. Thereafter, he worked briefly for a national chain of cookie stores, did some grass-roots political organizing, and dabbled in the world of campaign consulting. But his idealism soon led him back to business. "In politics, you build organizations and then tear them down," he says. Hoping to build something more permanent, he moved to Boston in 1981 and opened a cookie store on a busy downtown street.

The cookie store brought him into contact with Louis Kane, a fifty-year-old Boston businessman who had acquired Au Bon Pain in 1978 from a French oven manufacturer. Shaich was interested in buying croissants to sell in his store, but Kane had other things on his mind. His company was in serious trouble, and he did not know how to save it. His expertise lay in real estate, not food service. Impressed with Shaich, Kane suggested a deal: the two would merge their companies, with Shaich becoming a partner, president, and chief of internal operations. Kane would focus on external issues, selecting expansion sites and arranging financing. Shaich agreed.

At the time, Au Bon Pain consisted of three bakery-cafés located on prime Boston real estate and staffed by its own French bakers. It was an expensive operation, and it was losing money at a rapid clip. Beyond that, the company lacked any sense of purpose or direction. Customers were treated carelessly, as if they were intruders, and employee turnover was high, even for a fast-food operation. The situation called for dramatic action. In short order, the new management team got rid of the in-store bakers, eliminated the wholesale side of the business, and brought in Shaich's father, a New Jersey accountant, to design some financial controls. Then they turned to the stores themselves, replacing the old managers with new ones, whom they paid the going rate—about $18,000 per year.

But Shaich was not interested in building just another fast-food business. "I wanted to create a truly better food-service company," he says. Good food—"food you wanted to eat"—was a given, as was making money. He dreamed of a company built around a general, and passionate, concern for its customers. That, he realized, demanded a certain type of employee, "people who did things not because the boss was looking but because they really cared." In order to attract those people, he knew he had to create a different type of environment. "We didn't want to accept the low standards of the rest of the food industry," he says. "We wanted to show the big guys—Pepsi and McDonald's and Sara Lee—that the conventional ways of treating people were not the only ways. We felt we could do better. . . . I wanted an organization where *I'd* want to work."

With that goal in mind, Shaich began to tinker with the compensation system, setting up a program in which managers could earn monthly bonuses for generating sales above a budgeted level, provided the store stayed within bounds on its food and labor costs. It was an idea he borrowed from the famous business-school case study of Lincoln Electric Co., and it seemed like a surefire method of pointing managers in the right direction, thereby reducing the pressures on himself and the rest of the management system as the company grew.

And grow the company did between 1982 and 1984. As stores increased their volume, Au Bon Pain began adding units. Most weeks, Shaich worked ninety hours, spending the bulk of it in the stores, devising systems to handle the growth. Everywhere he went, he carried a message to employees—that growth, if properly managed, would create opportunities for those who took care of customers. "I did everything I could to make people feel that they wanted to be here," he says.

But growth also put strains on the company, strains that promised to get worse with time. For one thing, the Massachusetts labor market was getting tighter and tighter, making it more difficult to find new managers and crew. That situation created opportunities for employees, but dangers for the company. "We were promoting people left and right," says Shaich, "sometimes before they were ready."

By the beginning of 1984, the company had fourteen stores, generating annual revenues of more than $6 million, but the company's management resources were stretched perilously thin. The game plan, moreover, called for opening ten to fifteen new units in the next year and, at the same time, moving into the lunch market with a new line of soups and sandwiches. Shaich himself found that he no longer had time to give store managers the support they expected. So in April he brought in a regional manager from McDonald's Corp. as the vice-president of operations. "We wanted to give the stores the best leadership we could find," Shaich says.

It soon became apparent, however, that the addition of another top manager was not going to solve all the problems, many of which seemed to be related to the compensation plan Shaich had installed so optimistically in 1982. It wasn't working. In the atmosphere of constant change and growth, the company could not come up with meaningful budget targets for managers. Beyond that, the systems for recording operating results were overloaded, and people were constantly being moved before their actual numbers came in. As a result, the compensation plan had lost its integrity. Managers realized that their bonuses really depended not on their performance, but on Shaich's perception of it. Not that he was stingy. In the absence of clear guidelines, he tended to give something to everybody, but on such a discretionary basis that the system became known as "pennies from heaven."

To make matters worse, the new vice-president was busily destroying whatever lingering credibility the compensation system had. To fill the slots in the new stores, he hired new managers, many of them from McDonald's, at salaries $6,000 or $7,000 above those of the old managers. The latter were understandably furious, and they told Shaich so; a few even left. But he didn't intervene. "I felt I needed to give the guy the freedom to do his job." Unfortunately, it soon became clear that the guy wasn't doing his job very well, at least when it came to providing support for store managers, whose morale continued to plummet. "He managed downward," says Shaich. "He expected their loyalty but didn't feel he had to earn it. And he showed no interest in taking care of them as people."

By the end of 1984, Shaich began to have the feeling that the company was coming apart at the seams. Customer complaints were increasing, and the turnover problem was growing. Hard as it was to recruit new employees, the average stay had dwindled from one year to a mere seven months. The company also lacked adequate operating standards—governing, say, where to keep the lettuce for sandwiches. Per-unit operating profits, meanwhile, were deteriorating badly, even as sales continued to rise, and some of the worst performers were the new managers brought in by the vice-president of operations.

"Everywhere I looked," Shaich says, "there was another mess to clean up." He was frustrated, but no more so than his managers. They told him bluntly that they didn't trust the company anymore. Finally, in June 1985, Shaich did what he had to do, firing the VP of operations, putting the brake on expansion, and calling his father back to help rebuild the company. Once again, he took charge of operations—and tried to figure out where he had gone wrong.

* * *

"Things were worse than they had ever been," Shaich says, and he had a point, although on paper the company looked just fine. With thirty-one units from New Hampshire to Texas, it had annual revenues of $15 million and was still highly profitable. There was plenty of cash available, thanks to the recent sale of a franchise and Kane's success in raising $11.7 million from private sources. Perhaps most important, Au Bon Pain had established a clear identity for itself in the market. With a sandwich menu featuring tarragon chicken and ham with Brie, it could never be mistaken for another burger chain.

But all that was in jeopardy, Shaich realized, thanks to rising turnover, sinking morale, and operational chaos. He moved quickly to reverse the trend. Hoping to boost the managers' spirits, he raised the salaries of the capable ones and returned to the old policy of promoting from within. To aid the recruitment of crew members, he hiked starting wages 50¢ above those of competitors and began giving free televisions to employees who brought in new recruits. Those new people who stayed got college-scholarship assistance. And in case any managers failed to get the message, Shaich sent them all a memo telling them to holler whenever they had to work more than fifty-five hours a week. More than once, they did, and he dropped everything to go lend a hand.

But important as these measures were, they did not address the company's underlying problems, as Shaich was well aware. Somehow he had to regain the confidence of the people who judged the business every day: its customers. Again, he turned his attention to developing a compensation system that would keep managers focused on the all-important goal of satisfying the customer, but he found that he scarcely knew where to begin. The bonus system had been a dismal failure. What else was there? Looking for ideas, Shaich called a professor he knew at Harvard Business School, who put him in touch with a young colleague by the name of Len Schlesinger.

Schlesinger was a budding expert in the field of organizational behavior. He and Shaich met once, and again, and Schlesinger spent a few days at the company, talking with employees. Shaich liked him. "Len was somebody I could talk to about the business," he says, "and he really seemed to care." So Schlesinger was invited to join the company as a partner and executive vice-president.

For Schlesinger, accepting the offer meant giving up the likelihood of tenure at Harvard, not to mention a lucrative consulting business, but Shaich was persuasive. It was an opportunity, he said, "to build a company—to create a system you *care* about." Schlesinger says that, in the end, his decision came down to one question: "Was I willing to believe my own bullshit?" The answer was yes.

His first job was to help the company come up with a new compensation system. After the "pennies from heaven" fiasco, Shaich wanted a program that would be simple to explain, easy to sell, attractive vis-à-vis competitors, and equitable within the company. It also had to encourage managers to focus on customer satisfaction.

Schlesinger began by assembling a compensation committee from among the company's managers. Together they explored the options. "People were tired of inside deals," he recalls. "So we wanted something that was very mechanistic, something we could defend." In the end, they came up with a simple system under which managers would be paid according to their level of responsibility and the sales activity of their stores.

Under the plan, every store's general manager would earn a base salary of $375 a week. Salaries would then rise as weekly volumes increased, up to $633.75 a week at the highest-volume store. "We were willing to pay more for the high-volume store," says Shaich, "because it was worth more to the company."

Managers responded enthusiastically to the new system, but—unfortunately—it did not accomplish what it was intended to do. Very quickly, managers figured out the fastest way to make more money was to be assigned to a higher-volume store. "The guy we wanted to be focused and caring was spending a lot of his time lobbying for a transfer," says Shaich. "What's more, we *needed* to move them through the system, so they usually got their way." As a result, the new system had minimal impact on the actual performance of the stores.

The situation was further aggravated by continued turnover among crew members, which was running 40 percent to 45 percent in the summer and fall of 1985, despite the fact that the company paid hourly workers a premium wage. Nothing they did succeeded in stemming the tide. "We'd run big help-wanted ads," says Shaich, "and we'd get maybe two or three replies for an opening." Often the entire corporate staff—some fifty strong—had to help make sandwiches and serve customers at lunchtime. And there was no end in sight.

"The pressure was really on," Shaich recalls. "I remember thinking, 'Why aren't we located in the Southwest? Why is all this happening to us?'"

In October 1985, Shaich and Schlesinger took a break from the crisis to fly down to Orlando for the annual meeting of the Multi Unit Food Service Operators. Both of them felt battered and weary. They could take some solace in spending a few days with people who were struggling with similar problems, but that didn't help them forget their own. During one of the afternoon sessions, Shaich began doodling on a piece of paper, listing all the company's failings. Soon the page was filled with loops and arrows. The analysis went something like this:

It was hard for managers to find quality recruits, and when they did, there was no time to train them. The result was substandard work. Managers operated on the assumption that recruits wouldn't stay long, and they usually were right. When employees left, managers filled in at the counters, thereby ceasing to be managers. Eventually, they burned out. But though the system kept most managers from succeeding, they were promoted to other stores anyway—where the cycle repeated itself.

And that's exactly what it was, Shaich and Schlesinger agreed: a cycle of failure. Suddenly, 1,000 miles from home, the nature of their troubles seemed crystal clear.

It was a revelation, albeit a rather depressing one. That evening, however, they had a revelation of a different sort. They were having dinner with Ed Eynon, then vice-president for human resources for a company called Golden Corral Corp., headquartered in Raleigh, North Carolina. A chain of 435 steak houses, Golden Corral had a reputation as an unusual food-service operation. Listening to Eynon, Shaich and Schlesinger quickly found out why.

Several years back, Eynon said, the company had come up with its own solution to the challenge of running a restaurant chain: it had given unit managers a piece of the action. In addition to a modest base salary of $16,000, a typical manager owned 20 percent to 30 percent of his restaurant. Some wound up earning $100,000 a year or more; none required much supervision; and turnover among hourly workers had been cut in half. Shaich and Schlesinger could hardly believe their ears. Says Eynon, "I felt like I was bringing water to thirsty men in the desert."

Quenched though they were, they doubted such a system could work in Boston. Nevertheless, the conversation did offer hope that there might be a solution to their problems, and they returned home determined to break the cycle of failure once and for all.

During the next few months, the two inundated the company with resolutions, exhortations, and memos. Schlesinger advocated a coordinated program to attract high-quality people, with clear incentives, better training, and more timely performance reviews. Shaich followed with proposals for a $1 increase in hourly pay; time off to participate in comprehensive training; and additional bonuses to crew members who stayed on board.

As time went along, however, they began to develop nagging doubts that more bells and whistles would do the trick. Burger King, they heard, had tried similar ploys, to no avail. The cycle seemed to have a life of its own, impervious to adjustments and modifications. Au Bon Pain's own director of planning had to confess at one point that he would have difficulty recommending the place to his brother. On reflection, Shaich himself realized that he could not conceive of working as a store manager at Au Bon Pain—not under the current system.

But the gravity of the situation did not really come home to him until January 1986. One day, he was visiting a Boston-area store, and—before he had a chance to identify himself—a customer came in and ordered a turkey-and-Brie sandwich on a croissant. The employee behind the counter rang up the order, then realized that the store was out of croissants. Fine, the customer said, make it with another kind of bread. That wasn't possible, the employee said; the other bread could only be sold in whole loaves. The manager appeared and asked what the problem was. The employee explained. Well, said the manager to the customer, we can give you your money back. A disappointed customer left the store empty-handed.

There you had it in a nutshell, Shaich thought. The company had gotten so far away from its purpose that customers were being turned away to avoid slicing up a loaf of bread. All Shaich's efforts to develop operating standards had succeeded only in rendering store managers unable to think for themselves. They followed policies and procedures instead of common sense.

New policies and procedures were not the answer. (Who cared if the lettuce was on the left side of the counter instead of the right?) Nor were more stringent appraisal systems or better policing, piecemeal incentives or bigger bonuses. He could provide his staff with all those things, and the customer would *still* leave the store disappointed, without his turkey-and-Brie sandwich.

At last he saw the problem clearly. It was a waste of time to try to tinker with the system. A year from now, he and his district managers would still be baby-sitting store managers, solving the problems that they seemed incapable of solving themselves. Somehow, the system had to be turned around 180 degrees. Store managers had to want to solve their own problems. They had to be able to decide for themselves that a satisfied customer was worth a couple of slices of bread.

"We had to turn assembly-line foremen into shopkeepers," says Shaich.

Says Schlesinger, "We had to bust the system wide open."

The revolution began in early 1986. Schlesinger and Shaich read everything they could find about the innovative management techniques of successful food-service companies—Chick-fil-A Inc., in Atlanta, for example, and Luby's Cafeterias Inc., in San Antonio. They also hired a Lincoln, Nebraska, consulting firm, Selection Research Inc., to help in their search. Then, in April, they flew to California to visit a company called Harman Management Corp., based in Los Altos, that had the distinction of being the first Kentucky Fried Chicken franchisee in the United States.

Executives of both Golden Corral and Selection Research had mentioned Harman as a model of effective management, but Shaich and Schlesinger were skeptical as they pulled into the company's parking lot. They already had doubts about applying to Au Bon Pain the techniques developed by a company operating in such places as Utah and Colorado. When they saw Harman's cinder-block office, their hearts sank. It looked more like a chiropractor's office than the headquarters of their industry's most innovative leader. Inside, their skepticism mounted. There, in the lobby, was a copy of the company's yearbook. "It was incredibly hokey," recalls Schlesinger—filled with pictures of smiling Harman's employees and their families at company outings.

Then they sat down with Jackie Trujillo, Harman's vice-president of operations, and their skepticism began turning to wonder.

She told them that the company's 200-odd stores did, on average, 20 percent more volume than company-owned Kentucky Fried Chicken units. Turnover, she said, was not a problem, nor was supervision. Store managers were responsible for watching their own costs, recruiting their own crews, and making their units successful. How was this possible? Well, the managers—like those at Golden Corral—were owners, getting a salary of $18,000 to $20,000, with opportunities to earn a share of profits on top of that. What's more, they had the option to buy 30 percent to 40 percent of the stock in their stores. The company's role was to cheer them on with banquets, rankings, and awards.

Schlesinger was furiously taking notes. He and Shaich could not help but contrast the situation to their own. Harman's stock-purchase agreements with managers were three or four pages long; Au Bon Pain's directives to managers often ran to twenty pages. Au Bon Pain was spending $250,000 a year on help-wanted ads; Harman spent almost nothing. But perhaps the greatest contrast was between themselves and founder Leon W. "Pete" Harman, whom they met later that day. A homespun fellow in his sixties, he seemed to have all the time in the world. They spent an hour chatting leisurely, without a crisis or an interruption. He said lots of people came to see him, searching for solutions to the same kinds of problems. They listened, but they seldom followed his advice, which he found a little baffling. "You know, at a private company, you don't have to be greedy," he said. "You can share it with your good people, and it all comes back to you."

Schlesinger, the former Harvard professor, was impressed. "Here was a guy with maybe a high-school education, and he seemed to have it all figured out. It was the most humbling experience of my life."

That evening, they visited two of Harman's Kentucky Fried Chicken stores and several other fast-food outlets in the same neighborhoods. Again, they were struck by the contrast. At Harman's, if not elsewhere, the bathrooms sparkled, and the crew members were well dressed and upbeat. Indeed, one of the assistant managers tried to recruit them, saying how great it was to work there, and pointing out that the manager was making $100,000 a year. "You could feel it," Shaich says. "Everything we had been talking about was real."

Two weeks later, Shaich and Schlesinger were back on the road, this time heading to Raleigh, North Carolina, to visit Golden Corral. It was the same story all over again. There, managers worked as hard as their counterparts at Harman's, and the best of them had incomes to match. "The big difference between them and us," says Shaich, "was that they had adjusted the reward level to the point where it was worth all the pain."

By the time the pair returned from North Carolina, they had seen all the proof they needed. There were but two remaining questions: Would it work in Boston? And if so, how? Schlesinger spent two full weeks tinkering with profit-and-loss statements from individual stores. He tried to apply the profit-sharing formulas from Harman's but found that many of Au Bon Pain's stores had too wide a range of volume to produce meaningful incentives. Then it hit him: why not tie the store manager's incentive to "controllable" profits (that is, profit less rent and depreciation), instead of store profits? A manager, after all, could do nothing about his rent. But he *could* adjust his use of labor, shrinkage, and controllable expenses depending on the level of business he did. If the manager took care of his crew, used them when he needed them, and watched his other costs, the stores could become more efficient and profitable than ever. "Our basic premise," says Schlesinger, "was that it was a lot more important to control outputs than to control inputs." It all made sense, and—unlike Harman's system—it seemed equally applicable to low- and high-volume stores.

So they decided to put their plan to the test. The six-month trial period began on July 15, 1986, at two Au Bon Pain stores, selected because their managers were, at best, average performers. One store, managed by Brian McEvoy, was located in a Hartford office building. The other, in a shopping mall in Burlington, Massachusetts, was managed by Gary Aronson.

Schlesinger, who supervised the test, explained the rules to each of the managers. The company was, in effect, leasing the stores to them. It gave them goals for labor and food costs, but agreed to split the controllable profits on a 50–50 basis. They understood and went to work.

Almost at once, the stores began to change. Aronson got rid of one assistant manager to save on overhead, and hired his wife as a crew member. He and his remaining assistant began working longer hours, as many as eighty hours a week, and looking for ways to control costs and boost volume. They reorganized the store to increase its seating capacity; they developed wholesale and catering accounts; and they raised employees' wages. McEvoy took a different approach, holding his own hours to fifty-five hours a week, but increasing staffing during peak periods to assure prompt service. He also introduced a telephone express ordering service.

Schlesinger was amazed at the speed of the change. Overnight, managers began solving the problems they had previously dumped on the company. "We finally had a system that didn't accept excuses," Schlesinger says. "My role was helping them to build sales." Shaich was equally impressed when he paid a surprise visit to the Hartford store. The place was spotless. "I know when a store is running well," he says. "I could feel the difference. It was everything I had hoped it would be."

The numbers were just as exciting. Crew turnover at Aronson's store, for example, fell to almost nothing. Meanwhile, both stores were beating their targets by substantial margins. By the end of the six months, McEvoy had exceeded his sales goal by $74,000, and his controllable-profit goal by about $27,000. At that rate, he could expect to earn at least $55,000 a year. Aronson did even better: he was ahead by $54,000 on sales and around $45,000 on controllable profit—meaning he was earning close to $75,000 a year. "We were convinced," says Shaich.

The next step was easy. In January 1987, they began rolling the plan out to the rest of the company.

It is a Friday afternoon in April 1987, and Ron Shaich is sitting with Len Schlesinger in an office at the company's headquarters. A store manager named Jim Morgan walks in. Morgan, an effervescent fellow of twenty-six, has been with the company for four years, and right now he is in a hurry. The Boston Marathon is being run the next Monday. He just wants Shaich and Schlesinger to know that he'll be there at the finish line, selling croissants and beverages from his Au Bon Pain pushcart. Does he have the necessary vending permits? Oh, yeah, he took care of that himself. Will he need any help? No, no, he's convinced some friends to give him a hand. The bosses can relax. The situation is wired.

Perhaps nothing better illustrates how profoundly Au Bon Pain has changed in the past year. Time was when Shaich would have had to plead on bended knee to get a manager to take a pushcart to the Boston Marathon. Indeed, he had often pleaded with managers to take pushcarts to the Bayside Exposition Center south of Boston, but his entreaties went unheeded. These days, he doesn't give it a thought. Gary Aronson, who now manages a store in downtown Boston, has decided to cover Bayside. He expects to be there sixty to eighty days a year.

The new compensation system is working. It is already installed at ten of the forty company-owned stores, and those operated by manager/partners are outperforming the others by a wide margin. During the first three months under the new system, partner stores as a group ran 40 percent ahead of their profit goals, while the nonpartner stores were pretty much on target. So the company is going full speed ahead with plans to convert the remaining stores by year end. Meanwhile, experienced managers from other food-service companies have begun applying for jobs, and Schlesinger and Shaich are extending the concept to district managers and others.

To be sure, the system entails certain risks, especially for store managers. Each of them gets a base salary of $25,000 and a chance to win or lose. Even if the manager wins, and earns the monthly bonus, half of it (up to $7,500) goes into a reserve fund that is not paid out until his or her contract expires, thereby locking successful managers into their stores for the duration. "They're in the same position as company owners," says Shaich. "They can't just walk away." And like company owners, they have to solve their own problems, hire and fire their own people, set their own wage scale, cut their own deals. What they can't do is to compromise on food quality and customer service, which the company regularly monitors through in-store audits and visits by unidentified "mystery" shoppers. Aside from that, they're on their own.

Some managers will no doubt fail and have to be replaced. After all, the system is not for everyone. But for Au Bon Pain it is working so well that even Shaich finds the results hard to believe. The company projects sales of $35 million for 1987, and the stores have never run better, or with less support from headquarters. "We're out of the picture," he says. "It's a closed loop." The loop is so closed that he and his partners feel confident about letting the company grow at the rate of twelve new stores per year for the next few years.

Not that Shaich feels they have solved all the problems. The journey has been too long, with too many valleys and swamps, for him to believe it is finally over. But now, at last, Au Bon Pain meets his own test for a business. "This," he says, "is the kind of company I'd like to work for."

—BRUCE G. POSNER

I UNCHAINED
MY CHAIN
OF COMMAND

When I began my data processing service, the Thomas National Group, in 1968, I was determined to delegate authority. So I set up a management structure under which our managers reported to our vice-presidents, and our vice-presidents reported to an executive vice-president. The executive vice-president reported to the president, and the president then reported to me, the chairman.

All I had to do was sit back in my ivory tower and feel like a monarch whose kingdom is being run by others. I could get all the glory for the company's successes, and I didn't have to take the blame for any of its problems. The only trouble was, I felt less and less like the company was mine. I had no sense of achievement, the fire that a small company chairman needs to keep him going. What's worse, my people didn't have it either.

There's a right way and a wrong way to delegate authority, and in my company the vertical chain of command was definitely the wrong way. Today, now that we've restructured our management system, I'm exhilarated by my job. I'm able to plan for the company—to review personnel policies, to look into business opportunities, to discuss new products, and to work toward the public offering we hope to make in the next three years—without stepping on anyone's toes. I have time to do more creative work, and I enjoy my job a lot more. The same can be said, I think, for the seventy people who work for me.

For the first seven years of our company's growth, the vertical system worked pretty well. Between 1968 and 1975 growth was slow: it took us that long to reach $2.8 million in sales. But the advent of minicomputers made the services of data processing bureaus less necessary, and by the mid-seventies we began looking for a field in which to specialize. We developed a software program to help administer profit-sharing/thrift plans and another for processing of medical and dental claims.

The first of these, ImpleFacts, took off like a rocket. Eli Lilly, Polaroid, Xerox, Chemical Bank, and Colgate–Palmolive were among our first customers. Our sales have grown dramatically; they were over $8 million in the year that ended in February 1981.

But along with the growth came problems, and by the time our first program was ready for the market back in 1975, our people were overworked, cash flow was a headache, turnover was too high, and about 10 percent of our orders were being delayed.

The vertical management structure didn't allow us to deal efficiently with those problems. It didn't grant the vice-presidents enough authority or responsibility for their departments' successes or failures. No one was responsible for finding out what was causing delays, cash problems, or high turnover. And under the strict chain of command, I was inaccessible to everyone but the president, so I couldn't find out what was causing the problems, either. If I called a vice-president in for a discussion, I was stepping on the toes of his superiors, the executive vice-president and the president. A vice-president couldn't approach me with a problem without appearing disloyal to his bosses—and risking his job.

The trouble with the structure became clear to me one day in, of all places, the stock room. I casually asked one of the vice-presidents why a certain very talented programmer had quit. Practically in a whisper, he told me that an explosive situation was being created in his department by the policies his superior had dictated. I listened in amazement, not only at the policies he described, but also at the fact that he couldn't come to my office to tell me about them.

"Management," he told me, had refused the programmer's request for three days off, after the programmer had worked long and hard on a project, and had done it well. The programmers didn't even know who "management" was. What's worse, neither did I. When I tried to find out who was responsible for turning down the programmer's request, I discovered a set of rigid, rubber-stamp policies that enabled everyone to escape the blame for unpopular decisions.

Employees were not being treated fairly or with sensitivity. People were being good soldiers, following orders, playing the game according to the rules. The high degree of morale and motivation any small company needs to see it through a period of dynamic growth wasn't there. I was determined to see that the situation changed.

It took me several years to create the horizontal management structure that I finally implemented in mid-1979. I did a lot of thinking about what each of my managers was contributing to the company, and became convinced that no executive is good at everything. If 90 percent of a manager's effectiveness is in one area, he or she shouldn't have to stretch to do the other 10 percent.

Under our new structure, eight vice-presidents of our wholly owned subsidiary, Erisco, which administers benefits programs, report directly to me. Job descriptions were completely rewritten, to maximize each vice-president's talents. The vice-presidents of systems and operations were given full responsibility for profit and loss and for daily operations including scheduling. Each of them knows that when there's a delay, I'll be in his or her office asking why.

The vice-president of development for the ImpleFacts division, Charlie Hanlon, and the vice-president for marketing, Charlie Klein, no longer have to think about nickels and dimes. They're top planning and marketing people, and it's their job to bring in the business.

My second-in-command, Pat D'Amato, plays a role roughly equivalent to a president, but our vice-presidents still have direct access to me to discuss their problems. When I revamped our management structure, I made Pat part of the four-person staff that works directly under me in the parent company, Thomas National Group, to administer the Erisco subsidiary. Pat is best at putting a deal together for a customer so that the customer stays with us. He's a terrific marketeer. He also has an excellent feel for product development and is a great sales manager.

Under the old system, Pat had been responsible for the daily business—following up on problems such as arguments between employees and scheduling. He'd also been responsible for profit and loss, for examining the financial statements each month to see which jobs were most profitable, for discipline, and for firing people when necessary. These were all activities that took him away from what he loves to do and does best. Under the new system, those jobs have gone to the people who do them best.

The vice-presidents of the two divisions, ImpleFacts and ClaimFacts (our health-claims processing division), meet once a week. I read the minutes of those meetings and decide which problems I want to get involved in. As it turns out, I'm less and less involved in problems because the areas of responsibility are clearly—and *appropriately*—defined. Because people are doing what they do best, problems get solved quickly.

For example, there used to be a lot of animosity and jealousy between the technical staff and the marketing staff. The technical staff is made up of creative people who need a lot of freedom. The marketing people too often tried to get the programmers to do things their way, and on their schedule. Our vice-president of systems for ClaimFacts, Tony Bellomo, has suggested and implemented changes in working conditions for the programmers that have all but eliminated that hostility. Bellomo started at the company as a programmer, and he helped me realize that programmers are like artists; they can't be endlessly driven to produce.

We put all the programmers under Bellomo in a new office where they can wear jeans and don't have to stick to a nine-to-five routine. They're given time off after they've put in a certain amount of overtime. We've also upgraded the salaries of the technical staff so they're averaging about $10,000 a year more than they did several years ago. When it's appropriate, we'll even send a programmer and his or her spouse off on a short vacation at company expense. Now that they know they'll be rewarded, programmers are more motivated to get out the work that our clients need.

The problems that led me to restructure the company have also been taken care of. Before we changed, about 10 percent of our orders were delayed. Since mid-1979, fewer than 1 percent are delayed—and never for long. They're rarely delayed because everything's too visible. If a customer complains about a late order, the salesman is instructed to report the delay directly to me. Under the vertical management structure, people could sweep such a report under the rug. The people in charge of scheduling are also responsible for delays. If someone is consistently late in getting orders out, that person will be fired—and everyone else will know why.

Our accounts receivable have been reduced from an average of fifty-six days outstanding to an average of forty-three days. Under the old system, if an account was 120 days outstanding, the president had the responsibility for collecting, and he in turn had to put pressure on the people below him. Now, the controller, Jeffrey Sauerhoff, comes directly to me when accounts are more than forty-three days outstanding and I hand them over to our vice-president of marketing, who is responsible for collecting.

We've also reduced turnover because management is more responsive to individual needs. Between 1968 and 1977 we kept about one of every three people we hired. We now keep at least three of every four.

I'm aware that not every company can change its management structure as radically as I did. I had to wait for an opportune time, when I put our ClaimFacts and ImpleFacts products under the Erisco subsidiary. This made it possible for me to present the management changes to both executives and employees in a neutral way—as part of a companywide realignment designed for greater efficiency. Executives could see why the changes were being made, and there was less reason for them to be upset by changes in their job descriptions or to feel that authority was being taken away from some of them.

Even a company that has a vertical structure, I now see, can do certain things to make it work more efficiently. If I hadn't been able to change the structure of our company, I would still have reviewed the policies and procedures that had been established. I firmly believe the head of every company should review policies with top management at least once every five years. For example, I found that each manager had a different interpretation of our sick-leave policy. My original intention had been that sick leave would be granted only for illness. But some managers felt that employees were entitled to compensation if they didn't take sick leave. Others felt that sick leave and personal time were the same thing. A periodic review clarifies policy and eliminates inequities that can affect morale.

I had to give up a lot of illusions to make our management structure work. One of them was that delegating authority meant withdrawing behind the scenes and just pushing buttons whenever I wanted to tap into our daily operations. I also learned not to confuse our products with the people who create and sell them. Managing people takes at least as much attention as making and marketing a product. Today, our people are getting that attention.

—THOMAS BARREA

THEY ALL SAID
BILL SAUEY
COULDN'T LET GO

I was killing myself trying to manage 500 employees spread out in five plants around the country, running three shifts a day," says Bill Sauey, sitting in an office cluttered with plastic toys, housewares, sporting goods, and industrial parts. "After twenty-five years of keeping everything under my control, I decided there *had* to be a better way."

The better way Sauey found was to chop his company, Flambeau Corp., into pieces and turn over control of the pieces to a group of independent general managers. Before Sauey made the change at the beginning of 1979, Flambeau was highly centralized. The company, which manufactures plastic products, had grown steadily to $24 million with Sauey running the whole show. But as Flambeau got larger and larger, the pressure to continue that growth became too much for one man to handle. Today, Sauey presides over a company with six independent divisions under six managers—and sales have jumped to $35 million.

But Sauey is delighted by much more than just the boost in revenues. "I feel more in control now than I ever did," he says, flashing a catbird smile. "The divisions are really separate companies now. I have very little direct control over them, and the surprise is, I like it! My biggest regret is that I didn't do it sooner. I'm sure that we'd be a much more successful company today if I had."

This comes from a man who used to fly into a rage if his managers did anything without consulting him first. One manager remembers a typical incident back in 1975. Sauey was out of town when his company received an unusually large parts order from Chrysler. In his absence, the managers at the Baraboo, Wisconsin, plant reviewed their already tight production schedule and accepted only half the order. When Sauey returned and heard the news, he went wild. "No one turns down business around here except me," he shouted. "No matter what!"

As crazy as that refusal to rely on others may sound to him now, Sauey always made all the decisions about everything that was going on at Flambeau. He learned self-reliance while growing up on a northern Wisconsin farm as one of nine children of Norwegian immigrant parents. "My parents instilled down-to-earth values in us," he says.

One of the most important of those values was hard work. Sauey started Flambeau Corp. in 1947. This was one of the few times he looked to someone else for help with his business. At age twenty, he was still too young to incorporate a company on his own. So he asked his older brother to come to his aid.

From that point on, he guided Flambeau single-handed. By 1965, it had reached $10 million in sales. Sauey signed all the checks, bought all the plant equipment, interviewed all potential employees, and played a role in developing and selling all of Flambeau's products. The company was a testament to his persistence and his conviction that he could solve any business problem. So he continued to manage the company in his own tightly controlled way even though there were signs that this style wasn't working so well anymore.

"My biggest weakness was my inability to listen," he says. "When I felt strongly about something, like my business, I wasn't really hearing what others were saying."

For instance, by 1969, Flambeau's product designers were telling Sauey they had to begin selling their houseware products in colors like pink and turquoise to keep up with changing American tastes. No way, Sauey told them. People shouldn't buy wild colors like that. So Flambeau didn't produce them, and later, retailers like Sears and K mart began buying less of Flambeau's beige and off-white housewares and more foreign products produced in bright colors.

Sauey's desire to make all the decisions and to keep everything under his personal control led to other mistakes. In 1970 he learned that a motorcycle-helmet manufacturing business was for sale in California. Sauey loved the idea of making it a part of Flambeau. "I thought I had looked at all the angles, and besides, I felt that whatever I did was best for the business," he says.

His managers thought otherwise. The helmet business didn't fit into what the company was already doing, they argued. Also, it was too far away to manage properly, and it was currently unprofitable. Sauey disregarded his managers' advice again and bought the company. Four years later, he had to sell it at a loss of $300,000.

But if Sauey wouldn't listen to the people who worked for him, he was making up for it by listening to his peers at the University of Chicago's Executive MBA Program. Even though he was working time-and-a-half to keep his company running, every week for two years Sauey raced down 189 miles of interstate highway from Baraboo to Chicago to attend classes.

In the classroom with other company managers, Sauey began to see that maybe he didn't have all the answers. "That's a rude awakening," he says. "You think you're so damn smart and never make mistakes. But you begin to realize that you're not infallible."

Classes he attended in 1969 and 1970 planted the seeds of transformation in Sauey. But before he had time to make any changes, disaster struck in the form of the oil embargo. Flambeau was dependent on petrochemicals to make its plastic products. Sauey opened a new plant in Monroe, Georgia, in 1973 and watched it soak up cash while machinery and workers sat idle when he couldn't find raw materials. Meanwhile, Flambeau was also losing money because customers hurt by the recession weren't paying on time, and because market conditions were changing as consumers bought fewer and higher quality items.

To keep growing, Flambeau needed more cash, so Sauey tried to raise it by taking the company public. But the stock market took a nosedive in October 1973, just before the offering was made, and he withdrew the offering. No longer could Sauey contemplate making changes in the way he managed the company. Instead, he had to struggle for survival as, for fifteen months, Flambeau lost money.

To make things worse, Sauey was frustrated by what he felt was a lack of support from his managers. He had built his company as a strong, central organization that gave little authority and no bottom-line responsibility to the five plant managers. As a result, Sauey found his managers covering up and avoiding problems that threatened the profitability of their plants, instead of trying to resolve them.

At one point, Sauey found two plastic injection molding machines that the company needed badly. He bought them without seriously consulting the managers responsible for their operation. When the machines produced fewer pieces per day than expected, the response was, "Don't look at us. Sauey bought those machines."

To top it off, he couldn't find a manager to stick with the job at his Georgia plant. The problem was all too familiar to Sauey. In 1963 he had hired a talented young manager to run the company's then-new Wichita, Kansas, facility. Although the plant manager proved to be terrifically competent, Sauey had insisted on running the plant by remote control, making all significant decisions in Baraboo, 700 miles away.

"I didn't want to decentralize authority," says Sauey, "because I thought I'd lose the ability to get my message across and get the job done effectively." A few years later, the young manager quit, because he said he was "tired of asking for permission to go to the bathroom."

Now ten years later, things were the same. Sauey continued to make all important budgetary, sales, marketing, and production decisions for both the Georgia and Wichita plants, and he couldn't find a manager who wanted to work under those conditions.

As the effects of the oil embargo came to an end, Flambeau began to recover. Sauey felt he could look to the future again, rather than manage day by day. In 1976, he brought in a vice-president to organize Flambeau's financial systems and help get Flambeau moving again. Walt Smith had worked with lots of hard-nosed managers, and he knew what kinds of changes needed to be made in other parts of Flambeau's organization before the company could really grow. He didn't see any clear signs that Bill Sauey was ready to make those changes. So he commuted between Wisconsin and his home in New York and waited to see what would happen. "Bill was so involved with the details that he was losing sight of the important things," says Smith.

Yet it was the sheer weight of details Sauey wanted to keep under his control that finally led to an uncharacteristic decision—he gave up control over one part of the company. This happened in 1977 when Flambeau acquired Vlchek Plastics Co. in Middlefield, Ohio. In the past Sauey had always merged acquisitions into the central organization. "But I didn't this time," he says, "because I was so busy with the rest of the company—which by now had 500 employees working in five plants—that I knew if I brought it into our system, I'd screw it up."

Instead, he hired a competent general manager and gave him across-the-board responsibility, limiting his own role to a planning and advising capacity.

Two things happened. Vlchek's sales began doubling annually, and for once, Sauey didn't feel insecure about his lack of direct control. "I was really surprised at how little I worried about what went on at Vlchek," he says, his voice still registering amazement.

Despite this experiment in decentralizing part of the company, things continued much as they always had for the rest of the company. Walt Smith was still commuting from New York, and Sauey was still signing all of the company's checks. By late 1978, Sauey was running a company that produced and marketed everything from lawnmower parts to kitchen bowls to yo-yos. Everyone in the company had questions, and Sauey had set himself up as the only answer man.

"People were coming at me right and left with questions about new products and missed delivery dates and new market opportunities," he says. "I was going bananas trying to keep up with everything and I was losing credibility with my people, because I couldn't give them answers fast enough."

Unlike the early days, Sauey couldn't just work harder to make things go: he was already overworked and tired, and he was feeling the pressure of trying to hold the company together while the forces of growth were pulling things apart. That pressure finally pushed him into completing the experiment he'd begun with Vlchek.

"I was sitting at home one night after a frantic day at work, and I made up my mind. I just said to myself, 'By God, I've got to do it.' "

Things moved very fast after that. Sauey wrote up a reorganization manual that spelled out how he was going to decentralize Flambeau and give authority to general managers who would report to him, but have the freedom to run their divisions as they saw fit. The idea wasn't a new one. At the Executive MBA Program, he'd learned that giving authority to managers was fundamental to growth. It had taken him seven years, though, to decide that it was fundamental to Flambeau's growth.

When he first presented his idea for restructuring the company to his people, the skeptics came out of the woodwork. Everyone knew Bill Sauey could never give up control. He offered Walt Smith the job as general manager of the main Baraboo plant, but Smith turned him down. "I knew Bill would be right down the hall, and I didn't think he could keep out of the day-to-day operations," says Smith.

Sauey persisted with an "I can do it, fellas" attitude and proved as good as his word. Two months later he had appointed or hired six general managers to run Flambeau as six independent companies. Smith, finally convinced, became one of these managers.

Now, with sales at around $35 million, the changes at Flambeau are highly visible. But not even Sauey claims that he has completely reformed. Much to the dismay of his general managers, Sauey still controls all capital expenditures. Smith has been trying to get approval on a $10,000 conveyor-belt system for months. But even though Sauey's personality as a control person hasn't changed, he has at least changed his organization so that he can no longer get his hands on everything.

"It's the inability to change with circumstances that causes problems in a growing company," says Sauey. "You create concepts in your mind of how things must be, but if you run your business that way—as I did when I resisted producing our housewares in new colors—you miss out on opportunities that would help you grow."

And Sauey can admit now, too, that he fostered an atmosphere that made it difficult to change his conceptions. He tried to surround himself with managers who would support him and his goals for the company. But he never gave them the power that would allow them to do their jobs effectively. Now that he's decentralized Flambeau, Sauey has seen his managers become the responsible and motivated managers he always wanted, but could never seem to find or keep.

Recently, Roy Mason, Flambeau's corporate vice-president of engineering, went ahead and ordered a $17,000 machine, because he was tired of waiting for his boss's approval. A few years ago, he would have been the victim of Sauey's wrath for taking such an action on his own. But Bill Sauey can see things differently now. "You should have checked with me first," he told Mason, "but I guess you did it for the right reasons."

—DAVID DeLONG

WHO DO YOU TURN TO
WHEN YOU'RE
THE BOSS?

In early 1978, Joseph D. Simons, chief executive officer of Badgerland Equipment Inc., of Waukesha, Wisconsin, faced a dilemma. Salesmen were pressuring him to reduce prices of the company's aerial work platforms and other high-reach equipment, leased or purchased by contractors to lift workers and supplies at construction sites. But Simons's late brother Peter, who had founded the firm in 1969, had built Badgerland by providing prompt, excellent service, which allowed the firm to charge 10 percent to 15 percent more than competitors. Simons's instincts told him to continue that policy, but he had doubts. One salesman, for instance, complained that Badgerland had lost a $40,000 contract because its prices were too high.

Simons had faced such predicaments many times before, but that didn't make the decision any easier. Most often, as happens in many small firms, he had to rely almost exclusively on his own judgment. He had learned something about decision-making in a small firm: No matter how good a manager you think you are, sometimes you have doubts. Who do you turn to when your experience seems inadequate, when you're not sure if you're being fair or just? Who do you turn to when you're the boss?

When Simons faced his pricing strategy dilemma, he turned to John Komives, one of Badgerland's three outside advisers. If Badgerland cut prices, it would have to lower quality, Komives reasoned. And if it did that, the firm could destroy an image that had taken five years to establish. "Komives headed me off at the pass," says Simons. "I saw that it would be foolhardy not to keep our standards and our prices high."

That's the kind of advice and support that Simons has learned to expect from his three advisers, who are now members of Badgerland's board. Since 1977, they have helped Simons steer his small firm through a number of business storms. Badgerland's sales have grown 40 percent the past two years, to $5.9 million for the fiscal year that ended last January 31.

Simons urgently needed support and guidance when his brother Pete died suddenly in July 1976, and Joe, then twenty-six years old, became majority owner and CEO.

Pete had provided the entrepreneurial drive to build Badgerland. Joe, on the other hand, had the pragmatic, methodical temperament that Pete lacked. Joe joined the firm part-time in 1971, and he was happy to learn the business slowly, while working in Badgerland's service department. But when Pete died, Joe knew only how to run the garage, dispatch equipment, and handle repairs and maintenance. Finance, sales, and marketing were "totally bewildering to Joe," says treasurer Brian Kramer.

Joe Simons was scared, and he had good reason. Within a month of Pete's death, he received visits from the company's bankers and from a representative of JLG Industries Inc., the major supplier to Badgerland of aerial work platforms. "They asked tough questions," says Simons. Would the young CEO, they nervously wondered, run the company into the ground?

Fortunately, a settlement of a key man insurance policy put Badgerland on a solid financial footing. Fortunately, too, Simons had two experienced managers: Frank Jonkman, the sales manager, and Tom Langkamp, the chief financial officer.

He felt particularly lucky to have Langkamp, who was the minority owner of Badgerland, and whose relationships with the bank, the finance companies, and JLG Industries were vital to the company's health. "Tom had been my brother's right-hand man," Simons says. "I wanted him to be my right-hand man, too."

But from the outset, it was clear that Simons's and Langkamp's management styles and philosophies were different. Simons's methodical approach contrasted sharply with the entrepreneurial, high-flying style of Pete Simons and Langkamp that had characterized Badgerland in its early years.

The clash between the two was clear when it came to making decisions about growth and expansion. Langkamp urged the immediate opening of branch offices in warmer states to make better use of equipment during slow winter months. But Simons wondered if Badgerland had the managers needed for widespread expansion. Would the firm's service quality suffer if it opened too many branches? Simons didn't have the answers, and neither did Langkamp. For months, they talked in circles, and made no major decisions. "We weren't going anywhere," Simons says. "We were on dead center."

Even minor problems were not being solved. Brian Kramer, who was then controller, grew so frustrated in the summer of 1977 that he asked Richard Kaimann, professor of operations management at Marquette University and a small business consultant for fifteen years, to help solve a problem in the firm's delivery operation. After talking with Simons, Langkamp, and Kramer, Kaimann concluded that the problem he had been asked to solve wasn't the problem at all.

"I had a feeling that Joe didn't have a good hold on the business and that the company didn't have the management expertise it needed to grow," Kaimann says. He made a suggestion: Hire outside advisers to boost Badgerland's strength in finance, marketing, and sales.

Simons liked the idea. More and more, he felt isolated at the top. He recognized that he was trying to make decisions in a vacuum. He knew he urgently needed some objective advice to help him make the best possible choices. Still, he was reluctant to hire outsiders—especially at a fee of $65 an hour—until one day in August 1977.

At dinner that night, Frank Jonkman told Simons that Badgerland needed stronger leadership, and that he should resign. Simons was shocked and angry, and nearly fired Jonkman on the spot. But he didn't—nor did he give in. Instead he decided to take Kaimann's suggestion.

The sole charge of an advisory board, Kaimann told Simons, is to provide sound, objective, and competent advice. The advisers must have knowledge and experience equal or superior to the CEO's, especially in areas where he is weak, and they must be given freedom to criticize his actions when necessary.

Simons hired three advisers, all from Milwaukee, all with different strengths: Kaimann, John L. Komives, and M. Gordon Pederson. Kaimann, an operations specialist, took a systems approach to small business management, asking such questions as, "Is the necessary information available to make the proper decision?" Pederson, a management psychologist at Humber, Mundie & McClary, was expert at assessing the strengths and weaknesses of people and how they worked together. Komives, president of the consulting firm Lakeshore Group Ltd. and a director on ten small company boards, took a pragmatic approach, asking "Are prices high enough? Are receivables too large or too old?"

From the first advisory board meeting in August 1977, the board became "a network of support, a special kind of sounding board for Joe," says Pederson. Adds Kaimann, "He could use us to bounce ideas off of, to help provide him with information and alternatives to make decisions. But we certainly weren't going to make decisions for him."

Simons's resolution of an ongoing conflict between the service manager and the sales manager in the Iowa-Illinois branch office soon demonstrated the value of the board. Twice a week, Simons had driven the 250 miles between Badgerland's Waukesha headquarters and its Davenport, Iowa, office. But as soon as he left Iowa, the conflict would break out again.

Simons hadn't been sure what to do, and for months he vacillated between hiring a branch manager and continuing to run the operation from Waukesha.

Instinctively, though, he wanted to hire a branch manager. Finally he took his problem to the board.

Badgerland's growth to $2.5 million for the fiscal year ended January 1977, Kaimann pointed out, did argue for a switch from centralized to decentralized management. Simons couldn't effectively supervise all three branch operations. A properly trained manager could ensure that the branch operation met the firm's standards for prompt, excellent service.

Bolstered by the board's comments, Simons hired a branch manager,

CHOOSING THE RIGHT PEOPLE FOR YOUR BOARD

Joe Simons's feelings of isolation are common. "The small company CEO has probably the loneliest job in the world," says Stanley Vance, professor of management at the University of Tennessee's College of Business Administration and an expert on corporate boards of directors.

An advisory board or board of directors is one answer. It can be a "psychological crutch to help a CEO make important decisions only he can make," says Theodore Cohn, a West Orange, New Jersey, consultant specializing in small firms. After all, Cohn points out, everybody else in the company has a job to do. No one else can share the CEO's outlook because no one else has the same stake in the company's future.

Such a board can play many important roles: helping to formulate long-term plans, or critiquing existing financial, production, or marketing practices, for example. Yet perhaps its least visible and most powerful role is that of confidant, mentor, and peer.

Finding suitable mentors isn't easy. Who to consider? Avoid your key managers, suggests Leon A. Danco, a Cleveland consultant specializing in small, family-held firms. They tend to rubber-stamp the CEO's decisions, he says, and to inhibit frank comments by outsiders. After all, it's tough for a CEO or board member to candidly assess a top manager's performance if he's sitting at the same table.

"Also, it's not a good idea for members of your staff to know you're frustrated or don't have all the answers," says William Chisolm, president of Boardroom Consultants Inc., a New York corporate director search firm. "It weakens your leadership position."

Instead, choose only outsiders who won't be afraid to disagree or say no, suggests Danco in his book, *Beyond Survival: A Business Owner's Guide for Success.* Lawyers, accountants, or suppliers with a financial stake in the company should not be considered. Good choices include those engaged in businesses different from your own, who can appreciate and understand the risk of running a company. Overall, an adviser should have unquestioned integrity, good judgment, problem-solving skills, and a capability for action and risk taking. He should also show that he respects you, likes you, and wants you to succeed.

Finding such advisers can be a tremendous breakthrough for a hard-pressed manager, who learns he "can bare his soul and be met with empathy, not ridicule," says John Komives, a Badgerland director. "I've often seen CEOs develop new enthusiasm and confidence once they've developed a peer relationship with a small group of people whom they truly respect and who respect them, and who give support freely and openly in times of crisis."

Tom Foster, from competitor Hertz Heavy Equipment Rental, a subsidiary of Hertz Corp. Six months after Foster took over, branch sales had grown from about 18 percent of Badgerland's total sales to almost 38 percent.

Board members came to the advisory board's monthly meeting armed with tough questions. Badgerland didn't adequately break out expenses and revenues by division, branch, and function, the board said, so its financial statements were almost useless as managerial tools. A breakout revealed a problem: The delivery operation was losing about $8,000 a month. That didn't solve the problem, but at least now Simons knew a problem existed.

Komives zeroed in on another area, accounts receivable. How many bills were outstanding? How old were they? How did Badgerland's figures compare with the industry average? Once Simons saw the figures and understood their significance, he became concerned. Total accounts receivable for the six-month period that ended June 30, 1977, had more than doubled.

The dramatic jump in accounts receivable, caused primarily by increased sales, wasn't the problem, Komives pointed out. The real problem was that Badgerland didn't have the excess cash to cover outstanding bills. If there were ever a crunch and the bank called in the company's loans, Badgerland might not be able to pay.

Komives urged that Badgerland set a timetable for reducing receivables, a task Simons assigned to Langkamp. Langkamp agreed to do it, but he insisted that receivables weren't a problem, that the company didn't have a history of bad debts.

But by the end of January 1978, receivables outstanding more than 120 days had jumped from 10 percent to 20 percent of the total, and Badgerland's cash supply was shrinking. Langkamp insisted that no major problem existed, and that his efforts to reduce receivables were being hindered by a problem with a major customer.

Tensions were growing between Simons and Langkamp. They differed on Badgerland's future direction and on the philosophy of running a small company. What distressed Simons most was that the time he spent trying to resolve his differences with Langkamp took time from running the business. Objectively, he says, he could see that Langkamp's actions indicated "a lack of willingness to cooperate with me as CEO." Emotionally, though, it was tougher. Langkamp had made a significant contribution to the company. Simons resisted taking action.

Then, suddenly, the situation came to a head. Frustrated by the growing tension, Jonkman threatened to quit. He asked Simons to disband the advisory board, saying it was creating too much ill will.

Simons was thrown into a quandary. He didn't want to alienate his managers, to allow the board to create a wedge between him and them. Yet he found the board's help invaluable in becoming the kind of CEO he wanted to be—and he knew Badgerland needed. He discussed the problem with Kaimann and Komives. Put aside personal feelings, the two advisers urged, and simply insist that the managers fulfill their job responsibilities as you see them.

In early 1978 Simons sent a memo to Langkamp, demanding that Langkamp set up a system to yield more accurate branch and divisional statements. Langkamp refused and the situation worsened. But it was several months later, in the summer of 1978, before Simons could resolve the personal loyalty he felt to Tom Langkamp. With the board's help, he finally realized he had to put his company first. He asked Langkamp to leave and offered to buy his Badgerland stock. Even today Joe Simons talks about that decision as "the toughest one I've ever made."

Tough decisions come easier to Joe Simons today than they did three years ago when he first sought advisers. Simons is now hiring a new manager for another of Badgerland's branches. "It's been very different from that first time the board was involved in deciding to bring on a branch manager," says John Komives. "Then Joe asked us what he should do. This time he came to us with a description of the person he thought was needed, and reasons why. Then he asked for our comments. Joe has grown and matured into a top-notch manager right before our eyes."

The newest member of Simons's board (now a full-fledged board of directors) agrees. Dick Bertrand is co-owner and general manager of MSI, a Milwaukee-area contractor, a longtime acquaintance of the Simons family, and a close friend of Joe's late brother, Pete. "After Pete died, Joe would call and we'd talk about his fears of not being capable of picking up and taking over where Pete left off," says Bertrand. "Once he got the advisers, he was very excited about the fact that they could help him to do the job better. Now he can hold his own with anybody—a banker, or a competitor, or someone on the board. He's not afraid to have smart people around him, and he knows how to use them. Where he operated from the gut before, he operates from good business sense now."

Simons himself gives board members a big share of the credit, both for helping him develop that business sense and for giving him support and encouragement when he needed it. As he looks back, Simons says, "Without their support, I don't know if I would have made it."

—BILL HENDRICKSON

THE ADVICE SQUAD

I'm my own boss," is the entrepreneur's credo. At least it's the credo of Kenneth Hendricks, chief executive officer of ABC Supply Co., a building-materials distributor in Beloit, Wisconsin. ABC, founded by Hendricks in 1979, did $82.3 million in annual sales in 1984—a 76,075-percent five-year growth rate, placing it number two on the 1985 *Inc.* 500 list of America's fastest-growing private companies. Despite the size of the company—and the challenges that come with such fast growth—Hendricks sees no reason to establish a board of directors at ABC.

"The energy that goes into setting up a board, and then periodically sitting down with them, is a reduction in productivity," Hendricks says. "A board is a convenient way for an entrepreneur to shift responsibility to other people. I like being responsible for this company. I'm a hands-on kind of guy, and the buck stops here. I love the independent environment at my company, and I don't want to change it. Every day, it feels like a party around here." The forty-four-year-old Hendricks owns 100 percent of ABC, and there are no procedures, implicit or explicit, governing such long-range policies as succession. "I haven't thought about it," he says when asked who might take over should anything happen to him. "That's too far down the road. I'm having fun and satisfaction now."

Most people who start their own companies side with Hendricks when it comes to naming outsiders to a company board, even though the benefits to the business go well beyond planning for succession. In fact, the reasons to have a board are so sensible sounding that they are hard to dispute. Boards are an inexpensive way to get hardheaded, expert, objective advice. A board forces a CEO to drop back from day-to-day operations and to think strategically about the direction the company should take. Why, then, the reluctance on the part of so many CEOs? The answer seems to lie less with business tactics than with individual style. The very personality traits that lead people to start successful companies in the first place—a passionate concern about control; a bias toward action, not rationalizing and explaining; a desire to create a management style that is appropriate to the business, not one learned in an MBA program—are the same characteristics that make company heads chary of boards. When the subject comes up, the feeling that is voiced most often is fear of losing control of the company.

John Cross, chairman and former president of Elphinstone Inc., a $1.7-million Baltimore distributor and renter of construction equipment, has some strong opinions about why most heads of privately held companies shun boards. Cross, who joined the company in 1937 and became president in 1962, didn't set up his own board until 1979. "Entrepreneurs," he says, "tend to be secretive and trust no one. At the top of the corporate flow chart is the word 'me,' and underneath that is 'everyone else.' It's logical for entrepreneurs to have a board, but entrepreneurs tend to be ruled by their emotions, not by logic. That's why so many firms fail when the founder or driving force dies. The entrepreneur tends to put great faith in his own powers. He subscribes to the John Wayne image—the loner battling against impossible odds, the macho achiever. I've talked to many of my colleagues who don't have boards, and they say it's because outsiders are a threat. They're afraid they wouldn't be able to run their company the way they want."

David Boyd, associate professor of organizational behavior in the College of Business Administration of Northeastern University, finds much the same attitude. "For [the entrepreneur] to seek advice from something like a board is to admit weakness and vulnerability," Boyd says. "Entrepreneurs tend to compete with themselves. Relying on a board of directors is anathema to their desire of projecting an image of strength and omniscience."

Many small companies do have boards. But, as Leon Danco, president and founder of The Center for Family Business, in Cleveland, points out, most are rubber stamps. "The CEOs of most small businesses," he says, "either do nothing or pack their courts with shills. It's because successful entrepreneurs worship flexibility, i.e., 'freedom,' more than anything else—including, it would seem, survival."

That is a lesson that Victor Pomper learned well when he was head of marketing at H. H. Scott Inc., in Cambridge, Massachusetts. For two decades, the company, founded by Hermon Scott in 1947, was a standard-setter in the high-fidelity stereo equipment industry. "Hermon Scott was a genius," says Pomper. "He had an incredible, towering intellect. But he never shared his feelings, and he always refused to take advice. When imports started to eat away at our market share, and we started to get into trouble, he just couldn't cope. We'd come out with another brilliant engineering innovation, and we'd do well at first. But, invariably, our competitors would copy the technology and then undercut our price. Instead of cutting prices right along with them, he kept our prices up. He consistently traded market share to maintain profit margins. He was obsessed with our prestige. It was folly.

"Many times, I suggested we set up a board. But trying to get him to follow any advice was a knock-down-drag-out fight," says Pomper. "He was a strong man, but some strengths carried too far can become weaknesses." In 1972, the company finally went bankrupt. Scott, a broken man, died within a few years.

"I learned from Scott's mistake," says Pomper, who founded his Bedford, New Hampshire company, Satellite Data Corp., in 1981. "And what I learned was that a company is much better off with a board, preferably one that has a good number of outsiders sitting on it. A CEO needs a steady source of unbiased, outside advice."

William H. Chisholm, president of Boardroom Consultants Inc., a New York City consulting firm that helps companies recruit directors, agrees. "It's like putting inexpensive management consultants on retainer," he says. "But, typically, small firms have not resorted to outside directors, although that's finally starting to change." The change, though by no means a groundswell, is taking place most often at maturing start-ups. And it is giving birth to some boards that are as diverse as the companies that have created them.

"We hold over ten meetings a year," says Rick Terrell, president of Microware Distributors Inc., describing the board at his $15.3-million Aloha, Oregon, company. "That's an extremely high frequency for any kind of firm. But I depend on that many meetings. We're a fast-growing, dynamic firm, and we need to sit down and talk a lot. Not so much to discuss day-to-day operational stuff as to look at the strategic opportunities that are constantly presenting themselves." Terrell founded Microware—a distributor of microcomputer hardware and software, and number 350 on the 1985 *Inc.* 500—in 1979.

Microware's board has six members, who include three top officers and three outsiders. One of the key outsiders is Lou Manrique, a buyer for PacTel InfoSystems. "He's a retail man," explains Terrell, "who knows the buying patterns of our customers. He'll say: 'You don't want to start buying that. You won't find customers for it.' He's saved us from making many costly mistakes. This industry is changing every day, and I would have trouble keeping up with it without my board."

While the usual ratio of outsiders to insiders favors in-house directors, a number of small companies have taken a chance on a broader view from the outside. Richard Parker of Richard Parker & Associates, a $15-million direct-mail fund-raising company in San Francisco, recently set up a board composed of three outsiders and himself. "I don't want to live in my own little universe," says Parker, who is founder, CEO, and sole owner. One of the outsiders is an attorney. The other two are Aaron Adler, retired chairman of the board of Stone & Adler, in Chicago, and Pat Connolly, a vice-president of Williams-Sonoma Inc., in Emeryville, California, both recruited for their direct-marketing sophistication.

Parker says his four board meetings a year help him organize his thoughts and actions. "Just the process of meeting, and having to prepare ahead of time, helps me think more clearly," he says. "From having a board, I've discovered that if you can't logically explain what you want to do, it's probably not worth doing. Many entrepreneurs are too insecure about themselves to have a board. They're afraid they'll look naive in front of them. But I've gone into that boardroom and shared bad quarterly statements and bad moments with my directors that I wouldn't want to share with my mom. A board helps you face things a CEO would be tempted to deny or sweep under the rug."

George Clement, CEO of Clement Communications Inc., says straight out that before he created his outside board five and a half years ago, "I wondered if, under scrutiny of a board of sophisticated businesspeople, I could measure up. I wasn't so sure I wanted to be put to the acid test." Clement Communications, in Concordville, Pennsylvania, is a $10-million producer of posters and publications that help businesses communicate with their employees. The company, founded by Clement's grandfather, is closely held and family-owned. "When I thought about forming a board, I was afraid of losing control," he admits.

Despite his anxieties, Clement plunged ahead and set up a board consisting of himself and four outsiders. As his outside directors, he chose the company's legal counsel of twenty years for his long-range view of the firm; the CEO of a similar (but not competing) company for his knowledge of the publishing industry; a financial expert; and another CEO for his business savvy. Within a year, the board had convinced Clement to set up a system of bad-debt management that saved the company $190,000 before two years were up. The board also helped Clement Communications improve its financial reporting and, according to Clement, kept him from making foolish acquisitions. "My board has made me a better CEO," he says. "CEOs who don't use outside advice run the risk of internalizing too much. They never realize their full potential, and they miss a lot of opportunities."

Elphinstone's John Cross says the major reason he set up his board in 1979 was to establish continuity. "I'm sixty-eight years old," he says. "It would be irresponsible and selfish of me to not plan for the future. I don't want this company to fall apart after I go. I want a smooth succession. A company is a living organism, not an appendage of the leader's ego."

Cross set out very methodically to choose the four outsiders who would join three of his company's top managers as directors. First, he identified the areas in which he wanted advice from the outside. Then he and his management team drew up a list of candidates, which they pared down to four names. Cross sent each an invitation to join the board, along with a prospectus, a brief history of the company, a full set of financial figures, and a one-year and a five-year marketing plan. A sheet describing the duties of directors was also enclosed. Cross said he then phoned the candidates, explained what was on the way, and waited. All four accepted.

---

1 HOW TO MAKE THE MOST OF OUTSIDE DIRECTORS

Plan Ahead

The beauty of boards of directors is that their function can be whatever a chief executive officer decides best suits the company. That can be based on immediate needs, such as how to control costs, or projected needs, such as how to carve out new markets. Ideally, before setting up a board, a CEO will have thought through the direction he or she wants the company to take, and its current and prospective strengths and weaknesses. Just as important to the overall effectiveness of the board, the CEO will have assessed his or her personal strengths and weaknesses so that the directors will complement rather than duplicate talents.

John Cross of Elphinstone Inc. (see main text) was very clear about what he wanted from outsiders when he set up his board. He identified four areas in which he felt his construction equipment and supply distributorship needed more information on a continuing basis. He wanted to keep abreast of the latest developments in management techniques; he wanted financial advice; and he wanted to understand better the viewpoints of his customers and suppliers.

Once he had defined what he wanted, Cross recruited four outsiders to match his needs. They are Douglas Walker, a management and turnaround expert who is on top of the latest developments in management techniques; Karl Mullen—former treasurer of one of the largest rental firms in the area, and now a CPA with a computer software firm—who has the right financial background; William Hardy—executive secretary of the Maryland Highway Contractors Association and an expert on the state highway market for equipment—who could speak for customers; and Bernard Stang—head of a division of Ingersoll-Rand Corp.—who represents the suppliers' perspective.

Seek the Best

Once a chief executive officer has figured out what he or she wants a board to accomplish, that person should seek out experts, not college roommates or the company's lawyer or accountant. Some CEOs set up inhouse nominating committees, rely on consultants who specialize in finding directors, or solicit recommendations from peers.

Chester Kirk, CEO of Amtrol Inc., in West Warwick, Rhode Island, has an eight-member board that represents the kind of talent and experience that most entrepreneurs assume isn't available to them. Herbert H. Jacobi, for instance, formerly was an executive vice-president of Chase Manhattan Bank and is now a partner in Trinkaus & Burkhardt, a German bank. "The truth is, a lot of top-notch people are perfectly willing to sit on the boards of smaller companies," says Kirk, who founded Amtrol in 1946, when he was twenty-nine. "They're often very flattered to be asked, and they know that being a director at a small, growing company would be an education for them, too. But many entrepreneurs don't even try to recruit them. They're afraid those people will see their firm as unimportant. Entrepreneurs have more appeal than they think."

Money Counts

While the usual payment to directors of small companies is an annual retainer, a fee for attending specific meetings, or both, individual companies have worked out a wide variety of schemes for compensating their board members.

Rick Terrell, president of Microware Distributors Inc. (see main text) gives each of his directors a yearly payment equal to a certain percentage of the company's net profits after taxes. In 1984, this "bonus pool," as Terrell calls it, amounted to $1,800 each. "I want my board members to know how valuable they are," says Terrell. "I like the idea of tying their fortunes to the fortunes of the company. It makes them more committed."

Kirk, pays each director a yearly retainer of $8,500, plus travel expenses and additional fees for attending special audit, compensation, or planning-committee meetings. Board members can also buy shares of the company's closely held stock. Though the compensation plan is generous for a small company, Kirk sees it as a "bargain."

Laser Engineering Inc., a $2.5-million manufacturer of laser tubes and systems, in Waltham, Massachusetts, pays its board members neither a yearly retainer nor an attendance fee. Instead, Laser gives stock options. Each of the company's four outside directors currently holds an average of 2 percent in equity. "Equity makes directors more dedicated than money," says founder and president Robert Rudko.

Among the 31,000 companies surveyed in the 1985–86 *Growth Resources Officer Compensation Report,* an annual nationwide study of smaller-company officer compensation published by Growth Resources Inc., in Peabody, Massachusetts, the average retainer ranged from $1,175 a year at companies with less than $2 million in annual sales to $4,643 a year at companies with annual sales of $25 million to $40 million. Meeting fees among all respondents ranged from $100 to $1,000, averaging $534.

Cash-short companies may lean toward compensating directors with equity. The disadvantage, however, is that once a director holds equity in a company, he becomes an "insider," and may lose some of the objectivity that was sought in the first place.

Take The Time

One of the most common mistakes is to underestimate the amount of time a chief executive officer will need to spend with board members. Quarterly meetings—and the preparation that surrounds those meetings—are the bare minimum, if directors are to get psychically and emotionally involved with the company. In fact, the CEO faces many of the same motivational issues with board members as he or she does with key employees: how to involve them in decision-making; how to keep them fully informed; and how to make them feel an integral part of the company.

Robert Rudko, founder and president of Laser Engineering Inc., has pulled out all the stops in getting his four-member outside board involved. The directors meet every other month, and also serve on committees to tackle specific problems, such as incentive compensation. "Directors need a constant sense of purpose," says Rudko, who holds additional meetings with individual board members as often as once a week. He concludes, "They appreciate the fact that they're needed and given attention."

Cross's wife, Mary, a vice-president, attends every board meeting and lends her advice, even though she is not a board member. "Who cares more about your best interests than your spouse?" asks Cross. "She knows me better than anybody alive, and I trust her. It helps cure some of the loneliness that comes with being in charge. She doesn't have much marketing or financial knowledge or anything like that, but she has remarkably good hunches about personnel matters. We're a small company, with only sixteen employees, so she knows everyone here."

Recent hikes in directors and officers (D&O) liability insurance—and the difficulty in getting coverage—may put a damper on some small businesses' attempts to recruit outside directors. Premiums are from three to ten times higher than they were last year, and in most cases, higher premiums are buying less coverage.

A company can set up an advisory board, however, an effective alternative that also skirts the insurance and litigation problems that formal boards may face. "Many people in high positions are reluctant to serve on a formal board of directors because of possible legal hassles," says Howard Anderson, managing director of The Yankee Group, a consulting firm in Boston. "A board member is stuck with a hell of a lot of legal responsibility. If a company screws up, a stockholder, supplier, or customer can name that company's board of directors in a lawsuit. And an outside member of that board, even if he only attends a few meetings a year, is just as liable. Advisory boards, on the other hand, generally carry no legal liabilities. That means experienced, influential people are more willing to serve on them."

HoltraChem Inc., a $30-million chemical distributor in Natick, Massachusetts, set up an advisory board of two outside members last year, partly in response to the D&O insurance problem. The company was founded nine years ago by president Herbert Roskind and executive vice-president Ery Magasanik, who are co-owners. Roskind and Magasanik chose for their advisory board two men who have specific talents that they themselves lack. One is John Remondi, vice-president of finance at Fidelity Investments, in Boston, and the other is Glenn Petersen, retired president of a manufacturing company. Remondi's expertise in structuring deals is particularly valuable right now as HoltraChem tries to expand by acquiring other companies. Current plans, for example, call for the acquisition of a chemical-manufacturing company, in order to—in Magasanik's words—"integrate backwards." Remondi already has helped HoltraChem engineer a 1-percent reduction in the lending rate charged by its bank, a maneuver that might never have occurred to Roskind and Magasanik.

Such money-saving maneuvers have convinced many CEOs that they were smart to appoint outsiders to their boards in the first place. Increasingly, as John Cross predicts, the practice of setting up a board, formal or informal, is likely to become a matter of survival. "The rapid change in today's economy, the influx of computers, and the expanding information base are making entrepreneurs realize that they can't live in their own little universe," he says. "I think small business people are becoming less and less provincial. From now on, companies run by the seat of their pants will either see their market share shrink, or get destroyed by their competitors."

—JOHN F. PERSINOS

INDEX